Istanbul (Constantinople)

Troy Mudanya Brusa
Apollonia Asana
T. ARARAT Athens Izmir (Smyrna) Jasin TURKEY ANATOLIA
Konia (Iconi...)
Lystra
RHODES Silifke (Seleu...)

CYPRUS SYRIA Nineveh Teheran

MEDITERRANEAN SEA LEBANON Damascus IRAQ IRAN
ISRAEL Baghdad Isfahan
Baskale JORDAN

EGYPT SINAI Persepolis
Shiraz

SAUDI ARABIA

U.S.S.R. CASPIAN SEA

Sharrukin (Khorsabad)
Nineveh
Mosul KURDISTAN Teheran
Nimrud (Calah)
LESSER ZAB
GREATER ZAB
Calah Sherghat (Ashur) Suleimaniah

ZOHAB Hamadan (Ecbatana)
Taki-Bostan
Tekrit Kermanshah Behistun IRAN
Samarra

(PERSIA)

LURISTAN Isfahan

Baghdad ZAGROS MTS. Shushan
Ctesiphon KARUN R.
Babylon Kish TIGRIS R. Dizful Mal-Emir
Hillah Borsippa DEZ R. Shuster Kala Tul
Niffer (Nippur) Shush (Susa)
KHUZISTAN Lurdegan

EUPHRATES R. Warka (Erech) KARUN R. Ahwaz
Larsa
Ur Muhammera Abadan
Al Basrah (Basra)

KUWAIT PERSIAN GULF KERAK I.
Bushire

ROAD TO NINEVEH

ROAD TO NINEVEH

Novels (Junior)

HARD ALEE
ROVING ALL THE DAY
FATHOM FIVE
MAKE WAY FOR A SAILOR
REMEMBER THE VALLEY
JOEL
KING SOLOMEN'S NAVY
KING SOLOMEN'S HORSES

Non-Fiction (Junior)

THE FIRST BOOK OF ISRAEL
THE FIRST BOOK OF ARCHAEOLOGY

ROAD TO NINEVEH

The Adventures and Excavations
of
Sir Austen Henry Layard

Nora Benjamin Kubie

Doubleday & Company, Inc.

Garden City, New York

ACKNOWLEDGMENTS

I wish to thank first of all Dr. R. D. Barnett, Keeper of the Department of Western Asiatic Antiquities at the British Museum, for his assistance and information. The critical attitude toward the Trustees of the Museum which appears in the text is Layard's own reaction under very different circumstances and at a very different time from the present, and represents no criticism of the policies of the Museum today.

I should like also to express my gratitude to the Department of Press and Radio of the Government of Iran for various courtesies while I was there, to Mrs. Lael Wertenbaker for her freely offered editorial advice and encouragement; to Dr. Moshe Dothan for giving me the opportunity to learn about archaeological techniques "on the dig"; and to the MacDowell Colony in Peterborough, New Hampshire, where I was able to complete the book under the best possible circumstances.

With this book the author pays tribute to Barnard
College on the occasion of its 75th Anniversary.

CONTENTS

LIST OF ILLUSTRATIONS

NOTE

The major sources of this book are Layard's published works, (listed in the bibliography) and the Layard Papers in the manuscript collection of the British Museum. Direct quotations (including dialogue), unless otherwise noted, are drawn from these.

The English spelling of words and place names in such languages as Arabic, Turkish, and Persian not only differs in current sources, but was inconsistent in Layard's own writings. Also British spelling of ordinary words, as used in direct quotations, differs from the American usage as employed in the body of the text.

INTRODUCTION

In a main hall of the British Museum, two majestic monsters look down upon the passers-by. The pedestals bear identical titles: *Winged man-headed lion from a doorway in the palace of Ashurnasirpal, King of Assyria B.C. 885–860, Nimrud (Calah) excavated by Sir A. H. Layard, 1847.* The long gallery beyond, lined with bas-reliefs, is a history book carved in stone. There an Assyrian king, attended by officers and eunuchs, supervises the building of the palace these slabs once decorated; reviews his armies; receives a tribute of treasure, camels, cattle, slaves. A printed explanation in a glass case reads: *Layard also probed the great mound called Kuyunjik. This was the palace of Sennacherib . . . and the mound on which it stood was the long-sought site of Nineveh mentioned in the Old Testament.*

To the Hebrew prophets, Nineveh was the very symbol of decadence and luxury. "Arise, go to Nineveh, that great city, and cry out against it; for their wickedness is come up against me," said the Lord to Jonah. But Jonah fled in a ship, was thrown overboard and swallowed by Leviathon before he agreed to set foot in such a place. Nahum called it "the bloody city . . . full of lies and robbery," prophesying, "It shall come to pass that all they that look upon thee shall flee from thee, and say, Nineveh is laid waste: who will bemoan her?"

Nineveh fell to her enemies in 612 B.C., and was so thoroughly laid waste, so little bemoaned that by the nineteenth century of our era no one knew for sure where the city had stood. Mesopotamia

—modern Iraq—overrun by armies from Ashurnasirpal to Alexander, was mostly desert, the home of the wandering Bedouin. Here and there peculiar mounds rose from the level plain; according to Arab legend, those in the neighborhood of Mosul might (or might not) represent all that was left of the Assyrian capital.

Austen Henry Layard, though he knew his Bible, did not set out to prove its historical truth, nor was he determined from boyhood to discover Nineveh, as Heinrich Schliemann was determined to find Troy. He did not, like the methodical German, amass a private fortune before realizing an ambition in middle-age. Though called "Father of Assyriology" he was not a trained archaeologist, for the science of archaeology barely existed in his day. He was self-made, if any one ever was: an archaeologist whose knowledge came from reading books; whose methods developed through trial and error; a poor young man enchanted by the East, with a romantic thirst for adventure and courage amounting to recklessness. The qualities that brought him eventual success only made trouble for him at first.

Part One

ADVENTURES

Chapter I

A CONTINENTAL CHILDHOOD
(1817–1829)

The Layard family claimed descent—like many others, and somewhat mythically, says Austen Henry—from Raymond of Toulouse, and in the not-so-distant past, from a clan of noble Huguenot refugees named de Layarde. Doctors, army officers, and Church of England prelates were among his more immediate forebears; the family, though neither very noble any more nor very rich, was eminently respectable. His father, Henry Peter Layard, had gone out to Ceylon as a minor British official shortly after the island was taken over from the Dutch; he hoped to come away from it (as everyone was said to do) with a comfortable fortune. Henry Peter, however, came away only with chronic asthma which he blamed on the island climate, and with a small pension, just enough to marry his childhood sweetheart, Miss Marianne Austen, daughter of a banker of Ramsgate.

Peace had finally come to Europe with the defeat of Napoleon; the young couple thought it a good time to travel. The first of their four sons was born in a Paris hotel on March 5, 1817—just two years before another English baby, Victoria, who was to give her name to an era, was born at Kensington Palace in London. The Layards' first child was christened Henry Austen; some sixteen years later, at the request of his maternal uncle, the order of his given names was reversed. But the change did not take; he continued to be known by his friends, and in public life, as Henry Layard.

His first memory was of embracing a lion cub at the zoological gardens in Paris, to the horror of his nursemaid and the screaming terror of his infant brother Frederick. Aged three, he was already befriending creatures whose response, everyone assured him, would be fatal. His next recollection was of Italy, of nursery school in Florence, and a black poodle called Mouche that carried a lantern in its mouth to light the way after dark. And, even then, of visiting art galleries with his father, who pointed out to his small son the paintings that a man of taste preferred.

Into this happy childhood there now stepped for the first time Mr. Benjamin Austen, Mrs. Layard's brother, the very model of the perfect British gentleman. Henry's mother had beautiful blue eyes, gentle manners, and a sensitive disposition; her nervousness upset the masculine members of the family and herself. She was, according to her eldest son, "devotedly attached to her children and ready to make any sacrifice to promote their welfare"; hence, when her brother declared that Italy was no place to bring up young Englishmen, she agreed immediately. The family returned to Ramsgate in order that Henry might attend a dame school, of which he remembered only that he learned nothing. The dank Channel fog made life impossible for Henry Peter Layard; soon the family left England once more to hunt hopefully across Europe for a place where Papa could breathe.

First it was France again; at Moulins Henry was entered in a school where he was the only non-Catholic and the only English boy in a pack of small French villains who held him personally responsible for the downfall of Napoleon, their hero. *Ce cochon d'Anglais* was commanded to fall on his knees and kiss a cross chalked on the filthy floor. Staunchly Protestant and English to the core, Henry was not one to knuckle under even when it hurt. He managed to kick a few shins before his nose was rubbed in the chalk. Courage and a rather prickly pride were always to get him into scrapes as well as out of them.

But he was a warmhearted little boy who preferred to be liked, and was delighted to think his troubles at Moulins were over when his classmates appealed to him, as a bold fellow, for advice on how to get even with a brutal teacher. Though the only English school Henry had attended had been a gentle one, he knew what was expected of a young Englishman. "When I was a boy at Westminster," writes an eminent bishop, "the boys fought one another; they fought the Masters, the Masters fought them; in fact we were ready to fight anyone." So Henry told the boys at Moulins to throw things at the hated teacher—an idea they accepted with enthusiasm. Henry threw an inkwell, hit the blackboard instead of the teacher's head, and in the dead silence that followed, saw that everyone but himself was dutifully immersed in his lessons. Instead of popular acclaim, he received a beating with a heavy ruler, and was locked in a cellar for twenty-four hours on a diet of thin green soup. His parents were informed by the headmaster that their eight-year-old was corrupting the whole school; they could either permit him to be similarly punished in the future, or remove him. Kind, loving parents though they were, they adhered to the maxim of the day: spare the rod and spoil the child. Though Henry was not spared, he refused to be crushed. Attacked by the boys and beaten by the masters, he stuck it out until he horrified his mother one day by coming home with his cheek cut wide open by a blow. No wonder that after Moulins, so-called savages had no terrors for him.

The air of France had not agreed with Henry Peter either, and the family moved to Geneva. Though the Swiss school was an improvement, it was by no means smooth sailing. When Henry was not fighting for his honor with his fists, he was a ringleader in mischief. He bought gun powder for a friend's toy cannon, fired it, singed his eyebrows, and narrowly missed injuring the friend severely. Before he had learned to swim properly, he raced the others far out into the lake and had to be rescued, half drowned. The Swiss headmaster was a kind man who treated his pupils on feast days to fruit tarts and acacia flowers fried in butter, and during the holidays he took his favorites on a climbing trip to Chamonix. Henry reveled in the air and exercise, slept on a straw pallet in a peasant's chalet; drank milk fresh from the cow, and fell in love with mountains for the rest of his life.

Henry Peter Layard's health did not improve and he decided to return to Florence, where, on the earlier visit, he had been free of symptoms. For a family of modest means, the Layards traveled in what seems by modern standards high style. A large carriage with seats before and behind held the mother and father, four boys, a Swiss tutor, two English maids, and a French manservant named Pachot. To spare the horses, the boys walked across the Simplon Pass and up all the inclines with time to spare for catching butterflies. Brother Edgar, who was to become a distinguished naturalist, had a special passion for this common childish sport. Henry, curious about everything, was as keen for art and antiquities—his father's hobby—as for bugs and butterflies. When the entourage passed through Milan and Bologna, Mr. Layard took little Henry to museums and galleries. He afterwards remembered best (because it interested him most) the letters of Lucretia Borgia!

The young connoisseur was even consulted on the advantages and disadvantages of a flat which Henry Peter found for the family in Florence. It was in the Rucellai Palace, a masterpiece of Renaissance architecture sufficiently important to be in the guidebooks today. Henry approved the high-ceilinged rooms, the walls covered in silk damask and hung with old paintings in heavily gilded frames. A few English pounds went a long way in Florence under the Grand Duke Ferdinand of Hapsburg-Lorraine; impoverished nobility such as the Rucellai were delighted to retire to the upper floors of their ancestral homes and rent out the lower ones to the *Inglese*. One room only on those lower floors was forbidden. Henry's romantic imagination conjured up Blue Beard's wives behind that locked door, and one day when his parents were away, he persuaded Pachot to try out a bunch of keys. The door led to a chapel where the embalmed body of a saintly lady of the Rucellai family was preserved under glass—a relic which was a bit too antique even for Henry. He had nightmares about it for several months.

The tutor returned to Switzerland; Henry and Frederick were enrolled in Signor Rellini's *Instituto*, a day school for sons of good Florentine families and the foreign colony. Henry learned fluent

Italian and little else, but enjoyed himself enormously. A portrait of the time shows a little angel: round face framed by silky hair, turned up nose, innocent mouth, lovely eyes like his mother's. The little angel was an imp, but he charmed his teachers at the *Instituto* utterly. The only time he was in trouble was when Signor Rellini called at the *palazzo* to inquire after the health of his favorite pupil —to the astonishment of Mr. Layard. Henry, it turned out, had been skipping school to chase butterflies at Fiesole. His companions on such excursions were usually the children of Walter Savage Landor, the English writer, who had a villa there. It was a "joyous and happy company" that roamed the lovely gardens and groves, stopping at a peasant's cottage for *polenta* and a glass of sour red wine, or stretching out, when the sun was high, in the shade of an old olive tree, to chatter idly, to look down on the tawny houses of Florence, the rooftops which slanted every which way, the Duomo and Giotto's marble tower, as daintily colored as sugar candy. This was a golden time, an idyl he would never forget, which he was to dream of and yearn for in grayer days to come. He envied the Landor children because their freedom seemed more perfect than his; dressed in peasant clothes and barefoot sandals, they wandered about pretty much as they pleased. He envied their hit-or-miss home education; they could prattle ancient Greek as readily as English, and there was no Signor Rellini to check their school attendance. The Jovian figure of their father, his massive head and booming voice, impressed Henry, though the violent temper which he sometimes loosed on his children was embarrassing. The English Colony of Florence did not receive the eccentric Mr. Landor. Henry's father, a good Tory, considered Landor beyond the pale: the man was an atheist and a republican! Nevertheless he instructed his son to read Landor's *Imaginary Conversations* for its prose. Henry Peter could not conceive that the boy might be influenced (as he was) not only by the literary style but by such sentiments as these: "I have read whatever I could find written about the English Constitution; and it appears to me, like the Deity, an object universally venerated but requiring a Revelation . . . Despotism sits nowhere so secure as under the effigy and ensigns of Freedom."[1]

Henry Peter tried to make up for the inadequacies of the *Instituto* by reading aloud to his son from his own excellent library, especially from his favorite Elizabethans: Ben Jonson, Spencer and Shakespeare. Young Henry was encouraged to take down from the shelf any book except those which his father considered unfit to place in childish hands. Henry had his own favorites, one in particular, the title page of which read:

The Arabian Nights Entertainments
consisting of:
One Thousand and One Stories
Related by the Sultaness of the Indies
To divert the Sultan from the Execution of a Vow he
had made to marry a Lady every Day, and have her destroyed next
Morning, to avenge himself for the Disloyalty of his first
Sultaness, etc. containing
An Account of the Customs, Manners, and Religions of the
Eastern Nations, viz. Tartars, Persians and Indians.

Henry must have read this classic in the French translation of the Arabic manuscript made by Antoine Galland about a century earlier, for the first English translation (from Galland) did not come out till he was a grown man. The erotic elements of Sir Richard Burton's later version were not included in the early translations, or one can be sure Henry's father would not have allowed the book to be placed in childish hands. In spite of its purity, however, Henry was romantically affected: "My imagination was so much excited by it that I thought and dreamed of little else but 'jins' and 'ghouls' and fairies and lovely princesses, until I believed in their existence, and even fell in love with a real living damsel. I was deeply smitten with the pretty sister of one of my schoolfellows. I fancied I had a rival in an English boy of my own age. We quarrelled in consequence, and as we were both taking lessons of a fencing master, we determined to settle our differences in mortal combat with foils without buttons. How we were prevented carrying out our bloody intentions I now forget."

He would lie for hours on the marble floor of the salon, in the cool shadow of a great carved table, reading of those princesses with teeth like a cluster of pearls, eyes brighter than the morning star, and lips of coral, seated in pavilions hung with gold brocade curtains and furnished with cushions and couches embroidered in jewels. He read, too, of Sinbad, that intrepid traveler. His interest in the East, already stimulated by his father's stories of Ceylon, was thus supplemented in a grandiose fashion by Scheherazade. When he had spent years in the East himself, he still thought the truest and liveliest picture of its people and their customs was given in the *Arabian Nights;* he would reread it as an old man with almost as much gusto as when he had first read it as a boy. This was the book, he claimed, that had started him on the long adventurous road that led finally to Nineveh.

Though he dreamed often of travel in far places, the boy Layard found excitement and pleasure enough for the time being in Florence. Henry Peter Layard, with no need to make a living, amused himself by collecting illustrations for William Roscoe's *Life of Lorenzo de' Medici*, and young Henry was his father's research assistant. He read all the books on Italian history he could find; drew up a genealogy of Florentine nobility, and went treasure hunting, sometimes with his father, sometimes alone, in obscure quarters of the city, poking into second-hand bookshops, turning over battered volumes in street stalls. When he was lucky he would pick up for a few coins some torn and dusty print of a character mentioned in Roscoe. He grew to know every church and palazzo of importance: where each plot had been hatched, each assassination staged. His father's English visitors could find no better guide to Florence than this eager boy.

He knew his way about the art galleries as well. Henry Peter had taken his sons to the Ufizzi and the Pitti and to numerous private collections, and Henry could make a pretty good guess at the painter of every Florentine picture he saw. The palazzo in which he lived was full of fine paintings; an altarpiece by Filipino

Lippi was on the wall behind Henry's own bed, and there is still visible upon it today, as it hangs in a museum, the mark of a shoe Henry threw at his brother Frederick in a quarrel.

Some boys might have found the continual instruction in aesthetics a bore, or reacted from paternal pushing by having nothing to do with art. Henry merely carried his father's bent a step further by deciding to adopt the career of painter himself. An artist—a Bohemian in the family—was more than the elder Layard had bargained for. He cleverly arranged for Henry to take lessons from a threadbare and mediocre painter who lived in a cell in the Convent of Santa Croce. After copying bad prints of heads and horses for a while, Henry lost interest. But his talent in this direction and the brief training in draughtsmanship were to stand him in good stead.

Unlike the usual upper middle-class household in England, where children were relegated to the nursery and brought up by a nursemaid, the Layards enjoyed a close and intimate family life. When the parents visited Florentine friends in their country villas, Henry, who was a favorite with the Italian ladies, was brought along. The family spent two summers at Cortona. Nearby he had his first taste of field archaeology, watching the excavation of the mysterious Etruscan remains. (These were first studied early in the nineteenth century; the first grottoes with mural paintings were discovered in 1827.) Henry was taken also to Lake Trasimeno, the site of Rome's defeat by Hannibal. At night, with a frightened Italian gardener as his companion, he investigated a nearby ruined castle said to be haunted by ghosts of the slaughtered Romans. Henry met no ghosts and was disgusted.

In Florence the Layards kept open house for artists, writers, students touring Italy to finish their artistic education. One of the visitors was Byron's friend Trelawny. Young Henry listened "with bated breath" to Trelawny's tales of the Greek War of Independence: how with a Greek chieftain he had defended a mountain cave against countless Turks, and had married the chieftain's daughter. Though the Layard's was a Tory household, their oldest son was meeting a good many unconventional people and hearing a good bit about freedom of one sort or another. He envied the children of the scandalous Mr. Landor, without realizing that he himself was developing tastes, attitudes and opinions radically different from a boy of his class brought up in England. His Florentine boyhood caused this son of a conservative family to be, in an age of conformity, a thorough-going nonconformist. His uncle recognized the danger if the parents did not; Benjamin Austen wrote again, pointing out to his sister and her husband that their sons were growing up, and that neither the schooling nor the atmosphere of Italy were proper preparation for the life of an English gentleman. It was time to think of suitable careers for the boys, especially for Henry, who was now twelve. Since Henry's father had no prospects, his uncle promised "to do something for the boy." Henry must attend an English school; after that Mr. Austen would take him into his own law office, and if he did well, he might some day become a partner in the firm.

Once again Mrs. Layard, "the kindest, the most unselfish, and the most generous of women," allowed herself to be persuaded by her strong-willed brother. Her husband was also eager to do the right thing for his children, and felt, since his asthma was much improved, that he should not pamper himself. He agreed to escort Henry and Frederick to a boarding school in England; his wife would follow with the younger boys as soon as she had finished her packing.

They started on the journey almost at once. Not long after their carriage had left the outskirts of the city, Henry Peter Layard was so short of breath that his eldest son took charge of everything: arrangements, fares, baggage. His father was pleased and proud of him, and Henry was quite pleased with himself. But he was bitterly unhappy at leaving his beloved Florence.

Chapter II

"BRITAINS NEVER, NEVER WILL BE SLAVES"
(1829–1839)

Henry's new school was at Richmond, not far from London; a lovely country town with meadows bordering the river Thames. An English boy in an English school at last, he discovered that he was still a queer fish. Having been forced to fight his private, painful Napoleonic War at Moulins, he was now suspected of being a Frog-eater because he spoke French. Or else he was an organ-grinder's son, because he also spoke Italian. His taste for art was considered affected; his political opinions seditious. Again he was accused of corrupting the school. His punishment was to stand on a stool in the dining hall with his jacket turned inside out and give three cheers for well-known demagogues of the day—a punishment that, instead of shaming him, made him more of a rebel than ever.

The time of free-for-all fights was over; the English school system had been reformed. "What we must look for here," said the famous Dr. Arnold of Rugby, "is, first, religious and moral principle; secondly, gentlemanly conduct; thirdly, intellectual ability." This perfectly expressed the views of the Reverend James Bewsher, Henry's new headmaster. He was no worse than the average; kind enough as a rule; not much of a scholar. He did not, like the boys, poke fun at Henry's taste for art and literature; he knew nothing about them. A more unfortunate deficiency was the lack of training in the classics, which were considered unnecessary in Henry's case, since the boy was not going on to a university. Henry enjoyed the classics, when he could make them out on his own; he struggled for a while to turn a Greek tragedy into Latin verse but felt the results were sad. He was always to regret that he was not better grounded in Greek and Latin.

He had a gift for languages, and was, in general, a good student, quicker than most; he even won prizes and praise from the Reverend Mr. Bewsher. When he was not interested, he could not be bothered to study. The same was true in sports: he was a natural athlete but lacked the average British schoolboy's passion for cricket and football; he would far rather take out a boat on the river or walk across country with "Mousy," the French Master, who like himself was the butt of the boys' jokes.

Since his father had temporarily returned to Florence, Henry remained at Richmond during the summer holidays. With no boys to rag him, no teachers to interfere, he used the long summer days to go fishing or to sprawl on a leafy bank with his nose in a book. From a circulating library to which he subscribed from his small allowance, he borrowed travel books, historical novels, and romances of oriental life such as *The Persian Adventurer* by Baillie-Fraser, an adventurer himself. He read Hume, and Gibbon, who was then considered the leading authority on preclassical Mesopotamia, although his sources were limited to the Bible and unreliable Greek accounts. For a week or two Henry thought seriously of becoming an author himself, and began a romance of knights, ladies, and derring-do. He drew neat, precise little sketches of the church towers and thatched cottages in the neighborhood, but left the sketchbook half empty. Like many a talented youngster, he was trying himself out in several directions, jumping from one form of expression to another.

The Christmas holiday was spent in London with his aunt and uncle. Sara Austen was a beautiful woman, clever and ambitious, who fancied herself as a patroness of the arts and was an avid hunter of literary lions. When Henry was not listening eagerly to the parlor conversation among her guests, he haunted the British Museum, where, more than likely, he saw a collection, the first of its kind, of cylinder seals (then thought to be amulets) and bricks with curious decorations (cuneiform inscriptions) recently acquired from the widow of Claudius Rich, late Resident of the

British East India Company at Baghdad. Henry found utterly dreary Blackstone's *Commentaries on the Laws of England,* with which he was expected by Mr. Austen to spend his time profitably; he kept handy a book of history or travel which he could whip out when his uncle was not watching him.

He dutifully changed his name to Austen Henry at the request of Uncle Austen, who was his godfather and his guardian while his parents were out of England. In the autumn of 1833, aged sixteen, he was removed from school and articled as a clerk—apprenticed to the law—in Benjamin Austen's office. He was going to be a solicitor like his uncle because he had no choice. His parents wished it; Mr. Austen took it for granted; he himself had no training or the opportunity to be anything else. He was miserably conscious of being unfitted for the law also. Neither the *Instituto* nor Mr. Bewsher's Academy had provided him with suitable background or discipline. His miscellaneous reading had filled his head with bits and pieces of exotic information which had nothing to do with the law: Scheherazade and Baillie-Fraser only made it more difficult to concentrate on the practical and dull. He envied his schoolmates who were going on to Oxford, but he knew his father could not afford to give him a university education.

His father could send him only an allowance of eight pounds a month for board, lodging, clothes, and whatever else he might need. The "something" which Mr. Austen had promised to do for his nephew did not include spending money. He knew he should be grateful that he did not have to pay for his law training, as the other clerks did; and doubly grateful for the promise of an assured future if he applied himself. Without consultation, a back room was taken for him in a lodging house in New Ormond Street near the Foundling Hospital, within walking distance of his uncle's law chambers in Gray's Inn. An old neighborhood of law courts and offices, it was not then as beautifully kept up as it is today. Dickens, who was himself employed there, calls it "That stronghold of melancholy . . . Indeed I look upon Gray's Inn generally as one of the most depressing institutions in brick and mortar, known to the children of men. Can anything be more dreary than its arid square,

Sahara Desert of the law, with the ugly old tile topped tenements, the dirty windows, the bills To Let, To Let, the door-posts inscribed like gravestones, the crazy gateway giving upon the filthy Lane . . . the dry, hard, atom-like appearance of the whole dust heap?"

On his way to and from work, Henry must almost every day have passed the house at 48 Doughty Street where Dickens, five years his senior and later his friend, was then living. Dickens had long since escaped Gray's Inn, but for young Henry Layard there was no escape in sight. Benjamin Austen's old, well-established firm represented country solicitors in routine cases that came up to London; in all legal practice there could have been none duller. Henry arrived at nine each morning and was set to copying documents or running errands to the law courts. In every spare moment he was expected to read worthy legal treatises such as Blackstone, or *Coke-upon-Littleton*, which was written in the Elizabethan English of James I's Chief Justice. He had no money to spare for books that interested him, nor was he offered the use of the Austen's ample library. He ate dinner alone at a cheap eating place in Fleet Street, usually a six-penny chop and plain water—a beverage then considered less than palatable. After dinner, he was supposed to return to the office to read law till bedtime. Perched on a high, backless stool in a slice of a room that was freezing cold in winter, hot and stuffy in summer, his eyes burning from the dim lamplight and the dust rising from the pages of his book, he would fall asleep in spite of the best intentions. He honestly wished to please his uncle—and even more, his father—but the long paragraphs of legal verbiage seemed the most picayune of quibbling to this romantic boy. When he should have been memorizing precedents, his thoughts would wander to Petrarch and Boccaccio and the hills of Florence. He would never forget his uncle's expression of horror and disgust when, one morning, he owned up to this daydreaming.

He began to shirk the evenings at Gray's Inn; Uncle Austen, snugly at home by his fire, would be none the wiser. The other law clerks, friendly rough diamonds, would go off to a music hall;

Henry could not afford a ticket and didn't really care. He would walk back to his cold little room through streets where gas lamps made vague pools of light in a black fog which smelled of refuse, drains, and fried fish. The flute which he had learned to play at school was now his only solace. Thus, at just seventeen, he lived his own life, and if he ever thought that his uncle and aunt might have been more hospitable to a lonely boy in a strange city, he does not say so.

Noon dinner on Sundays, the one meal when he was invited to the Austens, was the high spot of the week. The food was undoubtedly solid, the company intellectual. Among the distinguished guests were Sir Charles Fellows, a famous traveler; well-known painters such as Turner and Eastlake; Isaac Disraeli and his son Benjamin. Mrs. Austen, a self-appointed literary critic, had encouraged "Disraeli the Younger" when he was almost unknown. She had induced a publisher to bring out his novel *Tremaine; or the Man of Refinement,* but denied rumors circulated by her friends that she had helped him to write the more successful *Vivian Grey.* To recover from the overwork involved in writing this the young author had gone abroad with the Austens, and had passed through Moulins, where Henry had met him. Disraeli's black curly hair, his affectations of manner and dress, had made a lasting impression on the little boy. Since meeting him again at his aunt's house, Henry had made a point of reading Disraeli's novels, which he admired enormously. Boyishly he fired questions at the author: What was it like to travel in the East? Were the orange groves of Corfu really so lush? Disraeli replied, with a sniff, that he really couldn't be expected to remember everything he'd written. Henry thought him conceited and unkind; nevertheless he continued to be fascinated by the man: by that ugly interesting face, and the witty remarks, to say nothing of the embroidered waistcoats, white pantaloons, and shoes blooming with red rosettes. At this time Disraeli had only just entered politics. Mrs. Austen liked to relate how, once when a discussion was raging, Disraeli said heatedly, "When I am Prime Minister, I shall do so and so." He was interrupted by general laughter. He paused in his pacing of the room, struck the mantelpiece with his fist, and cried, "Laugh as you may, I *shall* be Prime Minister." Some thirty years later, he proved his point.

It must have pleased the young law clerk to know that this brilliant man, who had been articled to a solicitor, had spent some time in Uncle Austen's office, and had also found it intolerable. He too had taken nonlegal books to chambers; had, in fact, been discovered reading Chaucer there. Mr. Austen had written to the culprit's father that since Benjamin obviously found the study of law repugnant, he should be allowed to pursue a literary career, which seemed to appeal to him. But poor young Henry did not have a wealthy father to support him until he should discover an appealing career to pursue.

Pointing out that it was a father's duty to supervise the education of his sons, Benjamin Austen had persuaded Henry's parents to return from Florence in the summer of 1834. They settled in a cottage near Aylesbury, now a London suburb, but then far enough out from the city for its air to be considered excellent for asthma sufferers. The Austens were spending the summer in neighboring Cheltenham, where Henry was invited to visit, and permitted to ride one of their horses over the hills—always thereafter his idea of the greatest sport on earth. He was happy to be reunited with his parents and to see his father apparently quite contented with his garden and his books. A short-lived contentment—Henry Peter Layard was taken ill with lung congestion brought on by his asthma and died, quite suddenly, early in October. The three younger boys were away at school; Henry, alone with his emotional mother, carried the double burden of comforting her and controlling his own grief. His father had been something more than the usual austere Victorian parent; he had been guide and friend, if not philosopher. After the recent years of separation, it was a severe blow to lose him again so soon.

During the following winter, Henry himself fell ill. He put it down to "the work and confinement in a lawyer's office." Emotional strain may also have been to blame; and the London climate, to which a boy brought up in the mild climate of Italy was unaccustomed. The London weather was no different and the comforts were fewer then than now. The cold was bone-chilling indoors as well as out; tiny grate fires or stoves that gave off more fumes than warmth were the only heat. Law clerks, trying to copy documents, sat hunched on their stools with mufflers around their necks, and hands too stiff to hold the pen. Henry would hurry from bleak law chambers to drafty courtrooms through streets where no street-cleaning department removed the ankle-deep mud and slush. At night the north wind whistled through the rotten old window frames of his lodging (no weather-stripping then) and damp penetrated the moldy walls. Henry's mother was convinced that her eldest son's health was delicate like that of his father. On the contrary, had he not been naturally robust, he would have come down with tuberculosis, which was common. The doctor, at any rate, advised "a change of air" during the summer holiday.

From now on, with such a good excuse, he went abroad every summer: to Switzerland for mountain climbing; to France and Italy for art and amusement; to Russia and the Scandinavian countries. In Copenhagen he looked over the recently formed collection of prehistoric northern remains; he does not tell us whether he realized at the time that an antiquarian revolution was taking place under the leadership of the Danish and Swedish scholars. The eighteenth-century taste for classical antiquities was beginning to give way to a quickening interest in things prehistoric; romantic explanations of early man were just beginning to be replaced (amid fierce protests) by attempts at scientific reasoning. Yet prehistoric archaeology could not be said to exist until the results of the Danish antiquarian revolution were spread throughout Europe, and the work of Layard and his contemporaries had taken place.

The young Layard was not particularly interested in prehistory; he thought the old Norse manuscripts describing Viking voyages to North America at least as worthy of attention as bones and primitive tools from the bogs of Denmark. But he found a bit of everything to suit a normal young man on these summer holidays. Returning again and again to his beloved Italy, he picnicked at Lake Maggiore, sang and danced by moonlight, flirted with a golden-haired, blue-eyed *Contessina*—so successfully that he barely avoided a duel with the lovely lady's jealous husband. He attended the secret meetings of Cavour and other young advocates of Italian independence, knowing he ran the risk of jail if discovered. He sat up half the night discussing the latest political treatises, including the works of Carlo Botta, exiled historian who had recently died in Paris. Some years later, under very different circumstances, he was to meet Paul Émile Botta, the historian's son.

Each winter he returned more reluctantly to Gray's Inn, to study the letter but certainly not to enter into the spirit of the law. In the evenings he read for pleasure, wrote articles for a monthly, attended the Italian Opera, and played second flute with amateur groups. He was beginning to find himself, to meet the sort of men he liked and do the things he enjoyed even if Benjamin Austen did not approve. He worked at research and translations from the French and Italian, using the money he earned and every cent he could save—often doing without the six-penny chop—to buy books, usually at auction. His little library in French, Italian, and English was as neatly catalogued as a museum collection.

Henry Crabb Robinson, a successful barrister and patron of the arts, whom he had met in Paris, invited Henry to Sunday-morning breakfast parties where the other guests were many prominent painters and writers. Among them was Wordsworth, "venerable and stately," and very kind to the unknown young man. Henry cherished for years a slip of paper upon which he had jotted down the translation of a Michelangelo sonnet as Wordsworth dictated it to him. His politics had always been liberal, and now his religious views followed suit; through Robinson, who called himself a Philosophical Radical, he met the celebrated orator, Anti-Corn-Law Leaguer and Unitarian minister, W. J. Fox. He began to attend the Unitarian Chapel. Benjamin Austen, a strict Church of England man, was horrified. He accused Mr. Crabb Robinson of unsettling Henry's mind, of turning him away from the law to frivolous pursuits. Sara Austen, instead, drew the cultivated barrister into her circle, and begged him to keep her wayward nephew on the right path. But Henry's dislike of the law only grew more acute as time went by.

He had served his five years as an articled clerk, and the thought of graduating into a solicitorship filled him with disgust instead of satisfaction. He could not hide his feelings, and it is not surprising therefore that his uncle refused to give him the partnership which had been more or less promised to him. All his friends also told him that he obviously had no bent for the law; even Crabb Robinson now took the part of Benjamin Austen. Henry was advised that he would be a failure if he attempted to set up for himself. He thought his talents might be better suited to a barrister's career, where he would be dealing in human foibles and crimes rather than in petty lawsuits and paper work, but his uncle discouraged this also, pointing out that Henry had no money for the additional training, nor to live on while he was acquiring it. Benjamin Austen was disappointed in him; Sara Austen, having decided that young Henry was a failure, no longer welcomed him to her salon. His mother was unhappy about him. She had always been over-sensitive to any setback—a "constitutional infirmity" which her son believed himself to have inherited. At this point he was so depressed and upset that he could scarcely function.

At the crucial moment, his paternal uncle Charles Layard arrived from Ceylon, where he had been for many years an important official. Several of his sons were also employed profitably in various capacities there. Uncle Charles told Henry that it was not necessary to be a barrister in order to practice criminal law in Ceylon; an ordinary law certificate would be sufficient. He suggested that his nephew join the other Layards in the magic island. Should he fail in the law, there were plenty of other excellent opportunities.

Even if Henry had not been, since childhood, under the spell of his father's stories of Ceylon, he would have seized any chance to escape London and his Uncle Austen. Moreover the perfume of the Orient, which so many Victorians were to sniff, was already in the air—had been, in fact, since Regency days. Who did not know Byron's *Destruction of Sennacherib*?

The Assyrian came down like a wolf on the fold,
And his cohorts were gleaming in purple and gold . . .

The grandiloquent poetry of the Romantics was based on Bible story, legend and pure fantasy. The Victorians were to come to grips with the East in actuality. The Queen had been crowned with pomp and circumstance in 1838; the festivities glittered with official representatives of the East as well as the West. "All this for a woman!" cried Sarim Effendi, the Turkish Ambassador, too dazzled to find his place in the ceremonial procession. The great days of the British Empire were just around the corner. In India, Persia, and the widespread Turkish dominions, Englishmen were already serving as diplomats, advisers, administrators and explorers—and writing books about their experiences. Young Henry Layard had read Claudius Rich's memoirs on Babylon and Assyria; a history of Persia by Sir John Malcolm, East India Company Representative to the Shah; James Morier's popular *Adventures of Hajji Baba of Ispahan*, and many others. It cannot be claimed that his love affair with the East was unique.

So he decided to try his fortune in Ceylon. Benjamin Austen was deeply offended. Although he could no longer promise a partnership to one who found the law so "repugnant" and whose mind was so unsettled, he felt compelled to warn his nephew of the risks involved. He pointed out that Henry was entirely ignorant of criminal law, and might find himself stranded without means of support, faraway from his family. Benjamin Austen, too, after his fashion, seems to have had a gift for unsettling minds. Uncle Charles Layard, on the other hand, was extremely helpful during his brief appearance. He not only encouraged his nephew, but he introduced him to a possible traveling companion. Having learned how to deal with the wily Oriental by working for a mercantile firm in Morocco, Edward Mitford was hopefully going out to Ceylon to be a coffee planter. Being "nearly a decade" older than Henry, he was somewhat taken aback by the youthful appearance of the prospective fellow traveler—smooth-faced, blue-eyed, with flowing hair à la Byron. But since it would be handy to have someone by "in case of danger or sickness in the barbarous regions to be traversed,"[1] the two were soon agreed.

Mitford's *A Land March*, the book about his travels written many years later when he was, in fact, a successful coffee planter, has little personality and none of Layard's humor. It resembles a dozen such narratives of Englishmen in the East, set down at the request of friends and family, and now forgotten. It is difficult to tell from it what sort of man Mitford was. He does not mention Layard by name, but as "my companion," although the companion, by the time the book was published, was a distinguished citizen. Perhaps this is the Victorian respect for privacy in print (though Layard in his own *Early Adventures* refers to "Mr. Mitford" frequently and favorably). Perhaps there was more friction than either would admit publicly; whenever there was a difference of opinion, Mitford was for the cautious (and sensible) plan; Layard for the risky one. But Mitford was also, according to Layard, "of adventurous disposition," and he was admittedly the initiator of the adventurous scheme they were to follow. Since he suffered from seasickness, he proposed that they make the trip overland through Europe, Central Asia, and India. For Henry, this realized his childhood dream of seeing the lands of the Tartars, Persians, and Indians, and Baghdad, city of Scheherazade.

Hardly anything was then known of Central Asia except that it was an unsafe place to be. Henry's family called the plan madness. Henry Crabb Robinson told him it was a wild-goose chase. Having made up his mind, Henry was not to be shaken; he had a mystic sense that the journey was the sole way in which he would find a career more suited to him than the law, and that he would survive its dangers. He could hardly wait to escape the continual arguments with his Uncle Austen, who still felt himself the moral guardian of his twenty-two-year-old nephew. Always on the liberal side, Henry now supported the agitation for the repeal of the Corn Laws, which labeled him as a radical, and to be a radical was, in the eyes of Benjamin Austen and his class, to be capable of any crime. Young Henry yearned to stand on his own feet and by his own opinions without so many family quarrels.

His first step was to get the certificate without which he could not practice any sort of law in Ceylon. He passed his examinations at the Law Institute without trouble. "I presume that I had not altogether thrown away my time," he comments drily. "On the 10th of June (1839) I received the order of the Chief Justice that I should be sworn, admitted, and enrolled an attorney of H. M. Court of the Queen's Bench at Westminster."

He next began to prepare for the wild-goose chase with practical thoroughness. He made a point of meeting a number of travelers whose experiences would be helpful to him. Sir Charles Fellows, a frequent guest at the Austens', who had discovered Greek and Roman ruins in Anatolia, urged him to take a hitherto unexplored route through the center of Asia Minor to look for more. Baillie-Fraser, whose popular books he had so enjoyed as a boy, filled him in on Persia. He consulted the Royal Geographical Society on itineraries, and asked if he could be useful. He was told that the Society would be delighted to receive any information he might collect, particularly in the eastern district of Persia on the border of Afghanistan, known as the Seistan.

Then, as now, spheres of influence in the Middle East were bones of contention, the chief contenders being Great Britain and Imperial Russia. Sir John MacNeil, who had recently withdrawn as British representative at the court of the Shah, urged the two young Englishmen, while in Persia, to see if they could learn what the Czar was up to. The diplomatic break might, of course, make it impossible for them to enter the country at all, and impossible to protect them if they did get in. Nevertheless, Sir John asked Layard and Mitford to take a route via the Seistan if they could. Alexander the Great, on his return from the Indus, had sent some troops through the region; since then no European was known to have penetrated it. Two English officers had recently been murdered in the attempt. But of course, any new route to India was of great interest to the Foreign Office. As bait, Sir John told Layard of a colony of fire worshipers and some remarkable ancient remains near the mysterious Lake of Farrah. Henry's enthusiasm for such things had not diminished since the days when he had explored the haunted castle at Cortona. He was too young and too healthy to worry about danger; Mitford, who had traveled in wild Morocco, made light of it also.

In a short time, their plans were set: "The result of our enquiries, and of the advice and information we received from these and other sources, was that we determined to proceed through Dalmatia to Montenegro; to cross Turkey in Europe to Constantinople; to traverse Asia Minor, and visit Syria and Palestine on our way to Baghdad. We were thence to enter Persia by Hamadan, to explore the mountains of Luristan, and to attempt, starting from Ispahan, taking the road by Yezd, to reach the Lake of Farrah and the Seistan. After exploring that part of Central Asia, then unknown, we hoped to visit Kandahar, to enter India through Afghanistan, and to traverse the whole of the Peninsula to its southernmost point, whence we could reach our destination without further difficulty. We calculated that it would take us about a year to execute this gigantic scheme."

Henry read whatever he could find on Persia, and the little then available on cuneiform and Old Persian writing. Among the Royal Geographical Society publications was a paper, "Notes on a March from Zohab to Khuzistan," by Major Henry Rawlinson, former military adviser in Persia. In the course of a punitive expedition against the ferocious Bakhtiyari tribes of Luristan, Rawlinson had learned of ancient remains in a mountain valley called Sûsan. Though unable to reach the place, he suspected it of being "Shushan the Palace" of the Prophet Daniel's vision. Henry promised the Royal Geographical Society to investigate Sûsan if it was at all possible.

Sir John MacNeil warned the two young men that they must expect to be held up in Persia. "You must travel as important personages with a retinue of servants and an adequate escort, or alone, as poor men, with nothing to excite the cupidity of the people amongst whom you will have to mix. If you cannot afford to adopt the first course, you must take the latter."

There was no question of which course to choose; neither of them had much money. When public transport was not available, they would go on horseback, find their own way with compass and maps, and employ a guide only when strictly necessary. Each bought a double-barreled gun for defense, for shooting game, and, in Mitford's case, for specimens of birds, which he knew how to stuff. For stormy weather and sleeping out, they had long woolen cloaks which could be rolled and strapped behind the saddle, together with a Levinge bed, which was a sleeping bag of sheets equipped with a mosquito curtain. They planned to travel without a servant, which was as unusual for young men of their class as it would be to travel with one today.

In order that his reports to the Royal Geographical Society might be accurate, Henry learned from a retired sea captain to measure altitudes, fix points, plot out routes. He bought a pocket sextant, artificial horizon, prismatic compass, aneroid barometer, thermometer, and a good silver watch, which, on the advice of Sir Charles Fellows, he painted black so as to make it less tempting. A doctor friend showed him the use of the lancet and the tourniquet, and the dressing of simple wounds; taught him the symptoms and treatment of diseases he would be likely to meet: dysentery, intermittent fever, and ophthalmia. He was also provided with a small medicine kit. Because he had always hoped someday to travel in the East, he had already studied the Arabic characters and a bit of Persian.

On July 10, 1839, Henry Layard, aged twenty-two, embarked for the lands of the Arabs, Tartars and Persians, via Ostend. As his ship steamed down the Thames, as the Tower of London faded away in the fog behind him, he had "mixed feelings." His relief at being free was tinged with second thoughts: What if Uncle Austen was right? How humiliating it would be to fail at this too. His parting from his mother, who had come up to London to see him off, had been difficult; she was anxious for his health, as usual, and for his safety; she wept. In her generous fashion she had provided him, out of her marriage settlement, with six hundred pounds. When this was used up, he would have to be self-supporting, because no more could be spared; she had other sons to bring up. Henry carried half the sum with him in the form of a letter of credit; the other half would be held for him by an agent in Ceylon.

He was too optimistic to think that he would fail utterly. But he felt guilty about leaving his mother, always so loving and so kind. "Had I remained," he writes, "I should in all probability have passed through life in the obscure position of a respectable lawyer."

Chapter III

ALL HAIL, JERUSALEM!

(July 1839–January 1840)

Visiting the art galleries and other conventional spots, Edward
Mitford and Henry Layard traveled down through Europe by
dusty *diligence* and post-carriage to Venice, where they stopped
for a few days at Danielli's Hotel before boarding a steamer for
Trieste. At Fiume, the last outpost of civilization, both young men
were delighted at the prospect of the new experiences ahead, "and
the risks which we were assured we were about to run, added not
a little to the charm of our position." They transferred to a rude
post-wagon without springs, which, on a rough road, shook up its
passengers so badly that Mitford remembered every uncomfortable
detail fifty years later. A day's journey beyond Spalatro (modern
Split) all roads vanished. They hired horses and Dalmatian guides,
heavily armed, who walked along singing national airs or carrying
on conversations with unseen shepherds high on the mountainsides. Out of the darkness one night came other voices, which
caused the guides to urge extra haste—these were dangerous men,
Turchi! They were probably only simple Bosniac Christian shepherds, Layard remarks, but to him they had the glamor of being
his first Turks.

The Englishmen had letters of introduction to important personages along the way, among them the hereditary Prince-Bishop
of Montenegro. The *Vladika's* stronghold at Cettigne was a shock.
Its tower was crowned by several dozen Turkish heads, sun-black-
ened and bloody, with long tufts of hair waving in the breeze like
pennants. The Vladika, Prince Danielo, all seven feet of him clad

in the black silk robes of a Greek priest, welcomed them in halting
French. They were royally entertained for several days in the primitive whitewashed palace, which contained, among other conven-
iences, an imported billiard table. When a fresh batch of heads was
rolled out at the prince's feet, he assured his guests that, as a cul-
tured man who had visited the capitals of Europe, he was trying
to educate his people, but some old customs were necessary to
maintain a warlike spirit in the holy struggle against the Albanian
Moslems. Layard, in spite of the "loathsome" head collection,
could not help but be impressed by the Vladika, with his gold
cross and his gun—and he was a poet besides!

On the way to the Albanian border, the traveling companions
had their first recorded difference of opinion. The Vladika had
recommended a visit to newly discovered underground caverns;
Layard was eager to explore them; Mitford refused to go below. On
re-emerging, Layard had to admit that the stalagmites and stalac-
tites had not been worth the risk of a broken limb (the rope on
which he was lowered had parted) or of getting lost in the underground passages.

At Scutari Layard entered at last the Eastern world of which
he had dreamed since early childhood. He was so agape that he
could hardly follow his guide through the labyrinth of his first
Eastern bazaar. Shafts of dusty sunshine streamed down from
openings in the vaulted roof; overburdened donkeys, swarthy men,
veiled women with kohl-rimmed eyes jostled him in the narrow
aisles; rugs, harness, copper pots and trays were piled on either
side, under a hanging frieze of embroidered vests, scarves, sashes.
Solemn Turks with fierce black moustaches sat beside their merchandise, drawing smoke through bubbling water pipes; and over
it all hung the pungent odor of broiling *kebab* and of spices in
bulging sacks. "The change since passing the borders of Christian
Europe was now complete," writes Layard, entranced.

A letter to the governor of Scutari produced post-horses and an
armed escort for the long overland journey across Albania, Bul-
garia, Macedonia and Thrace to Constantinople. Being anxious
to reach Anatolia before the cold weather set in, Layard and Mit-

ford rode as hard as the stony mountain trails and the endurance of their horses would permit (sometimes "at a wild gallop"). On September 13, they spied in the distance the dome and minarets of *Hagia Sophia*, once the greatest of Eastern churches. At the crumbling walls of old Byzantium, they had to pay a fee for something they would gladly have paid to avoid: fumigation (and near suffocation) by sulphur smoke against the plague. They entered Stambul by the Gate of the Seven Towers, rode through narrow dirty streets for almost an hour, crossed a bridge of boats, and found rooms at Roboli's Hotel in the European quarter of Pera.

Almost immediately Layard collapsed with a first bout of the malaria from which he was to suffer frequently thereafter. Known as the ague or intermittent fever, this illness was regarded as inevitable for both natives and visitors in the East. A young Armenian doctor, highly recommended because he had studied at Edinburgh, treated Layard in the approved fashion by bleeding with the lancet; after which he drew a circle on the patient's stomach with pen and ink and ordered it to be filled with leeches. Layard was in a high fever, delirious and close to death for several days. That he survived "the good doctor's" ministrations is a tribute to the constitution of Mrs. Layard's delicate boy. When his temperature finally subsided, he was too weak to travel. Mitford therefore went ahead overland around the Sea of Mamora with the three horses they had bought and Giorgio, a Cypriot Greek, as dragoman and cook. As soon as Layard could stand on his feet, he sailed across in a caïque to join them at Mudanya.

This was another climactic moment, for here a new continent—Asia—began. They would not follow the coastal roads, more or less well traveled, but, acting on the suggestion of Sir Charles Fellows, would plunge into the heart of Asia Minor, where there were few roads or caravansaries, guiding themselves by compass and maps. The Turkish authorities at Constantinople, after urging them not to go, had reluctantly supplied an Imperial *Firman*—the passport and permit issued to European travelers in the Turkish dominions —but it might prove to be worse than useless. Asia Minor was in a state of chaos. Mahemet Ali Pasha, the powerful Governor of

Egypt, had rebelled, sent an army north, and cut the Sultan's troops to pieces at Nizib. Disbanded Turkish soldiers and deserters were on the loose, living by robbery. No one knew where the loyalty of the population lay.

Layard and Mitford put their faith in the Turkish peasants and minor officials, by whom they had been treated with the greatest courtesy in European Turkey. But they held their guns ready as they rode out from Mudanya on October 6. In the saddlebags were the prime necessities: instruments, maps, ammunition; the third horse carried changes of clothing and a few other items, including a little tea, their only luxury. Spread over the packsaddle were the sleeping quilts, straddled by Giorgio, splendid in Greek kilts with a long knife in his belt. He was a typical Greek: quick-witted, brave, and with an independent manner (which Mitford considered insolence at times).

On the first day they rode nine hours, climbing heights which rose sheer from the sea, with the pine-covered slopes of snow-capped Mount Olympus above them. A track between classic olive groves and vineyards led towards Apollonia where they would carry out their first commission for the Royal Geographical Society: to map the true course of the river Rhyndacus. They slept that night in a shepherd's hut, cooking supper from their own provisions. Layard had never been happier. He was free at last: no Uncle Austen to denounce this as unfit for an English gentleman; no mother to fret over him. Only the extra charm of danger was lacking; the guns were never used against anything more ferocious than partridges for lunch.

Layard, as he jogged along, conscientiously kept up a notebook, ruled off into spaces representing each half hour's progress (about a mile and a half) in which he noted down compass bearings, names of villages and streams, the character of the country, crops, and other pertinent details. It was a demanding job, but it was also a form of entertainment when the pace of the horses seemed unbearably slow. This was his only admission that anything was ever dull. He was fascinated by the novelty of everything he saw, heard, and tasted, such as "a delicious sweet of honey and cream called *kymak*, made from the milk of the buffalo." He had untiring enthusiasm, an untiring eye, and a keen sense of humor about the foibles of others and the difficulties he got into himself.

Central Anatolia was largely a blank on the map he carried; when it was not, geographical details—the river Rhyndacus for example—were laid down in the wrong places. Nor was it easy to pry correct information from the natives. Once, when he and Mitford had been searching wearily for a town marked on the map, but apparently nonexistent, they asked a camel driver from where he had just come.

"From over there," said the man, pointing.

"But from what town did you come?"

"The town is there." He pointed again.

"But what is the name of the town?"

The most that they could get out of him was that it was a settlement vaguely in the direction of Smyrna (which was a hundred or so miles away). The typical Moslem dislike for giving a definite answer could be inconvenient when you were lost in unknown country—and trying to map it for the Royal Geographical Society besides!

They traveled from village to village; each community had an *oda*—a sleeping room set aside for strangers—and, for a few piastres, supplied the best supper it could produce. Layard enjoyed these evenings when the "honest, simple, and hospitable Turks" crowded into the oda to satisfy their curiosity about the Franks (a generic term, ever since the Crusades, for Europeans in the East). Mitford's reaction was different: "As long as one had information to obtain respecting the country and the roads, this is all very well, but it takes time to reconcile yourself to endure their smoke and stupidity, while you dress, wash, eat and write, until they have seen you fairly into bed."

Occasionally they camped out with the Ourouks, who were Turcoman nomads reputed to be brigands, and who proved to be the kindest of hosts. As soon as the strangers dismounted, women and children would bring brush for a fire, and a tray of stew, fried bread, cheese, and grape honey. Afterward the Ourouk men would gather around the fire to talk; most had never before laid eyes on a Frank. It was usually late by the time the guests lay down to sleep, warm and snug under fine, bright Ourouk blankets, with a starlit sky above and the fires of the wanderers sparkling on the mountainsides all around them. Before dawn the encampment would be awake, dismantling their white felt huts and loading up the camels. Layard and Mitford would politely decline an invitation to join the slow-moving group, and go on their way.

This same country of central Asia Minor, so wild and trackless, had been the site of a flourishing civilization until well past Roman times. The crumbling arches of Roman bridges spanned the streams; graceful columns rose from thickets alive with snakes; slabs of white marble inscribed with Greek letters were built into the walls of squalid village houses. Cliffs were pitted with the burial caves of vanished races. Stone lions at the mouth of a tomb suggested to Layard a necropolis of the Phrygians, who were contemporaries of the Homeric Greeks and Trojans. (New metaphors were added to the English language by two Phrygian kings: Midas of the Golden Touch, and Gordius, whose complicated skeins of power were symbolized by the Gordian knot.) In the same place there were crosses carved on the walls and the largest tomb appeared to have been used as a church, perhaps by early Christians in hiding. Layard spent a day copying Greek inscriptions at Konia (Greek Iconium), which Paul and Barnabas visited on their first missionary journey. Driven from Iconium, the apostles preached next at Lystra, where they were stoned. More successful on his second journey, Paul founded a church at Lystra. Destroyed down to the soil during the Arab invasion, only the stone lintels and ruined vaults of churches remained, scattered over a barren little valley on the lip of black volcanic mountains. The natives called it Bin Bir Kilisse—the place of One Thousand and One Churches. Mitford counted the ruins of twenty-three (more recent explorers, Gertrude Bell and Sir William Ramsay, estimated about twenty-eight). Shepherds were living in the underground crypts and sheltering their flocks in the aisles of Byzantine basilicas; the frescoed walls were well preserved at the time of Layard's visit, except that the saints' eyes had been scratched out.

A Turkish village of a few fever-stricken peasants stood on the site of Seleucia; time-worn sculpture and Greek inscriptions built into crumbling mediaeval walls were the only signs of the city that had once rivaled the wealth of Tarsus. In the Greek city of Soli, restored by Pompey and renamed Pompeiopolis, buildings, columns, tombs, and amphitheater stood in an impenetrable jungle inhabited by wild boars. Fields and brush filled what had once been a busy harbor.

From the Sea of Marmora, across the central tablelands, and down to the Mediterranean through the Taurus range by hitherto unexplored passes, the young Englishmen traced the scattered relics of Romans, Greeks, Phrygians, and even earlier peoples. Layard sketched, copied inscriptions, listened to local legends, made notes, and ventured some shrewd guesses as to the original names and histories of these lost cities. Yet he was distressed at his own ignorance. "Unfortunately neither my companion nor myself had sufficiently prepared ourselves for exploring regions so rich in classic and historic associations, and so full of objects probably new to science. I had turned my attention but little to archaeology, and I had but a smattering of scientific knowledge of any kind. I never regretted more the incompleteness of my early education. However the experiences I had acquired of Eastern life and manners and the information that I had gathered through intercourse with people, were to prove thereafter of use to me. I had seen much, and I had passed many happy and delightful days, not withstanding the toil and privations to which we had been exposed. And, above all, I felt and enjoyed my independence."

Asia Minor had been hard work, hard riding, and hard sleeping. At Tarsus the travelers returned to civilization as the house guests of Mr. Barker, a British resident of many years. Tarsus was crowded with the Egyptian soldiers of Mahemet Ali Pasha, improperly clothed for the cold Syrian winter, sick, and half starved. Since they had not been paid in twenty months, they supported themselves by breaking into houses and bazaars. The once opulent city was a pest hole; insects swarmed from its marshy, choked-up river; stench rose from the animal carcasses littering its streets. Conditions in Alexandretta and Antioch were no better, but the scenery of Syria was beautiful: orange groves in full fruit, flowing brooks and lovely gardens. And tombs and ruins and sculptures for Layard to sketch and puzzle over; and another comfortable English home to stay in at Suedia, where the father of their host in Tarsus had a villa. Layard was interested in the elder Mr. Barker's experiments with fruit and silkworms, and in his gossip about the eccentric Lady Hester Stanhope, who lived on Mount Lebanon in oriental style and was regarded as a mad prophetess by the Arabs. Mr. Barker organized excursions: to ancient Antioch; to rock-cut sculptures at Mount Silpius (later identified as Hittite); to the column upon which St. Simeon Stylites perched for thirty years. Layard measured the pedestal and agreed with Gibbon that the saint's seat was not so narrow as had been made out.

In Aleppo he had a recurrence of fever. He treated himself as instructed by the doctor in Constantinople, plus doses of quinine. Neither the illness nor its unpleasant corrective nor the "toil and privations" of the previous weeks cut down his phenomenal energy. By day he explored the city and at night enjoyed parties where Levantine ladies in costumes calculated to hide none of their fine points did stately dances to the dulcimer while their husbands discussed prices in the bazaar. "There was, of course, no conversation of an intellectual kind at such meetings," remarks Layard.

The worn-out horses were sold but the travelers hired donkeys and were only kept from visiting the ruins of Baalbek by heavy snow in the mountain passes. Layard made a side trip to the famous Cedars of Lebanon, cut his name on one, as many had done before him, visited Maronite convents and rejoined Mitford at Beirut in time for Christmas. Here Giorgio left them, worn out too. Layard and Mitford were delayed at Tsoor (ancient Tyre) by a howling storm and could not see the ruins that were visible on the sea bottom in calm weather. On the second day of the New Year, 1840, they set out for Jerusalem.

Layard was depressed by conditions in Palestine; he had never seen a more miserable population. An old Arab whom they met on the road told Mitford: "We have sold our carpets; we have sold the ornaments of our wives and daughters, our horses, and how are we to meet fresh demands? We cannot plough, for our children are taken as soldiers and none are left to work; we cannot deliver ourselves from oppression or strike a blow for our own, for we have no arms. Why do the Ingleez allow this? Where are the Oroos? Where the Sultan of the Franks? Will no one assist us to throw off this Pasha's iron yoke?"

A tragic tale of a different sort was told by the Franciscan friars of the convent on Mount Carmel. The visitor whose name was just above Layard's in the guestbook, a charming young French count, had died of poisoned coffee after dining with a neighboring sheikh; he had, unwittingly, insulted one of the sheikh's servants. These stories did not add to the joys of travel, nor did the fleas in the Arab huts where they were forced to spend a couple of nights after leaving the Franciscan hostel at Nazareth. Palestine, in fact, had little to recommend it but the wild flowers on the Galilee hills: scarlet anemonies, lavender cyclamen, and a carpet of tiny yellow, white and pink blossoms. And the graceful Arab girls in Madonna-like garments of blue and red.

Judea was a mournful and deserted land of "barren stony hills succeeding each other like the great rolling waves of the Atlantic," a land of empty villages ruined by the tax collector, a treeless landscape save for the wintery gray olives, a country of unrelieved solitude. No pilgrim crusader could have been more overjoyed than Layard when, after a weary three-day ride from Nablus, the dome of the Mosque of Omar and the Church of the Holy Sepulchre came in sight, followed by the walls and gates of the city, with Mount Zion in the background. Layard was reminded of a verse by Tasso:

> *Ecco apparir Gerusalem si vede;*
> *Ecco aditar Gerusalem si scorge;*
> *Ecco da mille voci unitamente*
> *Gerusalemme salutar si sente.*

(Behold Jerusalem in prospect lies!
Behold Jerusalem salutes their eyes!
At once a thousand tongues repeat the name,
And hail Jerusalem with loud acclaim.)

The first sight of Jerusalem is always a special experience, whether one is Unitarian or Church of England, Catholic, Jew, Moslem, or nothing at all. The Moslem minarets and Christian cupolas glitter in that clear air with a particular radiance; the Temple is lost but not forgotten. One is reminded that this city was thought to be the center of the center of the world. But when the two tired Englishmen pushed in through the Damascus Gate in a crowd of camels, donkeys, and screeching Arabs, their awe gave way to disgust. The Holy City had suffered grievously under both Turks and Egyptians; it smelled and looked even worse than Tarsus. Garbage collection was of course unknown; sewage was taken care of by the simple method of emptying chamber pots from windows into the narrow streets—and woe to the passer-by who did not watch out for it! Blind beggars whined for alms in the name of Allah on every corner; Jews beat their breasts at the Wailing Wall; and within the Holy Sepulchre, Roman Catholics and Greek Orthodox fought bloody battles over which sect owned the rights to the sacred places.

The political aspects of this struggle, as Layard reports them, have a familiar ring. Russia, through her consul and the Greek Orthodox clergy, was extending her influence in Palestine, Syria, and the Lebanon. Orthodox monks infiltrated the Maronite convents; the Russian Consul claimed to champion the cause of downtrodden native Christians. The opposition was represented by France, the Roman Catholic Church and its priests—a struggle for political power in the guise of religion.

Disappointed in the current scene, Layard turned his attention to archaeological sites, which held increasing fascination for him. He took daily walks about the city guided by the head of an English Protestant mission, but the identification of places mentioned in the Gospels, he observed, had been made on purely legendary and superstitious grounds. Little investigation was allowed. "Although I could not fail to be interested by my visit to Jerusalem," he writes, "I was not much edified by it. I was not sorry when the time came for me to leave it."

He was eager to see Petra, the mysterious Nabatean stronghold of which he had read in the works of Burckhardt, its discoverer. Johann Ludwig Burckhardt, known as the Sheikh Ibrahim, was a Swiss who became a Moslem. In this guise he had been able to explore many places forbidden to an infidel. Layard suggested to Mitford that they make for their next objective, Damascus, via the country east of Jordan. Some fifty years later he was considerably miffed to read in Mitford's book that he had left "for an excursion in the Hauran." He did not consider it an excursion lightly undertaken; his purpose was archaeological: "to visit Petra, Ammon, Gerash, and other ruins of ancient cities in the Syrian desert."

Mitford pointed out that midwinter was no time to camp in the desert. It was so cold in their Jerusalem quarters that they had to keep a charcoal brazier going all night and once were almost fatally overcome by its fumes. Mr. Young, the British Consul at Jerusalem, was strongly against such a trip; the wilderness south of the Dead Sea was infested with Arab tribes that were well-known thieves and murderers. Layard had read too many romantic tales of Arab hospitality to give the warning more than passing notice. Even if the rumors were not exaggerated, an unostentatious style of traveling, he thought, offered no temptation to robbers. Others beside the British Consul urged him not to undertake such a dangerous and difficult journey. He had heard those words before, all the way from London to Jerusalem, yet few Europeans would offer a complete stranger the kindness and courtesy which he had experienced among the brigand Ourouks and the poor Turks.

The upshot was that Mitford was "prudent"; Layard "determined not to be baffled." So they agreed to separate temporarily. Mitford would go, as everyone did, by caravan over a well-frequented route. Layard would make his way as best he could across the Wilderness of Hauran, and would meet his companion in Damascus on, or as near as possible to, a certain date.

Chapter IV

EAST OF JORDAN
(January–March 1840)

Not one of the Jerusalem guides would risk his neck where
Layard intended to go. By chance he came upon Antonio, a
nineteen-year-old Arab, convent educated but born near the Dead
Sea and therefore familiar with the desert, who agreed to act as his
guide and interpreter. The British Consul, having again warned him
many times over of murder and robbery, went so far as to provide
the rash young man with a letter from the Egyptian officials in
Jerusalem to their opposite number in Hebron. For this first stage
of the journey Layard hired two mules, bought a sleeping carpet
and a small second-hand army tent, and set out from Jerusalem on
January 15.

In Hebron, Yusuf Effendi, the Egyptian officer in charge, described even more graphically the dangers which the foreigner must
expect to meet if he insisted on carrying out his plan. When
Layard did insist, Yusuf Effendi shrugged off all responsibility and
sent for a desert sheikh to carry on. While awaiting this man's arrival at the Egyptian headquarters, Layard was treated to his first
sight of the *bastinado*, a common Eastern punishment. Poor
wretches who could not pay their taxes, or had otherwise incurred
Yusuf Effendi's displeasure, were strung up by the heels and
beaten on the soles of their feet with switches. Unable to watch or
listen any more, Layard took himself off to examine the so-called
tombs of Abraham, Isaac, and Jacob, which he classified as no
older than Byzantine.

Abu-Dhaouk, his guide to be, was a wicked-looking Bedouin,

black as a negro (though it was impossible to tell how much was skin color and how much dirt). Because there was a blood-feud among the Arabs in the Petra neighborhood, Abu-Dhaouk could offer the Frank no protection except from his own tribe. This, with two camels and two guides, could be had for only two thousand piastres (twenty English pounds, in those days about $100).

Ridiculous, said Yusuf Effendi, who was relaxing over a water pipe from a hard day of punishing local citizens. Perhaps a touch of the bastinado would make the price more reasonable? After an hour of such amiable bargaining, the sheikh agreed to send his brother next morning to guide Layard to his encampment near the Dead Sea. Later, when Layard was alone, Abu-Dhaouk called upon him to describe, with appropriate gestures, what happened to strangers who did not have the proper protection; other Franks had willingly paid forty purses of silver to be safe. Layard refused to pay the additional *bakhshish*, blissfully ignorant that the story was all too true.

Between Hebron and the Dead Sea was the Wilderness of Judah: parched stony hills and dun-colored earth crisscrossed by a labyrinth of tracks. It was very quickly apparent that his guide was not Abu-Dhaouk's brother but a Hebron camel driver hired for the occasion, who did not have the slightest idea where the sheikh's tents lay, save that they were in one of the numerous wadies running down to the Dead Sea. It appeared that Layard and he would have to spend the night in the open, lost in the bitter-cold desert. At sunset, by the greatest luck, they came upon a lone member of Abu-Dhaouk's tribe, who led them to the encampment.

The flocks were just being driven into a compound enclosed by black tents. When Antonio finally made himself understood above the bleating sheep, barking yellow dogs, and shouting herdsmen, Layard was invited to take a seat in the principal tent. In Abu-Dhaouk's absence, he was greeted by the sheikh's wife, and presented to his four handsome, filthy, half-naked little sons. The ritual of Bedouin hospitality, of which he had read, and which he was to experience many times over, then proceeded. A sheep was slaughtered; two hours later the feast appeared, in which Layard was joined by the important members of the tribe. There was a "great mess" of rice and boiled mutton, a bowl of camel's milk, flour, rancid butter, and unleavened bread swimming in grease. All dipped their hands into the dishes; the tribesman squatting nearest Layard rolled a tasty combination into a ball between his grimy fingers and offered it to the guest. He was lucky not to be offered that greatest delicacy, the sheep's eye. It would have been a deadly insult to refuse.

Afterward he retired to his own little tent, which Antonio had meanwhile set up. He sat at the entrance, gazing at "the strange and novel scene." This was another "first": his first Bedouin encampment. A full moon lighted up the narrow, desolate wadi, all black and white save for the yellow glow of fires in the Bedouin tents. The brooding silence was broken only by the hoarse moaning sound that camels make at night, and by the long mournful wails of the jackals, which seemed to be in the middle of the camp. This alone would not have kept him awake; he had a toothache.

By morning the pain was so unbearable that, with naïve trust, or Spartan courage, he put himself, for an extraction, in the hands of the tribal dentist. After two unsuccessful attempts were made on him with razor blade, hammer and awl, he "declined a third experiment," applied a creosote painkiller from his medical kit—and never mentions the tooth again. He was anxious to be off before the sun was high, but further dickering with Abu-Dhaouk, who had arrived during the night, made it ten o'clock before he could leave with two camels and two "villainous looking" guides, Awad and Musa.

 The landscape of this region is not likely to make one optimistic either. The Dead Sea shimmers in a white-hot haze; the mountains of Moab glare sullen red; to the south the salt flats lie, bleached as bones. Death has come to many who have challenged this land: to some from thirst, like the sheep whose skulls are scattered over the stones; to others at the hands of bandits. Such were the horsemen with their plumed spears silhouetted against the sky, said Antonio, shuddering. One group galloped up, but grew instantly amiable at the sight of guns pointed in their direction. Layard gave the

Bedouins bread, sat and smoked with them, and noted their names. Thus he began the practice of listing the tribes whom he met, with all their branches, clans, and families, his object being in part political, in part his undiminished curiosity and zeal for detail. When the men had left, Antonio, shaking with fright, told Layard that they had asked Awad and Musa to join them in plundering the Frank, who could not be traveling with less than fifty purses in his pockets.

The now famous Dead Sea caves were then hiding places of the worst thieves, and must be skirted at night. "Descending rapidly by a very rough and precipitous path down which we had to lead the camels, we found ourselves in a wild and weird glen, surrounded by rocks of sandstone of the most fantastic shapes . . . A more savage and desolate spot I had never seen, and the dark shadows in the moonlight added to its somewhat awful aspect." Awad and Musa swore to sacrifice a sheep and give its flesh to the poor if they emerged alive from this horrid place.

South of the Dead Sea is the desolate Aravah, the Valley of the Wilderness, a fault in the earth running all the way to the Gulf of Akaba and the Red Sea. The track to the Wadi Musa and Petra led from this great ravine up through sandstone mountains of red and yellow, eroded into nightmare-like forms. Water was scarce, and when found was brackish and nauseating; sleep was scarce because hiding places were few. It would have been hideously rash to call attention to one's whereabouts by shooting game, so the only food was boiled rice and unleavened bread baked in the ashes of the campfire—when it was safe to light a fire.

The Nabateans, an Arab people who dominated the desert for a few centuries before and after the birth of Jesus, founded their capital in a strategic spot. The only entrance to Petra still is the Sik, a defile between hundred-foot-high cliffs, half a mile long and so narrow that the rocks seem to arch overhead. At one end of the passage is the empty wilderness; emerging at the other one suddenly sees (oft quoted line from a little known poem) "a rose red city half as old as time":[1] temples and tombs hollowed out of the cliffs, some with elaborate façades and sculptured figures;

high places of early worship; a Roman amphitheater; mausoleums
rococo enough to be Venetian. All of it is carved from rock that
shades from pink to deepest garnet.

When Layard dismounted from his camel, a miserable ragged
mob swarmed like bats out of the caves to gather around him. On
request, they brought bread and milk, and watched in ominous
silence while Antonio prepared breakfast. A large sum was demanded for the privilege of examining the ruins; when Layard
refused to pay it, there was much screeching and drawing of
swords. He tossed down a coin for the bread and milk and calmly
walked off. Watched by a hundred pairs of murderous eyes, he
spent the day sketching and taking notes. He was deeply impressed
by the savage, lonely character of this strange place: "the rocks of
friable limestone, worn by the weather into forms of endless variety, some of which could scarcely be distinguished from the remains of ancient buildings; the solitary columns rising here and
there amidst the shapeless heaps of masonry; the gigantic flights of
steps, cut in the rocks, leading to the tombs; the absence of all
vegetation to relieve the solemn monotony of the brown barren
soil; the mountains rising abruptly on all sides; the silence and the
solitude, scarcely disturbed by the wild Arab lurking among the
fragments of pediments, fallen cornices and architraves which en-
cumber the narrow valley, render the ruins of Petra unlike those
of any other ancient city in the world."

He was not impressed by the architecture either of the Nabatean
or the Roman occupation, which he called "a bad period and a
corrupt style."

After the Wadi Musa, it was good to rest for a few days among
the Seydi'in Arabs whose tents lay in the high land of Moab, where
there was grass; where men and animals could slake the thirst,
which had tormented them for days, in clear mountain streams.
Layard bought chopped hay for his camels and a sheep to be
slaughtered for himself and his hosts. They were a fine-looking lot,
with sparkling black eyes, white teeth, and well-greased hair plaited
in many tails. The women, of whom there was only an occasional
glimpse, veiled the lower part of their faces with small triangles of

dark linen, and wore many bangles of silver on arms and ankles, and blue glass beads of Hebron about their necks to keep off the evil eye.

Musa asked leave to return to the tents of his family, since there was a blood feud between him and the Arabs of Kerak, whither Layard was bound. On the way, a minor sheikh named Mahmoud joined the party, tried to make off with Layard's saddlebags, and was disarmed. Because of his lean and hungry look, Layard gave the man breakfast, and ordered him to make no more trouble on pain of being shot. Near Kerak, Mahmoud's tribesmen suddenly appeared from all sides to pounce upon the party. What followed reads like "cops and robbers," or a Keystone Comedy, but it was no comedy for Layard, who was in imminent danger of losing his life: "A wild-looking fellow, whose name I afterwards learned was Beshire, approached me, menacing me with his spear. Awad seized him by the arm. His *keffiyeh*—the kerchief which the Bedouins wear on their heads—fell off. With his many plaited tails of black hair, half concealing his face, and his expression of mingled stupidity and ferocity, and his loud, guttural cries, he seemed a very devil. Releasing himself from Awad, he sprang upon an overhanging rock and again raised his spear, swearing that he would have my blood. The Arabs began throwing stones, and Beshire threw his spear at me. Fortunately it glanced by me. My assailants again drew their swords, and one or two fired their pistols at me, but they were too far away to reach me. I exerted myself with all my might to drag Sheikh Mahmoud towards Kerak, menacing him with death when he attempted to stop. The camels had become restive with the noise and confusion, and had turned back, so that there was, by this time, some distance between us and them. Some Arabs followed them, and began to plunder my effects. The others, probably fearing that they would not have their share of the booty, instead of pursuing me, joined their companions, and I could see them, as I hurried on with the sheikh, dividing the contents of my saddle-bags and my other property."

Rejoined by Antonio and Awad, who had run off, Layard set Mahmoud free at the foot of the mountain pathway which led to the dark tower and frowning walls of *Kala'at El Husn*—Kerak of the Crusaders. It had been a great fortress of the Hospitallers, mediaeval French in architecture, with oriental influences. Sixty years later, in more settled times, Gertrude Bell felt the brooding threat of the place and "half expected to see written over the arches, 'Be bold! Be bold! Be not too bold.'" Layard entered through the narrow vaulted passage lighted only by a few loopholes, climbing up and up broken steps to the center of the keep. Within the walls was a town, recently destroyed by the Egyptians, and the governor's home. Armed only with his double-barreled gun, a brave front, and letters from Yusuf Effendi, Layard lodged a strong protest at his recent experiences. Ahmed, the governor's son, who received him in his father's absence, agreed that the attack was an outrage, and said they would immediately go to Mahmoud's camp to demand return of the stolen property.

In Arab tents, no business can be transacted till coffee has been roasted, pounded, freshly brewed, and drunk. During this ritual, and during Ahmed's lengthy and apparently eloquent speech, Layard recognized many of the holdup men glaring at him through the pipe smoke. But Ahmed's mention of the Frank's powerful protectors—Yusuf Effendi and the Egyptian authorities throughout Palestine—had its effect. So did his denunciation of their sheikh's sin: Mahmoud had permitted the robbery after eating the Frank's bread! But to return the stolen goods was something else again. After a stormy session, the tribe agreed to search their tents for what could be found. Meanwhile there must be a feast in Layard's honor. In the midst of it, a young Bedouin staggered into the tent, clutching his stomach and howling that he had been poisoned by the brandy which the Frank secreted in his saddlebags. When the boy's mother begged for an antidote, Layard said that he could only prescribe it if his medicine kit was returned to him. The "brandy" proved to be the creosote toothache mixture; Layard administered an emetic, and remarked as the youth retched and vomitted, that thus did Allah reward a thief. Only a few more belongings dribbled in; Layard was told that he must remain overnight if he wished the remainder. His cloak was still missing; the cold and his uncomfortable thoughts kept him awake. This time the warnings he had so briskly brushed aside had been more than justified—and he was not out of danger yet. These Arabs, in whose tents he found himself were said to be the worst cutthroats east of the Dead Sea.

After another near riot next morning, the brutal Beshire sullenly threw Layard's cloak down before him. But his spare trousers had been tailored into a jacket, his second shirt cut up to clothe three children. Awad and his camels having left for the tents of Abu-Dhaouk, Layard had now to bargain with Ahmed for animals and guide. Again it was a tussle between crafty Arab and stubborn Englishman, in which the latter was the victor. Then Layard gave Ahmed his sword and tent, which he had intended to do right along, but not as the price of extortion. For the rest of his time east of Jordan, he was handed on from one sheikh to another, one guide to another. Sometimes there were outrageous demands for *bakhshish*, sometimes freely offered hospitality and the gracious manners which have charmed European travelers from Baillie-Fraser to T. E. Lawrence. Layard comments on "the double character" of the Arab. "The same man who at one moment would be grasping, deceitful, treacherous and cruel, would show himself at another generous, faithful, trustworthy and humane. The very opposite opinions which travellers have been led to form of the wild independent inhabitants of the desert may be accounted for by this mixture of good and bad qualities." Antonio remained loyally at Layard's side, in a constant agony of fear. It was pitiful to watch his face when the Bedouins whom they met discussed, in language the boy could understand but his master could not, whether to cut the Frank's throat or let him go in peace.

He was risking his life to see ancient sites, and he managed to reach all of the ones on which he had planned. Whenever it was possible, he measured and made charts of them. At Ammon, where Bedouin tents were pitched among the fallen masonry, he found the extensive remains of a large town: a magnificent theater cut in the side of the cliff, an arched bridge, temples, villas, public buildings of all sorts. He gave the credit to the Romans for con-

structing such a city, almost in the desert and so far from Imperial
Rome. Actually its history is far older. It was the capital of the

Ammonites, whom David conquered and tortured with "saws and
harrows of iron"; it was Philadelphia, one of the members of the
Decapolis, a federation of ten Hellenistic cities rebuilt in Roman
times. Today it flourishes again as Amman, capital of the Hashemite
Kingdom of Jordan.

After Ammon the desert was left behind for rolling fertile fields
with a settled population. Layard relaxed, thinking his troubles
over; Damascus, Mitford, and civilized society not far away. On
his way to Jerash, he and Antonio sat down with a group of Arabs
who were squatting on the ground near an old reservoir. He became
aware suddenly that this was a graveyard, and that he was in the
midst of a Moslem funeral. While the corpse was being washed
and wrapped in a winding sheet, he noticed its particularly ghastly
appearance, and inquired the cause of death. "The plague—and he
is the third who has died of it since yesterday," said the sheikh,
pointing to two other fresh-made graves.

Layard departed in haste. There was plague also in the encampment he reached at nightfall; plague was raging throughout the
country east of Jordan. No one who came from here, he learned,
would be allowed to enter the pashalik of Damascus! All communi-
cation was cut off; he could not even send word of his delay to
Mitford. He would have to get around the regulations somehow;
meanwhile he was not going to give up seeing Jerash (Greek
Gerasa) which was only two and a half hours away.

He left the plague-stricken encampment before daylight and
with the rising sun entered a narrow fertile valley literally filled to
the brim with marble ruins of a golden-pink hue. A broad paved
avenue, rutted by chariot wheels, ran from a fine gateway on the
north to a triumphal arch on the south. Flanking the avenue had
been a double row of columns; there was an oval colonnaded
forum, two theaters, many temples—the largest two being of the
Antonine period, with rich Corinthian decoration. Layard counted
two hundred and fifty columns still standing in various parts of the
ruins, and innumerable others, shattered or whole, lying on the

ground. He struggled through tangled brush and rubble to measure and draw a rough plan in his notebook. The accuracy of his reporting has been proved by twentieth-century exploration. Gerasa, too, was a city of the Decapolis. The two largest temples, to Artemis and Zeus, were built in the second century A.D.; the triumphal arch was built by Trajan, the gateway by Hadrian.

Layard slept in a ruined theater at Gerasa and by the next evening reached a miserable mud village where the rain was coming down so hard that he was forced to spend the night in a small dirty hut crowded with travelers from plague-stricken areas. They told him that it would be impossible to reach Damascus by the main road, which was thoroughly guarded. Time allowed of no shilly-shallying; he had been on the way from Jerusalem for over a month; the appointment to meet Mitford was already past. Under normal conditions the village was not much more than a day's journey from Damascus, but how was he to break through the *cordon sanitaire*? By detouring back into the desert, he might be able to find a less guarded border where he could slip through —but this would take another five or six days, and he could not expect Mitford to wait forever.

In the morning, since all Franks were known to be doctors, the sick and the dying were brought to him for treatment. If he remained he would surely catch the plague himself. His best chance, he thought, was to cross the Jordan and strike north through Galilee. But his guide and hired animals had left him, and he could find no mule or camel driver in the village who was willing to risk punishment by death or, at the least, the confiscation of his animals, for breaking the quarantine.

With his last piastre he finally persuaded a camel driver to take him as far as Tiberias. They set off in the pouring rain at a snail's pace across the muddy plain, crossed the Jordan by an ancient bridge, and two mornings later looked down on the black basalt walls and towers of Tiberias reflected in the calm waters of the Sea of Galilee. The guide yanked Layard's carpet and saddlebags from the camel, threw them on the ground, and precipitously departed; he was taking no chances of meeting a quarantine guard in Tiberias. Layard and Antonio hoisted the baggage to their shoulders and trudged into town.

On closer view, Tiberias, struck by an earthquake two years previously, was a heap of ruins. As Layard stood among the rubble, perplexed and forlorn in his damp clothes, with his baggage at his feet, and without money for animal-hire to carry him further, he was approached by a man in the long old-fashioned coat, broadbrimmed hat and ear-curls of the Polish Jew. Signor Haym inquired if the gentleman had, by chance, been robbed by the Arabs? Yes, on his way from Jerusalem, Layard answered. Haym took him home to a wooden shed among the ruins, found a horse for him to ride next day to Safed, where, he said, his friend Shimoth would be able to make further arrangements. He also loaned Layard ten pounds, saying he knew his money would be repaid, because, after all, Layard was an Englishman! Besides, it was his religious duty to succor the stranger at his gates. "This noble trait of generosity in a poor Jew made an impression upon me which will, I hope, never be effaced, and has given me a feeling of affection for his race," writes Layard.

Next morning he parted from his loyal Antonio, and rode off to Safed on its high mountain wrapped in mist. It was raining hard again; the horse stumbled and slid on the slippery rocks of the steep ascent. When the clouds lifted for a moment, there were glimpses of the lake below, green and tossing like the sea. He reached Safed after sunset, to find another ancient town lying in ruins; it too had been almost totally destroyed by the earthquake. Dripping and exhausted, Layard was glad to find shelter with Shimoth in another wooden hut. His detour across the Jordan had been useless, for the quarantine was tightly drawn around Damascus in this direction also. One more precious day was lost in trying to find a muleteer willing to run it, and papers from the authorities stating that Safed, from which Layard was coming, had no cases of plague. This was complicated the more because Layard was with a Jew and must therefore *be* a Jew to be vouched for by the head of the Jewish community. Though he grew increasingly worried over catching up with Mitford, he did not count it a day

"unprofitably spent." Safed, even now, is a picturesque town, a
center for mystics, sages and Cabalists who fled Spain at the time
of the Inquisition; a town where a miracle is the accepted thing—
not hard to believe in the narrow alleys where the bearded pa-
triarchs walk, constantly disappearing and appearing again in the
fog. The earthquake could only have added to its eerie quality.

After several disappointments, Shimoth found a muleteer for
Layard; in the morning, just before setting out, the man tried to go
back on his bargain because of fresh rumors of Bedouin robbers
along the road. He was afraid, too, of being taken for a soldier
by the Egyptians, or of having his mules confiscated, and would
only go when Layard assured him none of these things could happen while he was under the protection of a Frank sponsored by
Yusuf Effendi. They set out in a heavy downpour, across country
to avoid robbers on the road, plodding through thick sticky mud,
floundering through swollen watercourses. After a sleepless night
spent in an Arab hovel, there was more of the same. They were on
foot, looking for a place to ford a stream in full flood, when a pack
of Egyptian deserters set upon them. The muleteer ran off—something Layard either could not or would not do. He was seized,
stripped of his money belt with the remains of Signor Haym's ten
pounds, and of everything but the trousers and shirt he stood in,
the ragged cloak which by now was not worth taking, the compass,
books and papers for which the outlaws had no use, and the gun for
which they could get no bullets of the right caliber. When they had
gone off, the muleteer reappeared, delighted to find his mules in-
tact. Collecting Layard's few remaining possessions, which were
scattered about in the mud, they plodded on to the next village.

From a hill nearby, the gardens of Damascus could be seen as a
dark line upon the horizon. The villagers told the muleteer that if
he tried to get through the quarantine he would certainly be
seized, conscripted, and his animals taken from him. Terrified, he
flatly refused to go any further. "To be so near, and not to be
able to get to Damascus, without money and almost without
clothes, and not knowing where to go," writes Layard, "I was well-
nigh in despair."

The muleteer, who was "at bottom a good fellow," consulted with the village sheikh, and brought to Layard a man who guaranteed to get him into Damascus if he was willing to go on foot, at night, and obey orders unconditionally. He could pay after he had made contact with his friends in the city. But it was a considerable risk to take. If he was caught he would be quarantined in a filthy hole for forty days or so; if he did not chance it, he was trapped in this miserable village without a penny. It was almost two months since he had left Jerusalem; Mitford must think him dead. However if he reached Damascus in the morning, and did not find Mitford there, he might be able to catch up with him elsewhere. Risky or not, it was the only thing to do.

It was still some hours till nightfall; it was raining heavily and promised to be very dark, which was all to the good. Too restless to relax, Layard prowled the village and was rewarded by finding the marble foundations of an old building that the natives claimed had been built by Nimrod—the first time he heard this name, which was to mean so much to him, in connection with an ancient ruin.

As soon as it was dark, he and Ahmed Saleh set out, carrying his old sleeping carpet and almost empty saddlebags between them. His guide trudged steadily ahead in the pitch-black night and the rain, across rocks, loose stones; scrambling over walls, wading through swollen streams, creeping through ditches, wallowing through mud. The soles of Layard's shoes were worn paper-thin, and his feet were soon on fire, while his teeth chattered in the cold and wet. Sometimes they stopped for a few minutes when he was so exhausted that he could not go on. When the sky grew gray at last, Ahmed Saleh said the patrols had been safely passed. Layard sat down to rest, sniffing the gardens of Damascus on the morning breeze. A broad track lined with orchards and groves leading to the city lay before him.

He had scarcely got to his feet again when a Bashi-Bozuk (a soldier of the Turkish irregulars) came galloping up to question him. Layard slipped into the man's hand a small gold coin, which he had fortunately found in the bottom of a saddlebag, and presented his papers from the Safed authorities (which the Bashi-Bozuk, being illiterate, could not read, but protested long and loud that he ought to show to his chief). Finally he was persuaded to turn his back. Layard and Ahmed Saleh hurried on, leaving the main track for by-lanes, and climbing over garden walls till they reached the city gate. They entered unnoticed in a crowd of farmers bringing produce to the early morning market.

Mr. Wherry, British Consul at Damascus, was astonished to hear unmistakable British accents issuing from the mouth of a beggar at his door, a bedraggled figure, plastered with the filth of ditches, soaking wet, in ragged shirt, trousers and Arab cloak. And even more astonished to learn that this was Henry Layard, whom he had been expecting for weeks!

Chapter V

ACROSS THE GREAT RIVER
(March–April 1840)

Mitford had given his companion up for lost and had gone on to Aleppo; there he would again wait for a little while, hoping that Layard was still alive and could rejoin him. When Layard had learned this, his next thought was to get clean. He went to a Turkish bath, where he was scrubbed and massaged, smoked a water pipe, and made up some of his lost sleep. The consul's Janissary was sent to buy him a new outfit in the bazaar. Since no European clothes were to be had, Layard left for Aleppo dressed like an Egyptian soldier, in baggy pants, short jacket, a vest with many buttons, a gay-colored sash, with a red tarbush on his head.

He bought a mare at the Damascus horse market, and rode as fast as he could, and for the most part alone. He made only one long halt: to see the ruins of Baalbek. The lovely columns and temple of golden-colored marble impressed him more than ever with the energy and good taste of the Romans. He met no trouble along the road in spite of the usual warnings (which his experiences in Syria and the Hauran do not seem to have made him take any more seriously). It was spring, the air was soft and balmy, wild flowers covered the hills, and Layard felt marvelously happy at being his own master, without escort or any baggage but the little he carried in his saddlebags.

When he arrived in Aleppo, Mitford was again just about to give up hope and go on to Baghdad without him. Layard convinced him that traveling light was the best way to cover ground, and on March 18, after a few days' rest for the sake of the mare, they left Aleppo without servant, guide, or baggage horse, bound for Mosul. Layard writes: "I had traversed Asia Minor and Syria, visiting the ancient seats of civilization, and the spots which religion has made holy. I now felt an irresistible desire to penetrate to the regions beyond the Euphrates, to which history and tradition point as the birthplace of the wisdom of the West. Most travellers, after a journey through the usually frequented parts of the East, have the same longing to cross the great river, and to explore those lands which are separated on the map from the confines of Syria by a vast blank stretching from Aleppo to the banks of the Tigris. A deep mystery hangs over Assyria, Babylonia, and Chaldea. With those names are linked great nations and great cities dimly shadowed forth in history; mighty ruins, in the midst of deserts, defying, by their very desolation and lack of definite form, the description of the traveller; the remnants of mighty races still roving the land; the fulfilling and the fulfillment of prophecies; the plains to which the Jew and the Gentile alike look as the cradle of their race. After a journey in Syria, the thoughts naturally turn eastward; and without treading on the remains of Nineveh and Babylon, our pilgrimage is incomplete."

Stirred though he was by such thoughts, Layard had no idea of how important it was for his own future when, four days after leaving Aleppo, he crossed the great river in a small boat at Birejik. This was the spot where Colonel Chesney's Euphrates Expedition, sponsored by the government of George IV, had been launched in 1836. Two paddle steamers, brought overland in parts from the coast, had been assembled at Birejik for the purpose of surveying the Tigris-Euphrates basin; on the very first day, one sank with great loss of life in a sudden tornado; the second reached the Shat el-Arab (where the two rivers converge) and steamed back up the Tigris to Baghdad. It was generally concluded that the navigation of the Euphrates was not, for the time, practical.

Layard and Mitford had now to travel across "the vast blank," which was a no-man's land between the Egyptian and Turkish forces, and therefore an ideal playground for the Bedouin. They followed a little-known track through Orfa, Mardin, and the foot-

hills of Kurdistan. Often they came upon the still smoldering campfires of raiding parties, or the wreckage of a settlement which had
just been pillaged. They ran daily risks, but with their "usual good
fortune" were not attacked. They were entertained by Turkish
officials and notorious Kurdish chieftains, saw many ruins, lost
their way now and then, and three weeks after leaving Aleppo,
just as their horses were about to give out, sighted the crazily
crooked minarets and the gardens of Mosul stretching along the
west bank of the Tigris, with the snow-capped mountains of
Kurdistan beyond. On the left bank of the river, to the east,
a range of long smooth ridges stretched for several miles. Two
immense mounds, flat-topped and steep, with none of the soft
contours of a natural hill, rose above the rest. Layard, awe-struck,
realized that he was looking at the site ascribed to ancient Nineveh.

Whether the story was truth or legend, no one knew for sure.
After the destruction of Nineveh in 612 B.C. its very name vanished
for a time from history. Herodotus is said to have written of the
Assyrians, but if he did, his account is lost. Xenophon, who
passed that way with his Ten Thousand two hundred years after
the city's fall, does not mention it in the *Anabasis*. Later the name
of Nineveh reappeared in Greek and Roman writings, coupled with
fantastic legends. Although mediaeval Arab scholars were familiar
with the geography of Mesopotamia, and, indeed, mentioned a
small fort, Roman or Persian, called *Kalat Ninawi* (Nineveh
Castle) opposite Mosul, Europeans as a whole did not read Arab
works. Westerners knew of the country only through a very few
travelers such as the two twelfth-century rabbis, Pethahiah of Ratis-
bon and Benjamin of Tudela, who visited Jewish communities in
the East and wrote accounts, in Latin, of what they saw. "Nineveh
now lies in utter ruins, but numerous villages and small towns
occupy its former space," writes Rabbi Benjamin.

The mounds slumbered on, undisturbed except when the winter rains exposed some broken bit of alabaster which was promptly
seized by the local population for building material or to burn for
lime. Through the centuries, a handful of Europeans, many of
them Catholic prelates, wrote of travels in the East and of seeing

the mysterious mounds. The Danish scholar Karsten Niebuhr gave a detailed description of them in 1720. For the time being, that was as far as the investigation went. But when "antiquities" became a craze, hunters of such treasure multiplied. After Napoleon's raids on Egyptian ruins, the obvious Middle Eastern fields for further exploitation were Persia, where Persepolis and other monuments were still above ground, and Mesopotamia. Claudius Rich, appointed Resident of the British East India Company at Baghdad in 1802, was as much concerned with ancient remains as with the commercial and diplomatic aspects of his job. His *Memoir on the Site of Babylon*, appearing in a Viennese journal in 1812, set off more than a century of competition in the Mesopotamian field. Rich believed that the two largest mounds opposite Mosul, Kuyunjik and Nebbi Yunus (on which stood a village called Niniouah, a name resembling that of the ancient city), represented Nineveh. His posthumously published *Narrative of a Residence in Koordistan* includes a survey of the Mosul mounds, and the story of how his attempt to explore Nebbi Yunus was blocked by the fanatic guardians of the so-called Tomb of Jonah, a Moslem holy place. Except for this sort of reaction, neither the illiterate shepherds nor their corrupt Turkish governors cared what lay beneath the earth and grass.

Layard's first look at the mounds was from a distance and necessarily brief before riding on toward the massive walls of Mosul, parts of which dated back to Saracen times. From the center of the town sprouted the tall brown minaret of the main mosque. Only a few of the original blue-green tiles clung to the dome, and the tower had been a leaning one ever since, long ago, it had bowed down to the soul of Mohammed flying by on its way to heaven. The ground beside the walls was slimy with stagnant water and littered with bloated carcasses of camels and cattle. It was not an appetising introduction to Mosul.

The town was squalid and mud-built, with little charm, but Layard enjoyed his stay there. He and Mitford were guests of W. F. Ainsworth, who had been an officer of the Euphrates Expedition, and whose writings on Mesopotamia Layard had read; and of

Christian Rassam, "an Armenian gentleman of Chaldean origin,"
a native Mosuli, who had accompanied Colonel Chesney as interpreter. During the week that Layard remained in Mosul, he crossed
the Tigris by the shaky bridge of boats many times to spend hours
measuring, and hunting for bits of marble and inscribed brick
among the grassy ridges that covered the ancient walls. A clutter
of Arab houses crawled up the sides of Nebbi Yunus; Turkish
cavalry horses were grazing on Kuyunjik.

The scene filled Layard with a sense of mystery, and also with
curiosity. He wondered about the Assyrians: what had their civilization been like, their art? Even their history was a question mark
except for the fantastic accounts in Strabo, Pliny, and a few other
classical writers; and the Bible passages which told of their prowess
in war, their cruelty, their wickedness and splendor.

Here at Nineveh—if it was Nineveh—were none of the graceful
columns, the carvings, the legible inscriptions in Greek and Latin
of the ruins in Asia Minor and Trans-Jordan. It was easy to recon-
struct those cities in the mind's eye: one saw forums where politics
held sway and business had been transacted; theaters where Greek
tragedies had been produced; temples where known gods had been
worshiped. Here, in the Land between the Rivers, were no trees
and blossoming vines among the ruins, no running streams and
aqueducts, no distant views of a blue bay. It was a cruel land,
desolate even in spring—and how much more desolate it must be
when the long hot summer had scorched it to barren brown earth!
Here there was *nothing* to indicate what might lie beneath those
man-made hills rising abruptly from the flat plain. Layard could
not conceive the shape of the buildings—if there were buildings.
He was somehow sure that there must be. "It was believed that the
great edifices and monuments which had rendered Nineveh one
of the most famous and magnificent cities of the world had perished with her people, and like them had left no wreck behind.
But even then, as I wandered over and among the great mounds,
I was convinced that they must cover some vestiges of the great
capital, and I felt an intense longing to dig into them."

Ainsworth and Rassam invited their English guests to join them in an excursion to the ruins of Hatra, city of the Parthian kings who ruled the land several hundred years later than the Assyrians. Hatra lay in the oasis of Al Hadhar, in the remote Al Jasirah Desert, ninety-three miles southwest of Mosul, and had only recently been discovered by Dr. Ross, a physician attached to the British Residency at Baghdad. The oasis was known to be the camping ground of the Shammar Bedouin, a powerful tribe, fierce and warlike, and much given to *ghazous*, or raiding parties. Christian Rassam, however, having done favors for several Shammar sheikhs who came to Mosul occasionally to sell their wool and buy provisions, thought an attack on himself and his friends unlikely. In addition, the Pasha of Mosul graciously offered to send a single guard, or *cawass*, with the expedition. Layard accepted the invitation eagerly; he had been suffering from the ague for some hours, and felt that the dry desert air would cure him. This trip was to be a preview of two sites he was later to excavate: Nimrud and Kalah Sherghat.

The party rode out over rolling hills covered with scarlet ranunculas, pink stock, and white Star of Bethlehem, all of which Mitford knew by name; Layard noticed only that the wild flowers were beautiful. The first night was spent at Hammum Ali (the Baths of Ali), hot sulphur springs good for leprosy and skin diseases. Layard writes that the formerly prosperous village had been wrecked by the tax collector; Mitford says merely that the inhabitants had left for summer tents. The place was deserted, the doorways of the houses blocked with stones. They broke open one or two, but the swarms of fleas which greeted them made sleeping in an open shed preferable. Feeling stiff after the long ride, Layard wandered off to stretch his legs and climbed a small tel to admire the sunset. Not far away, on the other side of the Tigris, he saw a clump of mounds; one high cone towered above the rest, dark against the glowing sky, and beyond it faintly glimmered the yellow waters of the Zab. From its position at the juncture of the two rivers, Layard thought this must be the pyramid of Nimrud, described by Xenophon under the Greek name of Larissa. Even then, twenty-two centuries before, the ruins near which the Ten Thousand camped were considered the remains of a very ancient

city. According to local Arab legend, it had been founded by
Nimrod, the grandson of Noah. Verses of Genesis came to Layard's
mind:

*He was a mighty hunter before the Lord . . . And the beginning
of his kingdom was Babel, and Erech, and Accad, and Calneh, in
the land of Shinar. Out of that land went forth Asshur, and builded
Nineveh, and the city Rehoboth, and Calah, And Resen, between
Nineveh and Calah; the same is a great city.*

The land of Shinar, to which Scripture ascribed the earliest habitations of man, is Mesopotamia, the land between the rivers (modern Iraq). As darkness fell over the lonely mounds, Layard must
have wondered, as he so often wondered later, which of the cities
Nimrud represented. Perhaps this, and not the Mosul mounds,
was Nineveh?

Next morning the poor cawass, terrified of the Bedouin and of
being lost in the desert, galloped off towards Mosul and was never
heard from again. For the rest of the party, the trip was a delightful
picnic. The desert bloomed with thousands of tiny red and yellow
flowers; Mitford, the bird lover, noticed "turtle-doves and quail in
flights; flocks of sand-grouse and plover; white harrier hawks skim-
ming the plains in search of prey, hoopoes, green bee-eaters, and
blue rollers." Wild boars dashed out of a marsh near the river; the
party gave chase and Ainsworth killed an old sow. Its three sucking
pigs ran off, squeaking and grunting, till they found Mitford standing across their path, whereupon they stopped to sniff and examine
him. He grabbed two and carried one under each arm, "singing a
duet." Dinner was sucking pig, partridge, and hare, broiled in the
coals of the campfire. Hadj Ali, the Egyptian groom, was ordered
to watch the horses and keep up the fire all night for fear of desert
lions.

Even in the spring, the early morning air of the desert was bitter
cold; Layard, who still had a touch of malaria, was chilled through
after sleeping on the bare ground in a thin cloak; he was glad to
get going again at daybreak. Soon afterward they spotted in the

distance the great mound overhanging the Tigris called Kalah Sherghat, which Dr. Ross had marked on the map of his route to Hatra. They reached it in a couple of hours and spent the rest of the day taking measurements and hunting for the strange black stone figures which the Arabs claimed were buried there. Mitford made it out to be not quite three miles in circumference and a hundred and forty feet high at its tallest point. Judging by its size, Kalah Sherghat, like Nimrud, must have been a city of some importance, but the only traces of man's work which they could find were the usual fragments of pottery, a wall of hewn stones fitted together without cement where a small stream had washed away the base of the mound, and many red, black, and yellow burned bricks littering the uneven upper platform.

So far the party had been following the course of the Tigris; they now struck out into the desert itself along the compass bearing that Dr. Ross had given from Kalah Sherghat to Al Hadhar. After spending another night in the open and wandering all the next day without coming to the oasis, they began to think that the cawass's fear of getting lost was not so far-fetched after all. They camped that night in the pouring rain without shelter; by morning the desert was enveloped in a thick white fog. For two hours they picked their way along the banks of a small stream, and were considering whether they had better give up the search and turn back when a light breeze lifted the morning mist "like a curtain," and the ruins of Hatra were spread out before their eyes.

The Parthian empire lasted till the third century A.D.; Hatra had not yet been covered by the desert dust. Crumbled walls and towers loomed through the last wisps of fog, with sheep and camels grazing among them, and on all sides the black tents of the Shammar with the feather-tufted spears of the warriors planted before each entrance. The scene was so unexpected and so unreal that Layard, still lightheaded from fever, wondered if he was again in a delirium.

It was a dream not without danger; the Bedouin do not welcome unannounced guests. Christian Rassam, who knew Bedouin customs, urged speed in claiming the sheikh's hospitality before they

should be noticed and attacked. They galloped up to the largest
tent, which had the finest mares tethered before it and a spear
with the biggest ostrich-feather tuft at the entrance. Inside, a number of Arabs in long parti-colored cloaks and striped *keffiyehs* were
crouching around the embers of a fire. When the strangers entered,
they rose and gave the salute of welcome with a surly and suspicious air. Fortunately the sheikh recognized Rassam. He and his
friends were invited to sit down on the carpet and were served with
coffee, sour curds, and camels' milk to allay their hunger till a
proper breakfast was made ready by the women of the harem.

Layard, remembering the Hauran, was uneasy as the tent filled
up with men "whose savage countenances were rendered still more
ferocious by their bright restless eyes and their white teeth, which
gleamed through their lips." A tribesman demanded to know why
the Franks had come, how did Christians dare to venture into the
Shammar tents? The European passion for "old stones" and for
digging into the earth was a mystery to primitive people; their
explanation of it was one which Layard was to hear over and over
again, and which was to cause endless trouble for him: the infidel
knew where hoards of gold and silver were buried, and intended to
steal it from those to whom the country and everything in it right-
fully belonged.

Rassam and the sheikh tried to explain that the Franks had no
such intention in visiting Al Hadhar, but the attitude of the others
was so threatening, their language and gestures so violent that
Layard began to fear that he and his friends would have to fight
their way out. The whole crowd followed when they rose to examine the ruins, and worked themselves up into a fury all over again
when they saw Layard measuring and sketching, which they took
to be magic rites for locating the buried gold. By now he had
enough Arabic to understand what was being said: that the Franks
should be done away with because if they could not steal the gold
themselves, they would later send an army to take the country of
the Bedouin by force.

Fortunately the tribe was afraid that an Egyptian army might be
close on the heels of these particular Franks, and the more cautious

members won the argument. In the early afternoon tents were struck and the Shammar, with their flocks, moved off into the desert. Only the sheikh and one or two elders remained "to discharge the duties of hospitality" and, next morning, to see their guests safely back to the walls of Mosul.

During their absence, Texier, a well-known French traveler, had arrived from Persia. His drawings of Persepolis and other monuments whetted Layard's appetite to learn more about the great civilizations of the ancient East. Monsieur Texier also gave Layard useful information on the country that was next on the itinerary for Ceylon. As far as the young Englishman knew, Mosul was just a way station en route; when he regretfully left the city, he did not expect ever to see it again.

But he could not put the thought of the mounds, those "vast and shapeless masses of earth," out of his mind. "After my visits to Kouyunjik and Nebbi Yunus, opposite Mosul, and the distant view of Nimroud, my thoughts ran constantly upon the possibility of exploring with the spade those great ruins."

Chapter VI

THE CITY OF THE CALIPHS
(May–June 1840)

Layard's second view of Nimrud was from a *kelek*—a raft of planks supported on inflated sheepskins—floating down the Tigris to Baghdad. Keleks traveled with the current; on reaching their destination, they were broken up, the wood sold at a profit, and the deflated bladders returned to the starting place by donkeyback—a transportation system in use since Assyrian times, as the sculptures were to prove. Small rafts made Baghdad in eighty-four hours, larger ones in six or seven days. In summer the water was low and the trip might take a month. It was a particularly pleasant way to travel now, in spring, when the melting snow of the Kurdistan mountains filled the river with swift, smooth-running water.

Rich passengers were sheltered from the sun by day and the cold at night in an odd little hut constructed like a wooden bedstead roofed with cane and felt. Poor passengers squatted amid the cargo around earthenware stoves they carried with them for heat, cooking, and pipe-lighting. If you wanted your own private kelek, you paid for it by the number of skins required to float you and your baggage. Layard and Mitford traveled in style on a kelek of fifty skins with two bedsteads, so that each of them sat like a pasha surveying the scenery as the raft glided along. They were feeling pleased with themselves because, on settling their accounts in Mosul, they reckoned they had spent less than four shillings a day between them since leaving Constantinople—not counting the sums that had been stolen from Layard.

Late in the afternoon the river ran close to Nimrud, so close that they could see the potsherds, broken bricks, and alabaster strewn all about it among the grass and spring flowers. The cone—curiously like a volcano to be man-made—rose from the northwest corner of a high plateau, steep-sided and furrowed with ravines caused by the winter rains. There was no stopping the raft to examine anything now, for the racing current was carrying it toward a mass of half-submerged masonry upon which the water broke in foaming waves—an irrigation dam built by the Babylonians and destroyed by Alexander because it blocked the passage of his ships. The raft bent and groaned, and seemed about to turn over. The boatman, straining on his long paddle, called loudly on Allah for help.

Fortunately he also steered with great skill. When the danger was past, he explained that the dam was called *El Awayee*, because the waters cried "wahi! wahi!" with the sound of weeping women. In autumn when the water was low, great square stones held together with iron could be seen, said the boatman. They had been placed in the river by Athur, the lieutenant of Nimrod, as a causeway from Nimrud to a palace across the way at Hammum Ali—the very spot from which Layard had first seen the great mound. While Nimrud faded off behind them in the gathering twilight, Layard again experienced a mystic sense, a determination that somehow, some time in the future, he would explore it.

He fell asleep to the murmur of the boatman's voice, telling legends of the old kings still related among his people, while the kelek glided on toward Baghdad. On the next afternoon, they reached Tekrit, a settlement that lived off the river traffic, where the passengers had to wait for an hour for the skins of their raft to be inflated by mouth, and for a new steersman. In the ruined castle on a crag above the river had been born the son of a Kurdish chieftain, Saleh-ed-din, known to European history as Saladin, the redoubtable Saracen warrior who retook Jerusalem from the Crusaders. The Kurds have ever been fierce fighters and are so today.

The river was a historybook with pages slowly turning as the raft drifted along. Each picture spoke of past magnificence and present decay: the solidly built Sassanian wall, standing alone; the shattered, early Islamic stone latticework; the decaying corkscrew tower of the Great Mosque at Samarra, once the City of Beautiful Palaces, built by the Abbasside caliphs. The only inhabitants of these riverbanks now were wild creatures such as the white herons that stood hunched in the shallows, the pelicans flapping overhead.

On the following day, the first date palms appeared, and orchards of pomegranate, and orange groves snowy with sweet-scented blossoms. The breeze was gentle and cool; the only sounds were the water sliding by, the melancholy cooing of doves, the creak of a water wheel, the cry of an Arab on the bank who stopped his back-breaking toil for a moment to stare at the lucky, lazy Franks. Layard thought he had never experienced anything so delightful; his boyhood dreams of Araby were more than realized.

That evening the raft was made fast near a village in the groves, and the Englishmen went ashore to buy supplies. They were agreeably surprised to discover that the poor villagers would gladly have given their melons, milk, and butter for nothing. The women, with unveiled, tattooed faces, wore single long blue garments like nightshirts, and the family savings represented by necklaces of old coins and cylinder seals, silver bracelets, anklets, and nose rings. Layard thought these Arabs "dirty but handsome," especially the slim and graceful young girls.

Next morning an early start was made, and by sunrise the glittering gilded domes and minarets of Baghdad could be seen in the distance beyond a band of feathery palms. Layard and Mitford told the boatman to pull over to the bank so that they might wash and spruce up before appearing in the cosmopolitan society of Baghdad. All neat and clean, in fresh clothes, Layard climbed back to the raft—and slipped, falling flat into the river. He arose muddy and soaked to the skin, and had nothing to change into but the Egyptian soldier's outfit, threadbare after weeks of travel. "But I was compelled to submit to my fate, and to trust that my character as an adventurous traveller with small means would furnish me with a suitable excuse for my forlorn and somewhat wretched plight."

The raft floated on between endless date-palm groves, "until, sweeping round a bend in the river, we came in sight of the city rising majestically on its banks—with its innumerable painted domes and minarets, its lofty walls and towers, its palaces and painted kiosks. It seemed to be all that I had pictured to myself of the city of the Caliphs and the sojourn of Haroun al-Rashid." In a few minutes actors emerged from the enchanting backdrop: "Horsemen and riders on white asses hurry along the river side; Turks in flowing robes and broad turbans; Persians in tall black caps and close-fitting tunics, the Bokhara pilgrim in his white head-dress and wayworn garments, the Bedouin chief in tasseled *keffiyeh* and striped *aba*, Baghdad ladies in scarlet and white draperies fretted with threads of gold, and their black horse-hair veils, con-cealing even their wanton eyes. Persian women wrapped in their sightless garments, and Arab girls in their simple blue shirts." Young Henry Layard had quite an eye for the ladies and gave de-tailed descriptions of feminine charms, but he was too discreet to tell if he followed the invitation in those wanton eyes.

Like the other Eastern cities, Baghdad on closer view was a disappointment. The most beautiful mosque, where Haroun al-Rashid had answered the call to prayer, was now only half a mosque, the other half having been carried off by the river. In the windows of a shabby palace, the Pasha of Baghdad could be seen reclining on a divan among his attendants, all of them wreathed in pipe smoke. Further passage of the raft was barred by a bridge of boats strung on an iron chain. Layard and Mitford transferred to one of the *guffahs*—round boats of skins stretched over reeds caulked with bitumen, described by Herodotus and unchanged since his day—which skimmed like waterbugs across the river. In a few minutes they stepped ashore at "a handsome building, not crumbling to ruin like its neighbors, but kept in repair with Euro-pean neatness," and the hearts of the young men, who had been away from England for almost a year, lifted at the sight of their country's flag floating overhead. They had arrived at the Residency of the British East India Company at Baghdad.

Chartered in 1600 as "the Company of Merchants of London trading into the East Indies," the concern had gradually assumed administrative powers in India, and in the eighteenth century its board of control, by act of Parliament, became a branch of the English Government. The "Indian" Army and Navy, officered by Englishmen, were its martial arms. When, in the early nineteenth century, England established direct political relations with the Turkish provinces of Arabia, the Company's agent at Baghdad, with the title of Resident, assumed consular and diplomatic powers. And the Residency was the center for Englishmen in Mesopotamia for whatever reason: scholars, explorers, ordinary travelers, merchants.

Claudius Rich, as Resident, believing that when in the East, one should *outdo* the Easterners, had organized the Residency staff in a manner calculated to impress Turkish officials. British prestige had risen immeasurably during his tenure, and the present Resident, Colonel Taylor, was not allowing it to decline. Layard and Mitford walked past a sepoy sentinel, stiffly at attention in the vaulted entry, and a number of cawasses and other attendants in varied uniforms, to a large courtyard surrounded by rooms which constituted the *Divan Khaneh*, or official part of the house. It was divided by a high wall from the *enderun*, or harem—a word which does not have the significance it has been given in lurid fiction; it simply means the family quarters. Since it was summer and already hot, Colonel Taylor received the two young Englishmen in the *sordaub*, an underground chamber, which was moderately cool. The Resident was a slight, weather-beaten little man with a gracious manner, who had no trouble in recognizing the gentleman under Layard's native wrappings, and promptly invited him and Mitford to be his guests in a cottage at the foot of the Residency garden for the duration of their stay.

Here they found the best of two worlds; the standard of the Residency was that of a great English country house plus oriental picturesqueness and luxury. Happy as he could be wandering alone in the wilderness, Layard took a young man's normal pleasure in conversation with intelligent men and charming ladies. The Tay-

lors kept open house for the foreign colony of Baghdad. Colonel
Taylor had served in the Indian Army, and, like Rich, was an accomplished orientalist; Mrs. Taylor was of Armenian descent, from
Isfahan. One of their daughters was married to Captain Lynch,
commander of the small steamboat that, when not at anchor outside the Residency, plied between Baghdad and Basrah, the embarkation port for India at the head of the Persian Gulf. Several
young officers of the Indian Navy were usually in attendance, an
alert and intelligent group, the most distinguished being Captain
Felix Jones, whose maps of Nineveh, Babylon, and other sites
were to be a major contribution to archaeological knowledge. Layard struck up a fast friendship with Dr. Ross, the discoverer of
Hatra, who was well known among the Bedouin and the mountain
tribes as a great *hakim* (wise man or physician). His courtyard in
Baghdad was always full of patients of all races and religions, rich
and poor alike, and Layard considered him "a wonderful promoter
of good-will for England in the East."

Colonel and Mrs. Taylor usually entertained unofficially in the
enderun. When it was hot, the air from the river made the roof
the pleasantest place to be; afternoon tea was served there, with the
servants using the flat chimney tops as sideboards. At night one sat
on the roof also as a rule, talking in the dark unless there was a
moon, for a lamp would have attracted thousands of mosquitoes.
On more formal occasions the Taylors welcomed their guests in a
beautiful vaulted room decorated with inlays of ivory, rare woods,
and mirror-glass mosaic which reflected the candle flames in dozens
of diamond facets. The Residency, which had belonged to a leading Mameluke, lacked for nothing in the way of Eastern comfort
and décor. Under the long windows of the salon, fronting on the
Tigris and its breezes, were low˙divans covered in gold-threaded
Persian brocades. Upon these the guests reclined after dinner,
smoking *narguilés* brought to each of them (including the ladies)
by Indian servants in native costume who glided silently on bare
feet across the tiled floor. However secluded or informally garbed
they might have been during the day, Residency staff and guests
emerged at dinnertime, like the night-blooming cereus, in the full

splendor of evening dress. Gentlemen wore white linen or uniforms; ladies were boned and stayed, dinner-gowned and kid-
gloved, no matter what the temperature.

The household took its exercise in the early morning on horseback, cantering out through the city gates with an entourage of
grooms, guards and cawasses. On the day that Colonel Taylor
brought Layard and Mitford to pay their courtesy call upon the
governor, they had an escort worthy of a reigning prince. Before
them rode uniformed cawasses carrying silver maces, the chief dragoman of the Residency in flowing silk robes and massive turban, a
guard of sepoys; other attendants followed on foot. The callers
were mounted on fine Arab horses with gold-embroidered trappings sent for their use by the Pasha. This procession clattered
through the heart of the bazaar, making a great commotion and
scattering people right and left—a performance which does not
seem to the modern reader as calculated to promote good-will for
England. But in those times it was considered the best way to uphold the dignity of Empire.

The Pasha's *Serai*, outwardly so mean-looking, as Layard had
observed, was even more beautiful within than the Residency.
The Pasha received his guests in "a chamber worthy of Haroun
al-Rashid in his prime." But the Pasha himself did not fit into the
picture. Because of the heat, he wore only a light jacket unbut-
toned on masses of pink flesh; flapping trousers, and neither shoes
nor stockings. One can imagine the disgust of the British, who had
arrived all buttoned up. Coffee and pipes were passed around;
the Pasha, mopping his shaved and shining skull, asked the usual
questions as to the health of his visitors, how they were enjoying
his delightful city, and so forth. When the proper clichés had been
exchanged, and suitable time wasted, the English contingent took
a polite leave and clattered back to the Residency in the same
high style as they had come.

Plague had devastated Baghdad less than ten years before Layard's visit; a series of corrupt Turkish governors had allowed it to
become a mass of ruins and a sinkhole of filth. Its common people
were half starved, and many of the once lovely houses of the rich

were empty, falling apart, their owners dead. Of the great Abbaside palaces, caravansaries, and baths, nothing remained but the pineapple-shaped dome of the tomb of Zobeide, Haroun al-Rashid's wife. (Gertrude Bell, who made a study of Eastern architecture, claims it could not possibly have been the original building, or any earlier than eighteenth century.)

Though he was distressed by such conditions, Layard, like many English visitors before and after him, found life in Baghdad fascinating. In spite of the climate, he was active as ever. He took lessons in Farsi, the Persian language, and practiced it on a brace of exiled Persian princes; he often rode out into the desert with them to hunt antelope and game birds in the eastern fashion, using hawks and greyhounds. One hot summer night he kept going till dawn, and saw silhouetted against the pearly sky just before sunrise a cluster of irregular-shaped heaps—the site of Babylon, which, unlike Nineveh, had never been lost. Over the centuries, travelers had pottered around in its rubble, hunting souvenirs to take home. This had suggested to Byron the satirical lines in *Don Juan*:

> . . . *Claudius Rich, Esquire, some bricks has got,*
> *And written lately two memoirs upon't.*

Bricks were not enough for Henry Layard; he wanted to know where they came from. On the ride back to Baghdad he noticed that the surface of the plain, white and glaring in the morning sun, was crisscrossed by choked, dry irrigation canals, which in Babylonian times had made this a market garden and granary instead of desert and fever-breeding marsh.

On another day he rode out to Ctesiphon, south of Baghdad, which had been the capital of the Sassanian kings of Persia who were masters of Babylonia in the sixth century A.D. He relates a story from the Arab geographers: a Caliph of Baghdad wished to tear down the palace at Ctesiphon, but its masonry resisted all attempts upon it. He asked his Vizier what he should do. "Desist," was the answer, "or the world will say the Caliph of Islam failed

to destroy what the king of the infidels was able to build." Whether
this is truth or legend, nothing remains of the city but the great
palace, completely surrounded by level sand. Layard had sent away
the muleteer with whom he had come, having arranged to return
on a little steamer due to pass that part of the Tigris shore in the
afternoon. He was so absorbed in examining the ruin, and in climbing to the top of the high vault above the central hall, that he did
not start for the rendezvous till he saw the smoke of the *Nicrotis*
in the distance. He was much too far from Baghdad to walk back
if he missed it. He then found that he had to wade through a
marsh, in water up to his armpits, which "a weakened condition
due to constant attacks of ague" did not make any easier. Again
he had got himself into one of those situations which seemed to
delight as much as distress him, at least in retrospect. He writes
how Captain Felix Jones, who luckily espied him, "used in after
years to speak of his surprise at seeing a man with his head above
water, in a marsh far from all human habitation and in the desert,
struggling and making the most desperate attempts to attract his
notice, and at finding, when he sent to his rescue, that he was an
English traveller."

Layard's Arabian Nights' dream had finally to end; more than a
month had been passed in Baghdad, and the year which he and
Mitford had allotted to their "land march" was nearly up. There
was much ground still to cover between Baghdad and Ceylon. The
journey through Persia promised to be the most interesting, and
at the same time the most difficult part of the entire plan. The
route through the Seistan to Afghanistan was not only of interest
to the Royal Geographical Society but, evidently, to the Foreign
Office as well. Even Sir John MacNeil, who had urged the young
men to attempt it, admitted that it was extremely dangerous. The
very crossing of the border into Persia was not without risk.
Though the Shah was not actually at war with England, the air
was full of rumors of war. Layard had obtained letters from the
Persian princes in Baghdad to notables of Kermanshah, which
should be helpful. He carried with him a copy of Major Henry
Rawlinson's paper on Luristan, and hoped he would be able to

follow up some of its hints for promising ancient sites to be explored. As he made ready, he was like one of Prince Timur Mirza's greyhounds on a fresh scent. The mounds of Assyria and Babylonia were behind him—but Shushan the Palace lay ahead.

Chapter VII

CARAVAN TO KERMANSHAH
(June 29–August 8, 1840)

Colonel Taylor and other Baghdad friends told the young Englishmen that if they *must* undertake the dangerous journey through Persia they should by no means attempt to do it on their own, even at the start. Wild robber tribes that preyed on travelers lived in the mountainous border country; no way to cross it could be guaranteed safe, but the least dangerous was to join a caravan from Baghdad to Kermanshah. From such knowledgeable advisers, Layard took the warnings to heart, though not to the extent of dropping Persia from the itinerary and heading for India by the usual sea route from Basrah.

Mitford and he were also warned of the fanaticism of Persian Moslems, who for the most part were of the Shi'a sect, far more given to excess than the Sunni branch with which the Turks and Arabs were aligned. During Ramadan, even the ordinary Moslems, made irritable by fasting, were apt to attack nonbelievers; Heaven help a Christian if he should be in one of the Persian holy cities during the fast, when the streets ran with the blood of the Shi'as, who gashed themselves with knives, whipped themselves with chains in their frenzy. Indeed few Europeans had penetrated Persia. The natives were unused to seeing them; European trousers and other items of normal attire were considered obscene, if not an insult to Islam. (In many parts of Persia today, a woman is subject to insolence if she is not enveloped in the tentlike *chador.*) To be less conspicuous, therefore, Layard bought a Persian costume: a tall black lambskin hat; an outer garment resembling a

long bathrobe, held in at the waist by a draped shawl; beneath
this, wide-bottomed trousers tied at the ankle when riding. Mitford
had strong convictions that a disguise exposed the wearer to suspicion, and should be assumed only in extreme emergency. "I always
wore English dress," he writes loftily.

They hired two mules as far as Kermanshah, and packed them
with saddlebags, sleeping carpets, and quilts. The first time Layard
attempted to mount by the single rope loop that took the place of
stirrups, the wooden packsaddle and all toppled over under the
mule's belly. But he could have repacked many times before the
caravan started. The time of its departure, like any important decision, was up to a *mulla*, a holy man, who arrived at it through
opening the Koran at random and interpreting the passage at the
top of the right-hand page. Several steaming hot days passed with
the whole caravan encamped at the gates of Baghdad before the
interpretation was auspicious.

It was the very end of June, and because of the heat, the caravan
traveled by night and rested by day. Layard wrote a long letter,
which was sent back to his mother: "We are at last on our way to
Isfahan. Our caravan is composed of a motley set, in all about
seventy persons and fifty-five animals. The procession is generally
headed by two old Turks abreast, perched on very small donkeys,
whose apparent duty it is to find the way during the early part of
the night when there is no moon. These pioneers are followed by
five or six men on foot, who keep up a chant far from melodious
during our progress. Next appears a *koujiava*, a pair of boxes, somewhat resembling the body of a sedan-chair, slung across the back of
a strong mule, each containing a young lady. They are the wives of
an old Turk, who keeps so good a look-out after them that I haven't
yet been able to find out whether any beauties may be concealed
by the obstinate veil which is down night and day. After the
koujiava follows the body of the caravan, each member on his own
peculiar animal, striving for precedence; and as the horses and the
mules are for the most part well-laden, and have only the halter
which does not guide them, the confusion and continual concussions are highly amusing. Our caravan is chiefly composed of poor

pilgrims and their wives. One or two, however, boast the title of Mirza, a writer (equivalent to our ancient term 'clerk') and consider themselves considerably above the common herd. They are attended by their hookah-bearers, a man whose sole employment is to light the hookah and present it to his master. This he does on horseback with great dexterity, carrying the pipe with all its frail appendages at arm's length, when at a full gallop. As these good priests and pilgrims are returning with a bellyful of religion, and the Persians are notoriously more fanatic than the Turks and Arabs, we are looked at with no little contempt."

It was not all so entertaining as Layard made out in his letter. His flowing robes did not fool anyone; Mitford, of course, was in English dress. The few travelers who were at first inclined to be friendly were soon frightened off by the mullas, who warned that True Believers would be contaminated by the touch of a Christian, and must wash themselves after any contact; it was safer to keep at a distance altogether. Women were told not to lift their veils; children to stay away. When the caravan halted for the day's rest, Layard and Mitford were not permitted to spread their carpets near the others, even though this might be the only shady spot for miles. Fortunately they had their own cooking utensils in which to cook their own food, for they would not have been able to borrow pot or pan; even boiling could not remove the Christian infection. When villagers brought jars of water to the travelers, the mullas watched lest the infidels taint the rims with their lips, and if there was no jar for their exclusive use, Layard and Mitford went thirsty. An Afghan who had been a *munshi* (secretary to an English official) agreed to give Layard lessons in Farsi, but was forced to desist because of threats. A mulla from the holy Persian city of Meshed rode along alternately chanting verses from the Koran and calling down curses on the *giaours*. Being called a dog and a pig and other insults got to be too much for Layard. The next time his carpet was kicked away, he laid about him with a stout stick. He expected to have his head broken in return. But the Persian bark, he soon realized, was worse than the Persian bite.

On the second evening, a group of Armenians from Isfahan, who had left Baghdad ahead of the caravan, were waiting along the road for protection, having heard of robbers in the vicinity. The male members of the caravan spent the remaining hours of darkness in firing off their guns at random, boasting between rounds of what they would do if any robber showed his face. On the following night, when the advance guard reported the approach of a body of horsemen, the bold warriors were in a panic. Only the two Englishmen made ready to defend themselves. The "robbers" turned out to be the escort of Monsieur de Sercy, the French Ambassador, who was returning to Baghdad from a mission to the Shah. Layard delivered some letters to him and enjoyed a few minutes of polite chitchat before returning to his mullas and pilgrims.

The track lay between bleak cliffs and ugly, eroded rocks, with the bare, rugged barrier of the Zagros up ahead. This district, called Zohab, had not always been so empty of civilization; Layard began to recognize ruins and sculptures described by Rawlinson. One day while the pilgrims rested, he explored a ruin by the river Holwan called Shirin-i-Khosrau after the lovers made famous "through six times ten thousand couplets" by the tenth-century poet Firdausi in his epic *Shah-Nameh*, a history of Persia in verse. Perhaps these crumbling walls, covered with rosy furze and spiked with white hollyhocks, were the very "golden bower" to which the Sassanian king Khosrau Parwiz carried off the beautiful Shirin, lost love of his youth, to make her his lawful wife. The king had built many palaces for "this fair-cheeked lady,"[1] of which the ruin by the river Holwan was said to be one.

A day's journey farther along the road, there was a tomb high up on a cliff; beneath it the sculptured figure of a Zoroastrian priest holding a scroll, undoubtedly the sacred Zend-Avesta. The natives of the place called it *Dukkani-Daoud*—David's Workshop—and fell upon their faces before it.

The road, climbing upward, dwindled to a narrow rough trail skirting a sheer drop. The night was black as pitch. The confusion and "constant concussions" ceased to be amusing, and on the descent, after crossing the Persian border at the top of the pass, the striving for precedence almost jostled Layard off the track and into the abyss. Without bridle, bit or reins, he could not guide his mule or jerk it up when it stumbled on the loose stones. One had to have a firm faith in God or in mules to survive a night like this.

With the dawn, the first Persian village appeared far below in a valley with vineyards, running streams, gardens, and a handsome caravansarie. But Layard and Mitford knew there would be more fleas than guests, and they preferred to collapse upon their own sleeping carpets under a fig tree in the garden. They ached in every muscle from hours of balancing on the unsteady wooden packsaddle, of hanging on without stirrups. They had been on muleback without a break for fourteen hours.

The respite was brief, and the hardest part of the journey was still before them. For the next two days the caravan labored through Luristan in constant dread of the savage Lurs. Nomads who pastured their flocks in the mountains in summer and migrated to the plains in winter, they were, and are, fiercely independent, resisting all attempts to settle them even now. Though divided into tribes of different racial origins, such as the Kashgoi, originally Turkish, and the Bakhtiyari, pure Persian (both of whom Layard was to encounter), they were united in their way of life, which, in Layard's day, was both pastoral and predatory. They were in open rebellion against the Shah, which made travel in their country even more unsafe.

Shivering with cold and fright, the two old Turks on the two little donkeys led the way across another spur of the Zagros at night on a trail called, with reason, the Pass of the Broken Horseshoes. In the early morning, the caravan descended at last to a cultivated plain ringed around with snow-topped, saw-toothed mountains. Another four hours brought them to Kermanshah, looking large and prosperous in its nest of walnut and poplar trees, orchards and vineyards. As Layard and Mitford rode into town, a raucous horn blast from the bathhouse roofs announced that bathers would now be received. In front of the caravansarie, the new arrivals were besieged by smoke venders and barbers who thrust pipes and mirrors into their hands.

The Englishmen hired a room and, a bit later, heartily enjoyed their first Persian dinner, brought to them from a cheap cookshop on a large pewter tray: "soup, one or two made dishes with savoury sauces, a very good pilau, delicious fruits of various kinds, including very fine apricots and plums, and an iced and delicately flavoured sherbet." Layard did not hesitate, as the contemporary traveler does, to sample exotic cookery from dubious sources. He could survive bad meals with the minimum of complaint, but he dwells on the good ones (such as this in Kermanshah) with as much loving detail as he lavishes on the dress of beautiful women.

The morning after their arrival, Layard and Mitford rode out to see the sculptures of Taki-Bostan, five miles from Kermanshah. Carved into the foot of a mountain are two deep, arched grottoes, the remains of a pleasure retreat and triumphal monument of the late Sassanian period. A spring of clear cold water pours out from beneath the recesses into a stone pool in a lovely garden. The garden had run to seed when Layard and Mitford saw it, but red roses, favorite flower of the Persian poets, still bloomed among the weeds. Flandin, a painter, and Coste, an architect, both attached to the French Ambassador's mission, were camping at Taki-Bostan in order to make drawings for their forthcoming book *Voyage en Perse*. Layard copied the inscriptions, which were in the Pahlavi script, and sketched the charming bas-reliefs of the royal hunt, which seemed to illustrate the very occasion on which Khosrau re-encountered the beautiful Shirin while he was engaged in the chase, accompanied by "three hundred steeds caparisoned with gold, seven hundred falconers with royal falcons, three hundred keepers of the cheetah . . . eight hundred hounds with golden leashes . . . five hundred camels," and much, much more.[2]

After a delightful day in this delightful spot, the Englishmen dined with the Frenchmen, and then returned to their lodgings in Kermanshah. They found themselves in trouble. Considering all the warnings, they should have expected it, yet they were surprised when the governor's secretary arrived to convey, with barely concealed threats, his master's astonishment that the strangers had not seen fit to call upon him. Though they hastily explained that,

as modest travelers, they hesitated to intrude upon so august a
person, Layard and Mitford wondered between themselves
whether a fanatical mulla from the caravan had not denounced
them. Layard also realized too late that his letters from the exiled
Persian princes had done him more harm than good, since the
munshi, acting as interpreter, had imprudently presented them
while the addressee, a Persian notable, was in company, which
"probably caused him some annoyance."

At six o'clock the next morning the secretary returned with a
guard to escort them to the governor—not in the style in which
they had visited the governor of Baghdad, but on foot, through
reeking bazaars and filthy streets. In a letter to his mother, Layard
describes this as outright arrest, and it may have been just that.
Persian officials were now more hostile than ever toward the English because Her Majesty's troops had occupied the island of
Kerak in the Persian Gulf, and it was rumored that they would
soon invade the mainland with the intention of deposing the Shah.

The governor, "squatting on his hams," smoking a water pipe
and sniffing at a cucumber (no doubt to shut out the odors of his
decaying palace) received them coldly, examined their passports,
and fired questions at them, which Layard, through the munshi,
tried vainly to answer. The interview was a dismal failure. They
were not, as yet, imprisoned, but they were kept under surveil-
lance, their every move watched for several days before they discovered that the munshi was again the major cause of their trouble.
He had spread the story that they were British agents whose pockets were stuffed with money to spend in bribing the Persian Army
and buying traitors to the Shah. They found a new interpreter and
protested their innocence. The governor, fearing British reprisal
should he openly maltreat British citizens, dared do no more under
these circumstances than deny them a permit to travel in Persia.
Considering their government's unfriendly attitude toward his, said
the governor, such a permit could be issued only by the Shah
himself.

Layard, who had learned that the Shah was encamped with his
army between Kermanshah and Hamadan, asked leave to apply

for the permit in person. The governor grudgingly agreed, with the proviso that a soldier accompany the Englishmen—supposedly for their protection, actually to keep an eye on the spies. The soldier was insolent; Layard threatened to report his behavior to the Shah, whereupon their escort precipitously disappeared. The "spies" gleefully mounted their hired horses and went on their way, unescorted.

Now the mountains again enfolded them: steep shoulders of pale green plush and shining rock on either side of the road—the same road that had been the military highway for Cyrus moving west to overthrow Babylon, and Alexander marching east to lay waste Persepolis. From those days to this it has been the main trade and invasion route from the plains of Mesopotamia to the Iranian plateau. Towering above it is the great Rock of Behistun, now known as Bisitun, where Darius the Persian caused to be carved a giant figure of himself with his vanquished enemies at his feet. Accompanying the figures is a trilingual inscription in cuneiform. Since these characters could not then be read, Layard and Mitford did not know whom the colossal figure represented. Mitford writes that some supposed it to be the Sassanian king, Shapur, with his foot on the neck of the Roman emperor Valerian; others thought it Nebuchadnezzar, with the vanquished Jews.

The inscription, later deciphered, gives the genealogy of Darius, the events of his reign, a list of his territories and principles of government. Whatever means the stonecutters used to climb to their work was afterward destroyed, for Darius intended his monument to be beyond human reach forever. Part of the inscription reads:

> *King Darayawaush proclaims:*
> *Thou who shalt read this inscription*
> *In the days to come*
> *Shalt see that I have caused it to be engraved in the rock*
> *Together with these figures of men.*
> *Efface it not nor destroy it!*
> *See that thou keepest it whole*
> *So long as thy seed shall live![3]*

The Rock of Behistun is probably one of the few tourist sights in the world that is *not* defaced by names, initials, and intertwined hearts, because it is still beyond the reach of human hands. Yet it became famous, and the proclamation of Darius, in a script long forgotten, became known again to the world because one man, Henry Rawlinson, *did* manage, at the risk of life and limb, to climb part of the way up, and dangle part of the way down, not to deface, but to copy the inscriptions.

Layard, as he rested beside the lovely brook at the foot of the cliff (where there is now a teahouse for tourists), and as he strained his eyes to see the inscriptions faintly visible high up on the rock, knew that Major Rawlinson hoped something would be learned from them someday, but nothing, not even the Persian inscriptions, had so far been published. During a discussion in Baghdad, Colonel Taylor, himself an oriental scholar, had said that he put no faith in pretended translations of cuneiform inscriptions so far made public: "Not only are there no letters which have equivalents in Western languages, but there is no division of words, no punctuation, and a variety of signs or points added to the letters; but admitting that the alphabet is discovered, and admitting that the words are disentangled, the next question is, what is the language, Arabic being the oldest Oriental language that we are acquainted with?" Layard, of course, could have no idea of the part he himself was to play in Assyriology, or how closely he and Rawlinson (whom he had not yet met) would work together on its problems.

Two days after seeing the monument of Darius at Behistun, Layard and Mitford watched from the side of the road the contemporary Shah-in-Shah, or King of Kings, passing by on the way to his camp at Hamadan. It would have been highly imprudent for two unknown Englishmen to intercept so gorgeous a procession merely to ask for a travel permit. Mohammed Shah was as much a figure of Eastern splendor as Darius must have been, or the Sassanian kings in their oversized turbans. Diamonds glittered in his tall black lambskin cap, on his wrists, on the trappings of his magnificent white horse. Beside him rode his handsome little son, also glittering; then followed his Grand Vizier, known as the *Hajji*; the ladies of his harem, heavily veiled, some on horseback, others in litters, and a vast retinue of ministers, officers, servants and hangers-on. Mounted tribesmen raised the dust, galloping round and about, and at the very end of the line plodded four painted elephants sent by the governor of Hamadan to welcome the Shah. A half-clad, bare-foot, undisciplined rabble of soldiers straggled along behind the royal entourage. Layard, with his keen eye and sense of social justice, describes a town where the army had camped: "Like a swarm of locusts they had eaten up and destroyed almost everything that came within their reach. The vines had been rooted up and the fruit trees cut down for firewood; the standing corn had either been trampled underfoot or carried away as food for the horses; the bazaars and private houses had been pillaged of their contents. The wretched inhabitants of the town whose provisions had thus been consumed, and whose property had been wantonly devastated, would have reason to remember for many a day to come the visit of their sovereign and his army."

The Shah was on his way back to Teheran, his capital. He had occupied the Turkish town of Suleimaniah as a trial of his strength, and had intended to attack Baghdad, but had been forced to give up the campaign against the Sultan by Russia's protests. Layard and Mitford, as they followed the Shah's troubled wake across the plain into Hamadan, celebrated an anniversary: the date was July 10, 1840—one year since they had left London.

On reaching Hamadan, they applied to the Minister of Foreign Affairs for a *firman* for travel in Persia. After a number of excuses and delays, they were brought into the presence of the Grand Vizier, who had been the Shah's tutor, and was the real power behind the throne. The Hajji was a small man with the face of a fox, simply dressed as befitted a mulla who had made the pilgrimage to Mecca. He was a devout Moslem, loving God and hating only three kinds of people: strangers, Christians, and Englishmen. Why, he asked, had Layard and Mitford not gone to India via the Persian Gulf like everyone else coming from Baghdad?

Layard explained politely that he and his friend were fond of travel and wished to see the great domains of the Shah, especially ancient sites never before visited by Europeans. Mitford added that he preferred a land route because he suffered from seasickness.

"How, then, could you travel on the plains of Baghdad which are known to be excessively damp?" asked the Hajji. A permit to the Seistan was out of the question. The present difficulties between Persia and England, he claimed, had been set off by the murder of an English courier; he was not going to be held responsible for the death of two more. Layard pointed out that he and Mitford were not government couriers but private gentlemen. The Hajji merely shrugged. After more argument, he finally agreed to let them go where they wished provided they signed a statement that he had warned them and was not responsible "if there should be an accident." Layard was ready to accept the offer till Mitford reminded him that such a paper would make a convenient assassination possible without fear of consequences.

Audiences day after day produced half-promises, speeches, but no firmans. "The present Persians are the vilest race that ever were collected into a nation," writes Mitford bitterly. "Unlike the old Persians, of whom it is recorded that they never told an untruth, these people find their greatest pleasure in lying gratuitously." He was increasingly irritated by Eastern evasions, and increasingly anxious to get on to Ceylon.

Layard, though he also fumed, employed his time to explore Hamadan. Once it had been an important city—Ecbatana, capital of the Medes. It still had considerable charm, nestling at the foot of the Zagros, and filled with the sound of mountain water running through the streets in open conduits. The air was refreshing after the steaming plains, the pine groves above the town a delightful place to walk. The houses, even of the rich, were outwardly ugly, with blank walls unrelieved by windows lest the women of the harem see or be seen by men. But if one were invited to enter, as Layard was by the few aristocrats who did not regard every Christian as a pig, there were lovely courtyards bright with flowers and cooled by sparkling fountains, beautifully painted and gilded rooms ornamented with latticework and mirror-glass mosaic.

The only remains of ancient Ecbatana that Layard could find were a few broken columns. The so-called tomb of Esther and Mordecai, though revered by the Jews, had been taken over by the Moslems and was "a recently built mosque . . . a vault filled with rubbish." More rewarding were the rock-cut tablets with trilingual cuneiform inscriptions, some three miles from the city. These were difficult to get at and badly worn; Layard did not yet know enough to be sure of what he was seeing, but he thought the Hamadan tablets important enough to remain for three hours, copying them as carefully as he could.

He and Mitford were soon fed up with Hamadan, for all its cool climate and charm. The Shah's soldiers were insolent; the mountain tribesmen would have hesitated little to murder a giaour; even the ordinary townspeople threw stones at the Englishmen as they rode through the streets. The permit for the Seistan was not forthcoming. Layard suggested to Mitford that they attempt the journey without permission, in disguise. Mitford would have no part of this, pointing out that the only sensible plan was to take the most direct route to Afghanistan. This too had its dangers, but at least it had been traveled before. If they would take it and get out of Persia in a hurry, the Hajji promised to give them not only a permit but an escort and the protection of the Shah.

Layard did not wish to get out of Persia in a hurry. If, instead, he went to Isfahan, he might be able, with or without permission, to join a caravan for the Seistan, and thus carry out his promise to Sir John MacNeil. So once more the two agreed to separate, this time for good. Though they were in brief correspondence later, there is no record that they ever met again. At Hamadan they applied for individual firmans: Mitford for the route through northern Persia, Layard for Isfahan. The Hajji was apparently so glad to get rid of them that the permits were more than generous, providing horses and supplies at public expense. On August 8, Layard sped Mitford on his way. "We had been together for above a year, and I much regretted that we had to part. He had proved an

excellent fellow-traveller, never complaining, ready to meet any
difficulties or hardships, and making the best of everything."

He is more generous than Mitford, who says: "My companion,
finding that we should not be able to follow the route we had intended, resolved to return to Bushire, on the Persian Gulf, while I
prosecuted my journey alone through Khorassan, Afghanistan, and
India." This statement hurt Layard's pride when he read it in Mitford's book of reminiscences. The implication that Mitford was the
daring one who went on alone while his "companion" retreated
rankled so much that Layard quoted it as a footnote in his own
Early Adventures, with the rebuttal: "I left Mr. Mitford because
I was determined to persist, if possible, in our original intention
of making our way through Yezd and the Seistan." He was indeed
not retreating to the coast, but plunging into the heart of Persia.

Chapter VIII

THE LAWLESS MOUNTAINS
(August 9–October 5, 1840)

Layard planned that the trip to Isfahan should answer further questions posed by the Royal Geographical Society. The site of Susa, ancient capital of Darius, was generally conceded to be a large mound at Sus not far from the city of Shuster, in the plain of Khuzistan. According to Rawlinson's paper (which Layard still treasured in his saddlebags) ruins described by tribesmen in the valley of Shushan, in the heart of the Bakhtiyari mountains, seemed like a more likely site for the Susa (Shushan) of the Bible. So far no European had seen this place. Layard hoped to cross the Bakhtiyari mountains between Hamadan and Shuster and recross them from Shuster to Isfahan—a roundabout way of getting there, but one which would enable him to examine both sites.

He had been advised by a Persian friend that the Hajji could not afford to admit that the government had lost control of the Bakhtiyari tribes, and therefore would not refuse Layard a permit to enter their country. This proved to be the case. Possibly the Hajji also hoped that the Bakhtiyari would get rid of this nuisance of an Englishman, while he could not be held accountable, since he disclaimed all responsibility. He did, however, provide Layard with a letter to the governor of Isfahan, and another to the great Bakhtiyari chieftain, Mehemet Taki Khan—the very man mentioned by Rawlinson as being not only powerful but more enlightened than most. It was Mehemet Taki Khan who had told Rawlinson of the many interesting ruins in his country.

Layard refused the Hajji's offer of a horse and bought his own in order to be independent, but he was not allowed to refuse the services of a *Ghulam*, an officer appointed to accompany him and care for his needs. The Ghulam, sent to spy on the Englishman, promptly found a method of making a profit from the journey. With Layard's firman in hand, he extorted more food from farmers along the way than two travelers could have consumed in months. Layard insisted on paying for his own supplies—but this made no difference to the Ghulam. Every evening he would engage a room for Layard in a village caravansarie, leave him, and return an hour or so later with a retinue of poor villagers bringing bread, meat, chickens, rice, eggs, butter, tea, firewood—everything they possessed for their own nourishment and warmth. This he would load on requisitioned donkeys and sell in the bazaar of the next town. Anyone who turned down his demands was *yaghi*, disloyal to the Shah, and would be suitably punished. Not only was this performance disgusting to watch, but every stop was longer than it should have been, and the pace of the heavily laden donkeys made progress even slower.

Turning aside from the usual road to Isfahan, Layard and his guide mounted into the hill country. One evening he was able to pass up a flea-bitten village caravansarie for the palace of his boyhood dreams, which stood deserted in a lovely garden, far from other habitations. "Painted life-size on the walls were figures of dancing girls in various postures, and of richly-clad ladies with almond-shaped eyes and black locks, as they are usually represented in Persian pictures, and hunting scenes, with horsemen bearing falcons on their wrists. The Palace was reflected in a reservoir of crystal water, about a hundred paces in length. As I wandered through this beautiful building, which was without a human inmate and as silent as the grave, I might have fancied myself in one of those enchanted palaces whose inhabitants had been turned to marble, as described in the Arabian Nights."

Most of the journey, however, was a far cry from his boyhood dreams. He must often have wished for a magic carpet to transport him from place to place with more speed and comfort. The further he and the Ghulam penetrated the mountains, the more it became evident that the village chiefs did not care whether they were yaghi or not. The Ghulam made matters worse by backing his demands with threats of violence. On several occasions there was so much sword waving on both sides that Layard expected his head to be cut off by one or the other. And the antagonism of the villagers did not help him with his notes and his mapping; when he asked the name of a place, he was invariably given a wrong one.

Yet even these independent-minded people lived in dread of the Bakhtiyari. When Layard and the Ghulam approached the district inhabited by them, a villager who had been pressed into service with his packhorses refused to go on, and ran off without his animals rather than risk his life. Bakhtiyari chieftains led the life of mediaeval robber barons, constantly raiding one another, and levying a toll on all travelers. So Layard was not too happy when forced one night by a storm to seek shelter in the castle of such a chief. Nor did the sinister armed warriors lounging about in the courtyard give him a sense of security. He lay down to rest with his pistols primed and within reach. It would have been better for his weary bones if he had allowed himself a sound sleep, for he was not disturbed.

He was suffering from intermittent fever and dysentery. He no longer felt strong enough to cope with potential robbers, hard riding, and the Ghulam. The country, even in the mountains, was burned as brown as a clay pot; the heat was unbearable by day, and it was dangerous to travel by night. His only bed for weeks had been his carpet on the hard ground or an earthen floor; his only food sour curds, cheese, and fruit. He never dared to take off his clothes and refresh himself with a bath in a stream. And the Ghulam refused resolutely to go through the mountains to Shuster, describing in ghoulish detail what would happen to them if they tried. Layard could not get rid of the Ghulam, and he could not trust him. He was told by the villagers that, even if he managed to get to Shuster without being murdered, the heat of the Khuzistan plain was worse than anything he had so far experienced. He had come across no traces of ruins in the mountains. Shivering, feverish, suffering from cramps and growing weaker each day, he was forced to forego the exploration of both possible sites of Susa, to leave the high country and make for Isfahan by the most direct road.

It was a broad, dusty track bordered on either side by giant anthills—the entrances to the *kanats,* underground channels which since ancient days had brought water from the mountains to the arid Persian plain; some of the tunnels had been built by Darius. The ploughed fields and melon patches of the mud-built villages, and the lives of the village people, depended upon the kanats for survival (and still do, to this day). Even close to Isfahan, each village was surrounded by a wall, and had a mud fort for defense against the dreaded Bakhtiyari.

Isfahan was half buried in green trees—a welcome sight. At the outskirts of the city, the Ghulam departed for the bazaars with his laden animals. Constantly asking questions, Layard found his way through the high-walled, confusing streets of Julfa, the old Armenian quarter, to the house of Eugène Boré, for whom he had letters. Boré, a wealthy young zealot whose objective in Isfahan was the promotion of France and the Roman Catholic religion, invited Layard to be his house guest; Flandin and Coste, whom Layard had met at Taki-Bostan, were also in residence. The prospect of civilized company, a comfortable home, and a rest was a great relief. Layard, however, could not really relax until he had made a final attempt to obtain official permission to explore the Seistan. On the second day after arrival, still feeling extremely ill, he rode off to be presented to the governor, Menuchar Khan, the *Mu'-temedi Dowla* (one upon whom the State relies) commonly known as the *Matamet.* This gentleman's reputation for ingenious punishments had reached Layard at Hamadan. "Some prisoners were lately made at Isfahan," he wrote to his mother. "One of these had all his teeth drawn and then knocked into his head; another was shot with his own teeth, and then, having his head forced into a bag of hay, was thus left to die."

The governor's palace was crowded with petitioners, attendants, and *ferrashes*—soldiers who applied the bastinado (literally, sweepers). The roses in the courtyard were trampled, and the pool was being used to soak pomegranate switches in order to make their blows more stinging. The Matamet was enthroned in a beautifully ornamented room at the upper end of the court. He was a typical eunuch, short and flabby, with a smooth pale face, pendulous cheeks, a listless, pouting mouth, and a high shrill voice. Born of Christian parents in the Caucasus, he had been sold into slavery as a child, castrated, and converted to Islam. He took revenge for his crippled masculinity by an extra portion of ruthlessness, which, coupled with a clever brain, had raised him to a position of immense importance and influence with the Shah, who had made him governor of Isfahan province because it included the most difficult people in Persia: the semi-independent Arabs of the south and the wild Lur tribes. If anyone could keep these in line, it would be the Matamet.

After presenting the letter of introduction, and exchanging the usual polite commonplaces, Layard launched a vigorous complaint against the Ghulam. The reaction was startling. The Matamet screamed curses like a fishwife, calling the Ghulam and all his female relatives by every filthy epithet. Layard was assured that the man would be arrested promptly. Two days later the Ghulam hobbled up to Layard, weeping. "What good, sir, has the stick I have eaten done you? Who has profited by it? You and I might have divided the money and supplies that, as the Shah's servant, I was entitled by his firman to obtain for you on our way. The villagers would have been none the worse, as they would have deducted the amount from their taxes. Do you think that they will get back their horses, or their donkeys, or their money, their *tomans*? No, the Matamet has taken them all for himself. He is a rich man and does not want them; I am a poor man and do. He is the greater robber of the two. He goes unpunished and I have scarcely a nail left on my toes." Layard was sorry he had denounced the poor wretch.

The Matamet flatly refused to give Layard a travel permit to eastern Persia. British troops had occupied Afghanistan; the border country was in an uproar and the Agha Khan, a venerated religious leader, was marching against the Shah with the support of Great

Britain. It is small wonder that Englishmen were not popular with
Persian officials, but such was the military weakness of their country that even a malignant character like the Matamet feared to be
held responsible for an Englishman's death. Recently another of
Layard's compatriots, a Dr. Forbes, had been murdered in trying
to reach the Lake of Farrah, and the Matamet was convinced that
Layard would suffer the same fate should he attempt it.

However, if he still wished to visit Shuster, one of the Matamet's
own officers would accompany him there. A tall, handsome man
in Lur dress who was standing by confirmed the governor's statement that there would be no trouble in passing through the
Bakhtiyari mountains with a proper escort. He volunteered to present the Englishman to Mehemet Taki Khan's second brother,
who happened to be in Isfahan. Since it was obviously impossible
to go to the Seistan at present, Layard was delighted by the opportunity to pursue his second choice of plans.

Next day he found, with difficulty, the ruined palace in which
Shefi'a Khan, his acquaintance of the previous day, and the great
chieftain's brother were lodging. The courtyard was crowded with
fierce-looking tribesmen, black-bearded and black-browed, armed
with long matchlock guns, who eyed the *Feringhi* (European) in
Persian dress with curiosity and some suspicion. Shefi'a Khan presented him to Ali Naghi, a short stocky man of about forty, good-
looking but with a rather sly face. Layard was invited to sit down
on the carpet beside him and partake of iced wine and sweetmeats,
which he knew he must not refuse. They "soon became boon companions over the bottle." Ali Naghi was already quite drunk on
arak; he had spent some time at the court of the Shah as hostage
for his brother's behavior, and had caught some of the Persian
vices. He had also met and liked Englishmen. He suggested that
Layard join Shefi'a Khan's caravan, which would leave shortly for
Kala Tul, his brother's home. For Layard, this was the greatest bit
of good fortune. Though Mehemet Taki Khan was said to kill as
easily as he drew breath, he was the most powerful chieftain in the
mountains, the one man whose help was essential if Layard wished
to explore them.

As usual the start of the caravan was delayed. Layard, though impatient, kept busy with language lessons and the sights of Isfahan. He wandered about in the cool courtyards of the mosques, which are among the most beautiful in the world, covered inside and out with shining tile in green and gold, or brilliant blues. He walked across the great Maidan Square, where polo was played in the sixteenth century, when Isfahan was the royal capital. The stone goal posts still stand, as does the Royal Booth, a marble pavilion from which the Shah of those days, reclining on a jeweled throne-bed, had watched the game. At the end of the square are the booths of the coppersmiths and the huge, covered bazaar. From a balcony above its gate, a band of musicians used to greet the dawn each day. The merchandise must have been much the same in Layard's time as now: tribal carpets in glowing colors, hand-printed cotton goods, spices ground between millstones by a blind-folded camel; jewels, silks, and *gaz*, a nougat-like sweet whose base, according to Rawlinson, is "a glutinous substance like honey deposited by a small green insect on the leaves of the oak tree." This, and the pistachio nuts with which it is mixed, comes from the Bakhtiyari country.

Layard found the Royal Booth and the palaces of Isfahan deserted, their lovely gardens choked with overgrown roses. The finest Persian carpets were gathering dust upon the floors, and the walls, painted with "scenes of carousal and revelry" (Layard uses the very same words as the modern guide book), were fading and cracked.

While in Isfahan, he attended similar scenes himself as the guest of a Lur chief, and he describes them with relish: "Many of the girls were strikingly handsome—some were celebrated for their beauty. Their costume consisted of loose silk jackets of some gay colour, entirely open in front so as to show the naked figure to the waist; ample silk 'shalwars,' or trousers, so full that they could scarcely be distinguished from petticoats, and embroidered skull caps. Long braided tresses descended to their heels, and they had the usual 'zulfs,' or ringlets, on both sides of their faces. The soles of their feet, the palms of their hands, and their finger- and toe-nails, were stained dark red, or rather brown, with henna. Their eyebrows were coloured black, and made to meet; their eyes, which were generally large and dark, were rendered more brilliant and expressive by the use of 'kohl.' Their movements were not wanting in grace; their postures, however, were frequently extravagant, and more like gymnastic exercises than dancing. Bending themselves backwards they would almost bring their heads and their heels together. These contortions soon degenerated into outrageous indecency, for these dancing girls did not refuse the wine and arak that were liberally offered to them. These orgies usually ended by the guests getting very drunk, and falling asleep on the carpets, where they remained until sufficiently sober to return to their homes in the morning."

At Monsieur Boré's home, Layard enjoyed, as he had hoped, more civilized society. He liked particularly the distinguished architect Coste, of whose absent-mindedness he tells an amusing tale. One day while Coste was sketching, with his horse's rein looped over his arm, he looked up to discover that he was holding only a bridle; the horse had been removed. Layard went with him to complain of the theft. The Matamet laughed heartily. "That must be the work of a Bakhtiyari! No one else could have thought up or executed such a trick." Sure enough, the thief, apprehended and forced to return the horse, was one of Shefi'a Khan's men. Layard realized, and not for the first time, that, when he rode off alone into the wilds with the Bakhtiyari, he would have to keep his wits about him if he wished to keep his head on his shoulders.

The Matamet, who, it appeared, had been detaining Shefi'a Khan as hostage against taxes which he considered were due from the tribe, finally agreed that he might leave Isfahan accompanied by a revenue officer. The mulla announced an auspicious day, and the Bakhtiyari party, about fifty strong, assembled for the start. Though Layard was still congratulating himself on this opportunity to meet Mehemet Taki Khan, he was conscious of some tremors too. His Isfahan friends said he might get into the mountains all right, but they were dubious about his getting out of them. He had escaped death narrowly several times in the last months; would he always be so lucky? The Bakhtiyari, like other Persians, were orthodox Moslems; if, unwittingly, he did or said anything that offended them, they would not hesitate, as had the timid fanatics of the caravan to Kermanshah, to make him pay for it with his life. The Bakhtiyari, who claimed to be of pure Aryan descent, the original inhabitants of Persia, regarded the town-bred specimens as cowardly mongrels. Layard thought Shefi'a Khan's men seemed not *un*friendly—but how could one tell what these handsome, savage brutes were thinking? They were heavily armed; besides the long guns, they bristled with pistols and daggers, and the equipment of a small arsenal hung at their belts: leather flasks of gun powder, pouches for balls and wadding, molds for casting bullets, metal picks, iron ramrods.

On Shefi'a Khan's advice, Layard was armed in the same way, and had added to his Persian outfit some items of Bakhtiyari dress: a short outer coat of felt and an embroidered skull cap round which was twisted a scarf of striped linen. In the Persian fashion, the top of his head was shaven and two long locks dangled beside his cheeks; these and the beard he had allowed to grow were dyed a beautiful shining black. But even if his eyes had not been blue, he was under no illusion that he would pass as a Persian when he opened his mouth to speak. Being an optimistic young man, he could not believe that he would get into real trouble if he watched carefully and tried to conform to the tribal customs. He already knew that he must not ask too many questions, or openly make notes or take compass-bearings, because these things, in the East, were suspect. In small, weather-stained notebooks, in a tiny, barely legible handwriting, are the notes he made privately, from which he was able to write a memoir for the Foreign Office, and, many years later, his detailed and delightful *Early Adventures in Persia, Susiana and Babylonia.*

The Bakhtiyari caravan moved out of Isfahan at a smart pace, for the tribesmen were accustomed to such travel. Supplies bought in the bazaar had been loaded on mules with other baggage; on top of the packs jounced women muffled to the eyes in their chadors, carrying small children on their laps. Men on foot kept the animals going by beating on their rumps with matchlock butts.

For the first few nights they camped in villages. Shefi'a Khan and his men, having used up their cash in Isfahan, did not seize food as one might have expected, but ate only dry bread they had brought with them. Layard kept his cash hidden in a money-belt under his shirt and fasted too, for he had been told the Bakhtiyari would be mortally insulted if a guest offered to pay for anything during his stay with them. The revenue officer was the sole member of the party who slept in a room and ate a good dinner, requisitioned by authority of the Matamet.

After branching off from the highway to Shiraz, the way mounted into treeless hills rosy with heather. It was rough, steep going; occasionally, when Shefi'a Khan detoured to avoid meeting a hostile tribe, there was not even a trail. Nights were usually passed in friendly encampments where Shefi'a Khan and the other chiefs would sit around a fire till late, gossiping about the latest feuds, forays, and assassinations. Although the clans of this district acknowledged Mehemet Taki Khan's leadership, they could not be kept from fighting one another over pasture rights, family inheritances, or for other excuses. Layard was reminded of a Persian saying: "The life of a man is as the life of a sheep." The Bakhtiyari killed one as readily as the other.

At Lurdegan, a turreted castle "like a feudal stronghold of the Middle Ages," on the edge of a gloomy forest surrounded by rugged mountains, Layard had his first taste of real Bakhtiyari hospitality. "It was altogether a very picturesque and romantic spot, rendered even more so by the crowd of ferocious and savage-looking men, all armed to the teeth, who gathered around us. Two hours after sunset a procession of attendants, carrying torches, issued from the gates of the castle bearing trays on their heads, with an excellent and ample supper of pillaus, boiled and roasted meat, fowls, melons, grapes, sherbets, curds, and other delicacies, which did honour to the enderun of the chief whose ladies had prepared our repast." He was impressed also by the manly bearing and quiet dignity of his host, "so different from the false and obsequious Persians of the towns."

Though Lurdegan had never before seen a European, its people knew Franks to be skilled doctors. Layard was besieged by requests for medicines against intermittent fever, which he filled from his stock of quinine, and for charms to secure the love of a husband or the birth of a son (which, he explained apologetically, he could not fill). He had the greatest difficulty in escaping his patients even long enough to take a bath in a mountain stream, a luxury he longed for more than anything else, for his clothes had not been off his back since Isfahan.

One morning, after leaving Lurdegan, he discovered that his extra shirt and underwear had been stolen from his saddlebags during the night. For the remainder of the journey, he washed out what he had on, when he could, in some small river or brook, and hid stark naked and shivering in the rushes till his clothes were dry. On another day he was awakened by the cold (it was now October) to find that his quilt had been skillfully removed while he slept. But he was not the only victim. Others had lost pipes, caps, shoes. Shefi'a Khan blamed it on herdsmen they had met the previous evening, and swore he would punish them.

On the whole, Layard began to think the Bakhtiyari had been much maligned. He was aware of no overt hostility toward him. Two of the ladies, the wives of Ali Nagh Khan, had become friendly enough to drop their veils. One had a beautiful little five-year-old girl called *Bibi-Mah* (Lady Moon) who rode always on Layard's saddle before him, chattering away, and at rest stops sat on his carpet, playing with his watch and compass. If Mehemet Taki Khan proved to be as well disposed as the ladies of his family, Layard had nothing to fear. If, on the other hand, the robber baron took a dislike to him and decided to do away with him, no one would be the wiser. Another rash traveler would simply have been swallowed up by the Persian mountains, and no one would protest—least of all, the governor of Isfahan.

The highest, most rugged passes now lay ahead. Climbing the heights was agonizing; and in the valleys one had to push through thorny jungles and wade through icy, rushing streams. The largest and deepest of these was a tributary of the Karun, which had its source in these mountains, and, after many meanderings, emptied

into the Persian Gulf. From the last valley, two trails led to the
stronghold of Mehemet Taki Khan, one following the Karun across
the plain of Mal-Emir, and the other, more direct, over the steepest
pass of all. This was the one which Shefi'a Khan chose. The animals had to be pulled by their bridles, or pushed from behind,
over the sharp lichen-covered rocks, where they left a trail of blood
on the patches of snow. And the women, panting and stumbling
in their long, clumsy traveling cloaks, barely managed to reach the
top before they collapsed.

The view from the summit, when it was at last gained, was over-
whelming. Mal-Emir could be seen in the distance to the north;
almost at one's feet was a narrow valley bounded on three sides by
high mountains, and on the fourth by yellow hills, beyond which
Layard imagined rather than saw the vast alluvial plain stretching
to the Great River and the Persian Gulf. Far, far below in the
valley perched a small black speck: the Castle of Tul—a beautiful
but lonely sight to chill the spine of a solitary Englishman.

Chapter IX

CASTLE OF THE ROBBER BARON
(October–December 1840)

Animals and people slid as if on toboggans down the final steep
ascent, and then crawled through a narrow dry ravine to a moun-
tain-ringed glen in the center of which stood the castle on its
high mound. It was of brick and stone with five towers; the barrels
of four swivel guns showed between its battlements. Round about
it were pitched black tents and huts of boughs, and from these, as
soon as the home-coming party was spied, streamed women and
children crying out their joy in high shrill voices. Shefi'a Khan and
Layard mounted to the castle gate, where the elders of the tribe
and two of the chieftain's brothers, Au Kerim and Au Khan Baba,
welcomed them, saying that Mehemet Taki Khan was away from
home on tribal affairs.

Layard was escorted to the *lamerdoun*, a large vaulted room
above the entryway, reserved for guests. Others had already spread
their carpets on the floor: a *seyyid* (descendant of the Prophet)
who spent his time quietly reading the Koran, and two famous
hakims, specially brought to Kala Tul to treat the chieftain's ailing
little son. One, tall and black-bearded to the waist, was from
Shuster; the other, from Isfahan, was a small bright-eyed man
dressed in silk robes and green shoes with extraordinary high heels.
Layard's skill as a physician had been reported, and when patients
came to ask for his medicines, the Moslem doctors did not like it
at all, especially when he was sent for by Mehemet Taki Khan's
principal wife. This summons led to a series of events as romantic
as any Eastern fiction he had read—and which were to fill an entire volume of his *Early Adventures*.

The Khatun-jan Kanum was living in her summer home of woven boughs outside the castle gates. When Layard entered she rose from beside the pile of cushions on which her sick child was lying to greet him in the name of her absent husband. He was struck by her dignity and grace, and the sweetness of her face, which was not veiled. The sick boy, apparently about ten years old, was flushed with a high fever and barely conscious. The Khatun, whose large dark eyes were brimming with tears, said that he had been sick for some time; nothing the hakim prescribed seemed to help. Recognizing the symptoms of malaria at once, Layard gave her quinine from his medicine kit with instructions on its use. But the mother was afraid to administer it without first consulting the Moslem doctors. They, fearful of losing the rich gifts which they had been promised if they succeeded in curing the child, insisted on calling in the mulla, who was considered the wise man of Kala Tul. The verdict of the Koran was unfavorable to Frank remedies; instead the boy was to be bathed in melon juice, Shiraz wine, and water from a cup on which a text from the Koran had been written in pen and ink. In spite of this Hussein Kuli grew rapidly worse. He was soon so desperately ill that a messenger was sent to recall his father.

It was with some anxiety that the Englishman waited for his first meeting with the formidable Mehemet Taki Khan. On arrival, the chief leapt from his horse and seated himself at the castle gate to greet his guests, even before going to his wife and son. He was a man of about fifty, of medium height and a bit stout, with a handsome, proud face disfigured by a nose broken in battle. He wore the Bakhtiyari chieftain's war dress: a tight tunic to the knees over a silk robe, wide trousers fastened at the ankle with embroidered bands, a felt skull cap twisted about with a striped scarf. His weapons, which he was known to use skillfully and without mercy, consisted of a scimitar of Khorassan steel, a long-barreled gun, a jeweled dagger, and a highly decorated pistol. Strapped to the saddle of his blooded Arab mare was another sword and a heavy iron mace.

Layard presented the Shah's firman. Mehemet Taki Khan flung it from him, saying contemptuously that the Shah had no authority at Kala Tul. After a moment of suspense, the chief smiled, told Layard to sit beside him, and to consider Kala Tul his home for as long as he pleased. He then excused himself to retire to the family quarters in the castle, to which his wife and son had been removed. Soon afterward Layard was summoned there. The Khatun-jan and her ladies were on their knees, keening the high, plaintive "Wahi! Wahi!" with which Eastern women greet disaster. The father, himself sobbing unashamedly, offered Layard anything his heart desired: jewels, horses, greyhounds, falcons—if he could save the beloved child. The Moslem doctors had admitted that Hussein Kuli was on the point of death. The Frank's medicine was Mehemet Taki Khan's only hope.

Layard was in an uncomfortable spot. He knew with what jealous hatred his intervention was regarded by the two hakim. On the other hand, it was impossible to remain unmoved by the unhappy parents. He promised to do his best, on condition only that the other doctors should not be allowed to interfere a second time. The chieftain agreed, but as a good Moslem he would have to ask the advice of the Koran. This time the holy book was in favor of foreign medicines provided they were mixed with water from the inscribed cup. Layard gave the boy a powder to reduce the fever, and sat down beside him to await the results. He was well aware that if the boy died—as well he might—nothing would be easier for the Moslem doctors to say than that he had been poisoned. For hours he sat watching Hussein Kuli, fragile from long illness, almost too beautiful to be a boy. He watched the slight body toss and turn, listened to the shallow strained breathing which could falter and stop at any moment. Behind him in the chamber dimly lit by a flickering charcoal brazier, the parents and their attendants, the mulla and the hakim, crouched on the floor, watching too.

At midnight the patient's fever broke in a heavy sweat. Layard retired, leaving the boy in his mother's care. In the morning he began the doses of quinine; after a few days Hussein Kuli was out of danger. The parents' joy was as touching as their grief had been.

The Khatun had born her husband two more sons, but Hussein Kuli was the eldest, Mehemet Taki Khan's heir and successor to the chieftainship, and as such enjoyed special prestige. Mehemet Taki Khan always called his wife "Mother of Hussein Kuli." Mothers of sons in the East today are still so addressed.

The grateful parents insisted that Layard move into a room of his own, an upper room in a tower which formed one of the corners of the family courtyard. The chief gave him a thoroughbred horse to replace his, which had gone lame. The Khatun and her ladies made him a whole new set of clothes (also badly needed) in Bakhtiyari style, of cloth woven by themselves and beautifully embroidered. The most welcome gift of all was the chief's promise to help him in his search for the ruins of which Rawlinson had heard, particularly the place called Shushan.

Rawlinson had written in his paper: "From the accounts which I have received of it, it cannot be other than a sister capital of Ecbatana and Persepolis . . . On the right bank of the river, near the bridge, are said to be the remains of a magnificent palace . . . At a short distance from hence, to the north-east, is the tomb of Daniel, called Daniyali Akbar, the greater Daniel, in contradistinction to the other tomb at Sus, which is called Daniyali Asghar, or the lesser Daniel. The building is said to be composed of massive blocks of white marble. Adjoining the tomb is a large slab of marble engraved with a perfect cuneiform inscription."[1]

According to scripture, the palace of Daniel's vision was "by the river of Ulai." Rawlinson proposed that there had been two cities called Susa: the ancient capital of the Achaemenid kings—Biblical Shushan—being where "the greater Daniel" was buried, in the Bakhtiyari mountains, by the river Karun, the old name for which was the Eulaeus. Sus, on the river Karkeh near Shuster, would be Susa of the Greeks. Layard was eager to find out if Rawlinson's theory was borne out by the valley called Shushan, which lay north of Kala Tul, beyond the plain of Mal-Emir. Mehemet Taki Khan warned Layard that the Bakhtiyari of that district had little respect for his authority, for the rules of hospitality, or the Koran. As usual Layard turned a deaf ear to warnings. The Khatun-jan did persuade him to leave behind his money belt and the double-barreled gun which would be too much of a temptation for a self-respecting thief, but he refused to part with his watch and compass because he could not make his geographic observations without them.

Mehemet Taki Khan provided him with a guide and letters to two petty chiefs. Trouble began as soon as he reached the plain of Mal-Emir and the encampment of Mulla Mohammed (some of the Bakhtiyari chiefs, though neither holy men nor scribes, bore the title of Mulla). In spite of the letter sponsoring Layard, Mulla Mohammed objected to showing an infidel the rock-cut inscriptions nearby. Layard, who knew of them, found the place for himself, but he was so badgered and threatened by the tribesmen that he was able to make only a rough copy of the cuneiform lines. Had he only known it, the inscription dated from the time of the Achaemenians; Mal-Emir was included by the ancient Semites in the country they called Elam. All Mulla Mohammed's followers knew was that the name Mal-Emir signified "House of Treasure." Obviously the giaour had come to dig up the gold and steal it from the Bakhtiyari, to whom it belonged. He must be forced to tell them where it was buried. Without his gun, Layard could do nothing to drive them away.

He gave up, and retired to Mulla Mohammed's tent, hoping to make an early start for Shushan in the morning. At midnight he was roused and urged to set off at once in the dark—a gambit, he presumed, to facilitate the theft of his watch and compass, which his host had been eying avidly. The compass especially, for it would help the chief, as a good Moslem, to beam his prayers in the direction of Mecca. Layard refused to set foot outside the tent. He lay awake until dawn, expecting to be robbed, or killed if the watch and compass could not be obtained in any other way. He wondered if the ruins of Shushan were worth the risk he was taking—but he was too near them now to turn back. As soon as daylight filtered into the tent, he started out—and was promptly held up and relieved of the coveted items. Much as he regretted them, he felt lucky to escape with his life.

His second letter was to the chief of a tribe that camped at Shushan in summer, cultivating a few crops along the banks of the Karun. Layard explained to Mulla Feraj that he was a pilgrim to the shrine of the holy Daniel. The "white marble building" of which the tribesmen had told Rawlinson proved to be a mud-brick hovel similar to tombs of other local Moslem saints. Scattered about the valley he discovered rough masonry foundations no earlier than Sassanian, and a few small mounds—no columns, slabs, or inscriptions such as had been described. The most impressive thing at Shushan was a ruined bridge with massive buttresses which has withstood the swift-running river. Layard judged it to be older than Sassanian, probably very ancient. Leading up to it on either bank were traces of a paved road, such as he had observed further along the valley. The bridge and the road were probably part of one of the great highways constructed by Darius to link the plains of Susiana (Khuzistan) with the highlands of Persia and his palace at Persepolis. The road could be traced in many spots between Mal-Emir and Shuster.

It was impossible for Layard to sketch the bridge or examine it and the other ruins properly because of treasure hunters breathing down his neck and religious fanatics who interpreted his every move as desecration. On his return to the chief's tent, he was again met by a barrage of accusations: "The reasons which were assigned for my visit would have been as amusing as they were ridiculous had they not been seriously entertained and had they not endangered my life. According to one man I was employed by the Shah to examine the country with a view to its conquest and occupation. Another gravely asserted that I was the brother of the King of England, who was already at Baghdad on his way to take possession of the mountains of the Bakhtiyari. According to a third, my forefathers had buried a great hoard of gold in a spot which was described in the books I had brought with me."

Since he had left his saddlebags in charge of the chief, it was not surprising that the books, including Rawlinson's paper, had disappeared. After a great deal of fuss he managed to get them back, probably because no one could read them. He knew it was hopeless to attempt further exploration, and since a small caravan was about to set out for Mal-Emir, he left the tents of the inhospitable Mulla Feraj. Not far away were a few overgrown foundations, which his companions animatedly pointed out as streets, bazaars, and palaces—typical Eastern exaggeration such as had deceived Rawlinson. Whether the valley was Shushan of the Bible or not, it was impossible for Layard to judge. He could only say that it was a logical location for a city: easily defended, well watered, fertile. Though Daniel's tomb was not of marble, the Bakhtiyari tradition that held the spot sacred was very old—but so was the legend naming the Sassanian ruins "the Temple of Solomon." On the whole, Shushan was a disappointment.

He was welcomed back to Kala Tul as a member of the family. It was an unparalleled opportunity to observe the customs of a living, little-known people instead of the remains of a nation long since vanished. Mehemet Taki Khan himself was a fascinating subject for study. Many of the reports Layard had heard were true —yet there was another side to him. Though a savage warrior, the best shot and the best swordsman in the mountains, he was known to be a merciful and generous enemy. He did kill a man as easily as a sheep; in both cases when it was necessary. In a culture where politics inevitably involved treachery, his word could be relied on. Rawlinson, who had officered the Shah's army in an expedition against him, wrote of Mehemet Taki Khan: "At the outset of his career he was the acknowledged chief of his own single tribe, and he owes his present powerful position solely to the distinguished ability with which he has steered his course amid the broils and conflicts of the other tribes. The clans, one by one, have sought his protection, and enrolled themselves amongst his subjects. He collects his revenues according to no arbitrary method, but in proportion to the fertility of the districts and prosperous state of the villages."

Mehemet Taki Khan enforced a kind of peace in the mountains, though he could not altogether prevent intertribal cattle stealing or the brigandage which Layard had encountered. On hearing the story, the chieftain sent a horseman with the message that unless Layard's possessions were restored, he himself would visit Mulla Mohammed and cut off his nose. Next day the watch and compass were returned. It was easy to see why Mehemet Taki Khan's reputation had spread, not only among the Bakhtiyari, but throughout Persia. This, as Layard discovered later, had its dangerous aspects.

Life at Kala Tul followed a routine unchanged for generations. On waking in the morning, the men went outside, washed their faces, and rubbed their teeth with the right forefinger (left hands were reserved for less delicate ablutions). They then put on the few clothes they had removed for sleeping, said the morning prayer, and were ready for the day. The women made similar toilets inside castle or tent. Attendants brought in breakfast: rice pilaffs, boiled mutton, and bowls of sweet sherbet on a tray which was set on the floor where the family gathered around it.

After breakfast Mehemet Taki Khan left the enderun for the raised seat at the castle gate, where, with the elders of the tribe, he listened to complaints, settled disputes, and discussed future plans. Though the elders could advise, only the chief had the power of life and death. When business had been disposed of, Mehemet Taki Khan would order out his horses for inspection and choose one to ride that day while his attendants exercised the others. Round and round the castle they would gallop, practicing all the tricks common to horsemen from cossacks to cowboys. On other days the chief would invite his guest to hunt for ibex or lion. Light-colored lions were said to be Moslems, dark ones were *kafirs* (infidels). A Moslem lion would spare the life of a man who took off his cap with respect and said, "O cat of Ali, I am the servant of Ali. Pass by my house, by the head of Ali."

Mehemet Taki Khan did not ask mercy from lions, Moslem or kafir. An incident which went from mouth to mouth and became a legend in the tents occurred during Layard's stay at Kala Tul. The chieftain and he were returning empty-handed one day from the chase, when a big black-maned beast sprang from the bushes upon one of the attendants. The man, in falling, caught the robe of another and inadvertently dragged him down too, so that both were pinned under the lion's claws. Mehemet Taki Khan sprang from his horse and advanced toward the beast. "O lion!" he called out, "these are not fit antagonists for thee. If thou desirest to meet an enemy worthy of thee, contend with me." The lion raised its majestic head to stare back as if it understood. Mehemet Taki Khan walked up to him; the lion did not move. The chief then fired his pistol at close range, killing the lion. The body was carried in a triumphant procession back to the castle, where it was skinned. The pelt was presented to Layard.

When ibex or mountain sheep were shot, the meat was made into kebabs and served with rice, stewed fowls, and several kinds of sweets for evening dinner. After the meal, coffee and pipes were handed round; the guests played backgammon, or talked, or read and recited poetry. In the first days at the castle, while Layard was quartered in the lamerdoun, he, as a Christian, had been as much a pariah as ever, served separately while the seyyid and the Moslem doctors shared a tray. Now he ate in the enderun with the Khatun-jan, quite contrary to etiquette, for it was not considered proper for even a husband to sit at the same tray with his wives. Mehemet Taki Khan, who had an excellent sense of humor, joked about the introduction of European customs into the harem.

The greatest favorite in the family circle was the Khatun's younger sister, known as Khanumi (Little Lady). She was the beauty of Kala Tul, in fact the loveliest girl in the whole tribe, as fair-skinned as an Englishwoman, with delicate features, large almond-shaped eyes, and soft dark hair which curled around her oval face and fell down her back in a dozen long braids. The costume of the Bakhtiyari ladies was as flattering to the young and shapely as it was the reverse to the old and baggy. Even aristocrats like Khanumi wore outfits not unlike the Persian dancing girls: loose trousers of silk, a brief linen chemise looped at the throat but open down the front. (As a mark of respect to a husband or before strangers, a silk handkerchief was tied around the neck to hide the bosom.) On her head Khanumi wore a tiny cap embroidered in pearls; on her feet high-heeled slippers of soft green leather; she tinkled as she walked, with gold and silver necklaces, amulets, bracelets and anklets. She was dressed like a princess, which indeed she was: the daughter and sister-in-law of powerful chieftains. (Saroya, the beautiful ex-queen of the present Shah, was of Bakhtiyari blood. Had Khanumi been born a century later, she too might have graced royal society.) She was Layard's Persian Princess of whom he had read in the *Arabian Nights*, "with teeth like a cluster of pearls, eyes brighter than the morning star, and lips of coral" made flesh and blood. He reports that she was not only beautiful but "intelligent and lively."

To her, the young Englishman must have seemed like a prince from the *Shah-Nahmeh*, as dashing a horseman, as daring a lion hunter as any Bakhtiyari warrior. Added to this was the appeal of his background, the great mysterious world beyond the mountains —and he was handsome too, as the frontispiece of *Early Adventures* plainly shows. There he stands, blue-eyed and black-bearded, in a jaunty striped Bakhtiyari turban and three layers of embroidered robes, a curved dagger thrust through his red-tasseled belt, a silver-sheathed scimitar at his side and one hand on a long silver-mounted gun. In the background, dimly seen, is the castle on its high mound.

Mehemet Taki Khan and the Khatun-jan told Layard more than once that if he would become a Moslem and remain at Kala Tul always they would give him Khanumi as wife. "The inducement was great, but the temptation was resisted," he writes, too much the Victorian gentleman to say more. Those were not the days when one kissed and put it in a book. The Persian Princess must have had temptations of her own. Let us hope, in the light of her short and tragic history, that she did not resist them all during Layard's stay at Kala Tul.

Fatima, the mother of Khanumi and the Khatun, was a good friend to Layard, and a source of endless entertainment, for she had a stock of stories about blood feuds and internecine betrayals which she told in picturesque words with dramatic gestures and flashing eyes. Layard could by now understand and speak Persian, and had picked up the Bakhtiyari dialect, which the tribesmen claimed was *Farsi Hakim*—the language of the ancient Persians.

He took additional lessons from the seyyid, reading with him the poems of Hafiz and Saadi, dear to the hearts of their countrymen of every rank and time.

Each person in the enderun had a small sleeping carpet, a bolster, and a wadded quilt, which during the day was rolled up in a silk cover. At bedtime, the bundles were unrolled, the carpets spread, the men and women took off outer coats or jackets and loosened all strings, buttons, and belts. And so another day at Kala Tul ended.

It was in many ways an idyllic life. Even for the ordinary tribesmen, it had many satisfactions. They dearly loved their rugged country, the lush grass in spring, the clear cold water of the streams, the starry skies. Unlike other nomad tribes, they seldom left their mountains, but in winter merely moved from tents on the high slopes to dwellings in the valleys. The women cooked, cared for family and small animals, wove beautiful carpets in patterns handed down from mother to daughter. The men herded the flocks, raised a few crops, and raided neighboring tribes for their cattle. There were of course difficult periods in their lives, as there are for Persian nomads today: times of drought when the grass was poor, the flocks grew meager, and the people suffered from hunger. Mehemet Taki Khan, aware of this, had purchased lands and founded villages, and hoped that, by opening the land to commerce, he could turn his still lawless followers to the raising of saleable products.

He took a keen interest in modern discoveries, and asked Layard to describe the steam engine and other inventions to the elders of the tribe, and to explain science, astronomy and geology. He liked to pit the Englishman against the mulla, whom he would order to disprove Layard's statements. The best the holy man could do would be to quote a passage from the Koran in refutation of Sir Isaac Newton. Mehemet Taki Khan could not understand why Layard had left the comforts of his own country, the steam engines and gaslight and safety. He came to the same conclusion as the Persian authorities, that Layard was a British agent. But this was in his favor. Mehemet Taki Khan loathed the Shah's corrupt officials; anyone who was against the government at Teheran was the Bakhtiyari's friend.

The revenue officer who had accompanied Shefi'a Khan from Isfahan had been ordered by the Matamet to collect the sum of ten thousand tomans (approximately £5000) at Kala Tul. The chieftain did not have any such sum; the tribes had little use for cash and did not keep it on hand. Their flocks supplied them with meat and dairy products, hair and wool for clothing and tents; they raised fruit, flax, rice, barley, and corn in the valleys; the forests gave them fuel, nuts, and *gaz*. These products were bartered with itinerant traders or in the bazaars of the nearest towns for the few other things they required, such as coffee, and silks for the ladies. Mehemet Taki told Layard that he could only squeeze the ten thousand tomans out of his people penny by penny through the use of force and torture—a method he thoroughly disliked, and which would result in rebellion against his authority. He staved off the revenue officer with excuses for over a month; he could not delay his answer much longer. And now, in November, Ali Naghi Khan, again a hostage at Teheran, wrote that the Matamet had denounced the Bakhtiyari chief as *yaghi*, or worse. The Shah, who had heard exaggerated reports of Mehemet Taki Khan's wealth, and considered it should be his own, had authorized an expedition against him as soon as the mountain passes were open in the spring.

"The mud fort of Tul," Rawlinson wrote, "may be considered formidable enough among the Bakhtiyaris, but it could make no resistance against regular approaches." Its four pieces of artillery were scarcely more than oversized matchlocks; the castle mound stood in a plain, open to attack on all sides. The vulnerability of his stronghold did not seem to worry Mehemet Taki Khan; he had a low opinion of the Shah's fighting men. Rightly so, Layard must have thought, after what he had seen of them, but he could also understand why the chieftain was reluctant to have that swarm of locusts enter his country, to burn up the trees, trample the fields, pillage and steal. Mehemet Taki Khan had allowed his brother to be taken as hostage just in order to avoid such a catastrophe. No proofs of loyalty were sufficient, however, and more was involved than the question of taxes. Mehemet Taki Khan, as the lineal descendant of a Bakhtiyari chief who had made himself Shah of all Persia, was a threat to Teheran. Though the clan had not retained the kingship, it was regarded with special suspicion, particularly when one of its number grew too powerful. Such had been the case with Mehemet Taki Khan's father, who, as a result, had been taken prisoner by the Shah and blinded. This was a fate Mehemet Taki Khan dreaded more than death. He declared that he would fight to the death rather than suffer it.

Shefi'a Khan rode out to call upon the chiefs allied with Mehemet Taki Khan for as much money as they could spare. He was instructed not to ask for armed contingents or do anything else which the Shah could use as an excuse for an invasion. Mehemet Taki Khan was not optimistic, however, believing that the Matamet would invade in any case, for the sake of the plunder. He had only one hope: to enlist the help of England. He asked Layard if he would undertake a mission to the island of Kerak, where the British were said to be preparing an expeditionary force against the mainland. Layard was to inform the general in charge that the great Bakhtiyari chieftain was willing to swing the fighting men of all the semi-independent tribes under his jurisdiction to the side of England, against the Shah. (Rawlinson had noted that Mehemet Taki Khan could at any time bring into the field a well-armed force of between ten and twelve thousand men.) In return he asked only that he be protected from the Shah's vengeance, and declared officially the supreme chief in Khuzistan.

Layard gladly agreed to go to Kerak. Winter had set in; the rain poured down day after day; the stone-and-mud castle was always damp and cold, and he was far from well. The Khatun had nursed him through many attacks of fever; several times he had been delirious for hours. In the British garrison he would be able to get treatment from an army doctor, replenish his own medical supplies, and ask for medicines and advice on behalf of the chief's youngest brother, Au Kelb Ali, who was wasting away with tuberculosis. Also he was eager to know what was going on in the world;

he had been out of touch with civilization for months. And he planned, while at Kerak, to set in motion another of Mehemet Taki Khan's ideas: to make arrangements with some enterprising British merchant who would be interested in the Bakhtiyari products: indigo, cotton, carpets, wool, goat's hair, and the rest. His main purpose, however, and Mehemet Taki Khan's desperate hope, was that he would be able to enlist British military support against the rapacious Matamet.

On December 8 Layard said good-by to Khanumi, the Khatunjan, and the chieftain, and started with a guide for the Persian Gulf. He promised to return as soon as possible.

Chapter X

THE KISSES OF THE MATAMET
(January–August 1841)

Layard returned to Kala Tul in January, healthier but not happy at the news he brought from Kerak. Mehemet Taki Khan could look for no military assistance from Britain, which was in the process of settling its differences with Teheran. This was a bitter disappointment, for now, if ever, he needed help. The Governor of Isfahan was reported to be already marching into the mountains at the head of a large body of troops. The high peaks were still dazzling white against a sky of Persian blue, but in that latitude snow melts early; the passes from Isfahan were open. Nevertheless, as Layard remembered well, it was not easy country for men and animals to negotiate without a native guide. Who could be guiding the Matamet?

Layard joined Mehemet Taki Khan at Mal-Emir, where he was encamped with the minor chiefs who had rallied to him. Hundreds of black tents were pitched on the plain; arms and ammunition were stacked and ready. The monotonous beat of drums and the skirling, wilder than bag-pipes, of the *surnay* (a kind of oboe) made martial music that stirred the savage tribesmen to frenzy. They waited only on their leader's command to ambush the Matamet as, encumbered with baggage and artillery, his forces struggled through the narrow passes. But still Mehemet Taki Khan hesitated.

When darkness fell and campfires dotted the plain, the tales of other battles and other heroes were told. Layard never ceased to be fascinated by these performances. "I witnessed the effect which poetry had upon men who knew no pity and who were ready to take human life upon the smallest provocation or for the lowest greed. They would stand until late in the night in a circle round Mehemet Taki Khan, as he sat on his carpet before a blazing fire which cast a lurid light upon their ferocious countenances—rather those of demons than of human beings—to listen with the utmost eagerness to Shefi'a Khan, who, seated by the side of the chief, would recite, in a loud voice and in a kind of chant, episodes from the *Shah-Nameh*, describing the deeds of Rustem, the mythical Persian hero, or the loves of Khosrau and Shirin. Or sometimes a wandering minstrel would sing, with quavering voice, the odes of Hafiz or Saadi, or improvise verses in honour of the great chieftain. The excitement of these ruthless warriors knew no bounds. When the wonderful exploits of Rustem were described —how with one blow he cut horse and rider in two, or alone vanquished legions of enemies—their savage countenances became even more savage. They would shout and yell, draw their swords, and challenge imaginary foes. When the death of some favorite hero was the poet's theme, they would weep, beat their breasts, and utter a doleful wail, heaping curses upon the head of him who had caused it. But when they listened to the moving tale of the loves of Khosrau and his mistress, they would heave the deepest sighs—the tears running down their cheeks—and follow the verses with a running accompaniment of 'Wahi! Wahi!'"

Mehemet Taki Khan sobbed like a child. When Layard asked how he, who had seen so much bloodshed, and who had killed so many enemies himself, could be moved by mere words, he answered, "Ya, Sahib! I cannot help it. They burn my heart!" Behind that war-scarred face there was a heart easily touched by the troubles of others, and a deep love for his people. He hesitated to give the word to attack because he knew that war would mean chaos, lawlessness, and a plundered countryside. The Matamet's agents, through threats, lies, and bribery, had set tribe against tribe, brother against brother. Such divisive tactics succeeded because these were people torn by blood feuds for hundreds of years. It had been extraordinarily difficult for Mehemet Taki Khan to unite a number of chiefs under his banner, and already they were splitting off in pursuit of personal advancement. He foresaw that they would end up, not by fighting the Matamet, but each other. This, he felt, must be avoided at all costs—even at the cost of his own pride. He decided upon a policy of appeasement (a term which, of course, he had never heard). He would receive the Matamet at Mal-Emir as an honored guest. He would collect and deliver as much tribute as he could. He would (most humiliating of all) swear allegiance to the Shah.

When oboes and drums echoing in the gorge at the head of the valley announced the approach of the Governor of Isfahan, Mehemet Taki Khan rode out to meet him, accompanied by two of his little sons as tokens of his peaceful intentions. A show of strength however was not neglected: the track where the Matamet would pass was lined on both sides with matchlock men who fired salutes, and horsemen who staged a realistic mock battle.

First came the Matamet's ferrashes, clearing the way for their master by dealing out blows left and right; next the musicians, blowing away as if their lungs would burst; then buffoons, turning somersaults, and dervishes who called upon Allah to bless the head of their leader as they spun round and round. On Mehemet Taki Khan's order, sheep and oxen were slain before the path of the Matamet as he rode along. The Bakhtiyari chieftain dismounted to greet him, as a sign of respect; attendants lifted up the two little boys for him to kiss.

With a shock, Layard recognized that the guide who had led the Persian forces over the mountain passes was Ali Naghi, the chief's own brother. He had done it, he explained, because in return for his services the Shah had promised that the government of all Khuzistan would be given to Mehemet Taki Khan. The Matamet had no hostile intent but was merely passing through the Bakhtiyari country on his way to collect taxes in Shuster, Dizful, and other towns of the Khuzistan plain.

The Persians pitched their tents opposite those of the tribesmen, and for forty days the warriors faced each other suspiciously while their leaders negotiated. Promises, offers, rumors flew back and

forth; plans for secret attack and counterattack were made in the
tents while Mehemet Taki Khan wavered from decision to decision.
Ali Naghi claimed that only a little patience was needed before
they were rid of the Matamet. He, who had been at the court of
the Shah, ought to know more of diplomacy and tactics than his
backwoods brother. So Mehemet Taki Khan gave way to Ali
Naghi's advice.

While discussions were going on, Layard took the opportunity
to explore the neighborhood a second time. The valley of Shushan
was deserted, and no one interfered with him, but he found no
more palaces than before. He considered Mal-Emir the most remarkable place in the Bakhtiyari mountains. On all sides high
peaks rose almost straight up; at the eastern end of the plain were
the mounds he had not previously been allowed to examine, the
ruins of an ancient city, known as the Prince's House, or the House
of Treasure. Greek and Sassanian coins were frequently found
there. Bas-reliefs were carved on the cliff faces in four spots. The
most remarkable were in a small gorge north of the city: 341 small
sculptured figures and a perfectly preserved twenty-four line cuneiform inscription.

Mehemet Taki Khan gave a final lavish feast at Kala Tul for
the Matamet, and handed over on a silver platter all the money
he had been able to scrape together, with many gifts: five high-
bred Arab horses, twelve fine mules, a valuable Cashmere shawl.
In addition he had provided for the Persian troops during the
entire time they had been in the Bakhtiyari country. When the
Matamet demanded additional supplies, he had called upon the
other chiefs for their quota, which caused considerable discontent.
One can imagine with what relief the Bakhtiyari saw the last of the
mountebanks and dervishes dance off into the passes leading
south. Again it would have been easy for the Bakhtiyari, mobile
and accustomed to the rough terrain, to attack the clumsy procession in the narrow mountain defiles. But Mehemet Taki Khan was
a man of his word. Not so the Governor of Isfahan. Shefi'a Khan,
Ali Naghi, and a number of other chiefs who had been invited to
accompany the Matamet part of the way as a mark of honor were

barely out of sight of Kala Tul before they were seized, loaded down with chains, and imprisoned.

Once out of the mountains and safe in the castle at Shuster, the Matamet sent word for Mehemet Taki Khan to surrender his person. The chieftain refused. He was declared a rebel and traitor; a fresh invasion was prepared. Weakened by many defections of his own allies, Mehemet Taki Khan was back on the horns of the old dilemma. He had humbled himself; he had paid tribute to the Governor of Isfahan, and his country was to be laid waste anyway. Ali Naghi, his brother, and Shefi'a Khan, his most trusted friend, were already in the Matamet's hands. He offered to send additional hostages as proof of his loyalty to the Shah. Send me Hussein Kuli, your son, answered the Matamet.

Mehemet Taki Khan was beside himself. In order to save his people, he would have to give in to this request too. The Matamet swore that he would not harm the boy—and surely not even the most treacherous Persian would deliberately hurt a child.

Wails filled the harem from the moment of the father's decision. It had been hard to make; it was even more difficult to tear the boy from his frenzied mother's arms. Others, weeping as they did so, dressed Hussein Kuli in the silken robes of a Bakhtiyari chief and set him on his father's favorite mare. The Khatun broke from those who had been restraining her, pulled her son from the saddle and clung to him until an attendant was ordered to drag her away by force. Pitifully she turned to her English friend, who had saved the child once before, and begged him to accompany Hussein Kuli, and to protect him from the Matamet. In order to comfort her, Layard promised to do what he could—though he had little faith in his ability to keep the promise.

Hussein Kuli was close to tears—he was only ten. But he showed no signs of fear, and sat his horse like a miniature warrior. When the party rode out through the castle gate, Mehemet Taki Khan tore open his shirt and beat upon his naked chest with his clenched fist. The Khatun, wailing piteously, ran beside the boy, almost under the horse's hoofs. When she could run no more, she cut off her hair with her dagger and trampled it under foot. Hussein Kuli pulled his horse to a stop; the Khatun put her arms around her son once more and then, hiding her eyes, walked slowly back to the castle.

A number of Bakhtiyari warriors escorted Hussein Kuli and Ali Naghi's oldest son, also a hostage, to within a mile of Shuster. The two boys, their *lala* (tutor), and Layard mounted to the old castle built on a rock overhanging the river Karun. The Matamet was seated on the terrace from which he could watch a mock battle which was being staged on the plain by two Bakhtiyari tribes that were enemies of Mehemet Taki Khan. Layard saw at once that the wily Governor had no intention of renouncing his expedition against the father, now that he had the son as a hostage. "He could not conceal the smile of satisfaction and triumph which passed over his bloated and repulsive features when the children stood before him. He addressed Hussein Kuli sternly in his thin, shrill voice. 'Why,' he asked, 'have you not brought your father with you? Is he not coming to Shuster to see me?' 'No,' replied the boy, with an undaunted air, his hand resting on his gun. 'What if I were to send these soldiers' (pointing to the horsemen careering in the plain beneath) 'to fetch him?' rejoined the Matamet. 'Let them go to Kala Tul,' answered Hussein Kuli, grasping his dagger. 'They will all come back naked, like this,' putting his forefinger into his mouth and then withdrawing it and holding it up, a significant gesture employed by the Bakhtiyari to denote that they have stripped a man to his skin.

"The Matamet could not help laughing and admiring the boy's courage and calm intrepidity. But, addressing him in a menacing tone, 'has not your father,' he asked, 'got much gold?' 'I know nothing of such things, as I am a child,' was the answer. 'You know, however, the place where he conceals it,' said the eunuch, 'and if you do not tell me where it is willingly, I shall have to make you,' giving the boy to understand that he would be subjected to the bastinado or some other torture. Nothing daunted, 'It is not likely,' he replied, 'that my father should have shown me the spot where he hides his money. If I knew I should not tell you, and if I were compelled to do so he would not let you have it.'"

Seeing that he could get nothing out of Hussein Kuli through threats, the Matamet ordered him and his cousin to be kept in close confinement. Persian officers who had stood by without a protest followed the children from the room and covered them with kisses. Layard was disgusted, outraged, and helpless. On the same day, the Matamet sent word to Kala Tul that the boys would be put to death unless Mehemet Taki Khan surrendered himself. Layard rode to the castle, and back again to Shuster with the chief's brother, Au Kerim, to offer the Matamet fresh terms. While Au Kerim negotiated, Layard investigated ruins in the neighborhood of Shuster. But he was soon once more in the city, plotting with Bakhtiyari friends to rescue Hussein Kuli. All had been arranged; a servant of the Persian in whose custody the child had been placed was bribed; Hussein Kuli was to be spirited away disguised as a girl. At the last minute, the *lala*, fearing for the boy's safety, or for his own, would not let Hussein Kuli go.

Once more Layard started for Kala Tul, only to learn when he was halfway there that the chieftain had fled the country, thus doing away with the Matamet's reason for an invasion. With Mehemet Taki Khan gone, there was no excuse to seize the Bakhtiyari's ripening crops and leave the people to starve. Layard was told that the chieftain would seek refuge with his ally, Sheikh Thamer of the Cha'b Arabs, who lived in the southern marshes near the Shat el-Arab—the kind of country where pursuit would be extraordinarily difficult.

Layard turned around and made for Fellahiyah, the headquarters of Sheikh Thamer. His horse was stolen, but he still had his saddle. He found a boat down the Karun to Ahwaz, a village of mud huts (in ancient times an important town trading with India; thriving again today as an oil center). He was down to his last penny. The sale of his saddle brought enough for mule hire, and he rode thirty miles or so across wasteland. Though there were countless mounds strewn with bricks and potsherds, he did not stop to pick up a single specimen; for once he had lost all taste for antiquities. At Kareiba, a large swamp Arab settlement on the Jerrahi, a tributary of the Karun, he learned that the Bakhtiyari party had passed that way on the previous night—and that the Matamet was pursuing them with a large army. On Sheikh Thamer's orders, the country beyond Kareiba had been flooded by destroying the dikes. The mule driver, after one look, leaped on his animal and trotted back to Ahwaz, leaving Layard stranded on the steaming riverbank.

At dawn orders had come through to evacuate this village also, and as Layard watched, the reed huts were being torn down to make rafts. It was a frantic scene. Naked children chased after squawking fowls while their elders drove buffaloes and bullocks into the river to swim to the next place of refuge. Every few minutes the men would stop whatever else they were doing to join hands and do a war dance. All were screeching at the tops of their lungs. Everyone was too busy to notice a stranger, much less help him. One by one the rafts pushed off, loaded to the edges with people, furniture, caldrons, cook pots, quilts, sacks of corn and rice, the smaller livestock. By sunset the ground where the village had stood was half under water, and Layard stood alone on a tiny island. He would have to make a raft for himself as soon as there was a moon to see by. He collected all the reeds and mats he could find, lay down on them, and tried to sleep. Soon he was surrounded by howling, deserted dogs, while the jackals, invading the remains of the huts for offal, "added to the frightful chorus."

He sat waiting in the fetid, pitch-black night, keeping off the dogs and trying to keep off the mosquitoes, till the moon, orange with heat, sailed up over the rim of the desert. By its light he bound his mats together with twisted straw as he had seen the Arabs do, launched himself upon them, and pushed out into the stream with a tent pole. The dogs followed along the bank as far as they could, howling pitifully. Herds of buffalo, camels, and sheep swam by in the moonlight with their noses barely above water. Men were crossing the river to the western bank, which was considered safer, on inflated sheepskins, carrying children on their shoulders, and bundles on their heads. Women, minus their long blue shirts, were helping to rescue the household goods. Thamer's men were breaking down the remaining dikes and set-

ting fire to the crops. The riverbank was an inferno: flames crack-
led, children screamed, dogs howled, temperature and terror rose.
No one paid the slightest attention to Layard, who floated along
among the other refugees, guiding himself with his pole.

By morning he had reached a long avenue of date-palm groves
which extended for two miles on either side of the river. He came
to a spot where it divided into three channels, all of them as
clogged with rafts as a lock on the Thames with punts of a Sun-
day. Since this was no time or place for English manners, Layard
forced his way into the middle channel, which was the broadest.
Along these banks, reed huts stood undemolished, surrounded by
the security of the deep marsh. Early in the afternoon, the channel
narrowed to an alley of water, enclosed and roofed over with mats.
On both sides, Arabs were lolling on carpets while attendants
hurried about serving *nargilehs* and tiny cups of coffee. Layard had
poled himself into the reception hall of Sheikh Thamer.

The Sheikh sat at the far end on a fine carpet set off from the
rest of the *musif* by bolsters. Having known other Englishmen
through doing business with the East India Company, Thamer
welcomed Layard cordially, listened to the tale of his recent adventures with amusement, and ordered for him a repast of "mutton
boiled to shreds and bread soaked in sour milk." The sheikh was
a tall, ugly man with the coarse features, bulging forehead, and
dark skin of the Arabs descended from those who had married
their African slavewomen. Yet he was impressive in his gold-
embroidered cloak, with a gold-mounted pistol and sword at his
belt. Beneath the cloak he wore neither trousers nor shoes, being
a specimen of the type called by the Turks "kafirs without religion, without drawers, and without saddles." Actually many a Turk
was far less progressive than Sheikh Thamer, who encouraged agri-
culture by keeping the irrigation canals in repair, and commerce by
giving protection to merchants. Under his rule Muhammera, below Basrah, at the juncture of the Shat el-Arab and the Karun, had
been made a free port and had prospered thereby. At the same
time Thamer had a reputation for having shot to death more than
one guest in this very musif.

Layard asked Thamer, in private, for a guide to take him to Mehemet Taki Khan. The Sheikh swore by Allah that the Bakhtiyari chief had turned back to the mountains. Layard did not believe him. Next day, while walking through the bazaar of Fellahiyah, he recognized a Bakhtiyari in Arab dress. After some argument, he persuaded the man to take him to his chief's hiding place. It lay deep in the marsh; they had to swim canals, wade through thick black mud or water to the armpits for hours. Layard was weak from fever, dizzy with the sun, and just about to give up when the guide pointed out a lonely group of tents squatting on the bank of a small canal. The most cheerful thing about it was the thought that the Matamet would have a hard time finding it.

"The Sahib has come!" cried the guards. Mehemet Taki Khan rushed out to embrace Layard in glad surprise. The women wept happy tears; they had not dared to hope that he would follow them into the swamps. Questions poured out. When had he left Shuster? Had he seen Hussein Kuli? What had become of the chief's brother, Au Kerim, who had been sent to negotiate with the Matamet? Hussein Kuli, as far as Layard knew, was well; Au Kerim was a prisoner.

Mehemet Taki Khan told his story. Several thousand tribesmen who had followed him into exile had been cut off by flooding spring streams. Only the family and their personal attendants were here among the swamp Arabs. On the way from the mountains they had been robbed of all they had managed to bring with them; little remained of the chief's so-called wealth. It was fate, *Kismet*, and as a good Moslem, Mehemet Taki Khan must accept it. The Khatun-jan called Layard into her tent to give him the few small things he had entrusted to her, which she had hidden safely even when robbed of her own jewels. "Ah, Sahib," she said sadly, "the Khan now repents him that he did not take my advice and refuse to give up Hussein Kuli, for he loved the boy better than his life. He will never again be happy now that he has lost him."

Mehemet Taki Khan was not totally without hope of returning to his mountains. Away from them he hardly felt it worth the struggle to live at all. The steaming dampness of the swamps choked him; the monotony of the flat expanses of water wearied his eyes. Pointing to the blue peaks on the far horizon, he said to Layard, "We shall, *inshallah,* drink snow up there together before the summer."

Thamer had sworn that he would fight to the death before he gave his guest up to the Persian dogs. For days his tribesmen had been gathering at Fellahiyah from the surrounding swamps. Almost naked, black from the sun, they danced in circles about their standard bearers, screaming war cries and chanting impromptu verses: "Thamer is a burning fire! Thamer is a lion of war!" The dancing and the yelling, the matchlocks blasting away, the war-songs and drums and oboes went on day-after-day, night-after-night.

The Matamet was now only twelve miles from Fellahiyah. Mehemet Taki Khan's trusted friend, Shefi'a Khan, arrived as an emissary from his captor, with the same threats, the same promises, and the same oaths that this time promises would be kept. Mehemet Taki Khan had only to prove his loyalty by coming to the Matamet's tent, and all doubt about it would be removed, all punishment forgotten.

The Khatun knew it was a lie. "You have taken my son from me," she said to her husband, "and now you would leave me and your other children without protection. Look at these families; they would not desert you in the hour of danger, and will you now desert them? How can you trust to one who has already over and over foresworn himself? Remain here and fight like a brave man, and wallah! wallah! there is not a woman here who will not be by your side."

Matamet sent a high priest of Islam, and his nephew Suleiman, an he had no fear for himself, but he did not wish to involve Sheikh Thamer in a bloody and probably disastrous war for his sake. The Matamet sent a high priest of Islam and his nephew Suleiman, an Armenian Christian, both of whom swore on their respective creeds that the Governor meant what he said. To a good Moslem it was unthinkable that an oath on the Koran could be broken.

Mehemet Taki Khan embraced his wife and embarked in the boat which had been sent to bring him to the Persian camp.

Layard was witness to the final betrayal. No sooner had the Bakhtiyari chieftain stepped inside the glittering pavilion of the Matamet than he was accused of treason, loaded down with chains, and dragged away by the ferrashes. He had not been allowed to say one word in his own defense. And again Layard stood by, helpless.

He slipped out of the Matamet's tent and hurried back to Sheikh Thamer's headquarters at Fellahiyah. A war council there decided to rescue Mehemet Taki Khan through a surprise attack by night. To Layard's mind the engagement was more like utter chaos than a battle: "The camp of an Eastern army has rarely any proper out-posts, and we were almost in the midst of the Persian tents before our approach was perceived. A scene of indescribable tumult and confusion ensued. The matchlock men kept up a continuous but random fire in the dark. The Arabs who were not armed with guns were cutting down with their swords indiscriminately all whom they met. Bakhtiyari and Arab horsemen dashed into the encamp-ment, yelling their war-cries. The horses of the Persians, alarmed by the firing and the shouts, broke from their tethers and galloped wildly about, adding to the general disorder. I kept close to Au Khan Baba [a brother of Mehemet Taki Khan] who made his way to the park of artillery, near which, he had learnt, were the tents in which his brothers were confined. I was so near the guns that I could see and hear Suleiman Khan giving his orders, and was almost in front of them when the gunners were commanded to fire grape into a seething crowd which appeared to be advancing on the Matamet's pavilion. It consisted mainly of a Persian regiment, which, having failed to form, was falling back in disorder.

"Before the Bakhtiyari and the Arabs could reach Mehemet Taki Khan, he had been taken from the tent in which he had been con-fined. The Persians had removed him as soon as the first alarm was given."

Au Kerim was set free; Shefi'a Khan also managed to escape. But the Cha'b Arabs had suffered severe losses, including several of the principal sheikhs. It seemed useless to continue. In the Bakhtiyari camp, many had lost husbands, sons and brothers; the tents were filled with the sound of grief. The Persians had also lost a large number of men, and were thoroughly discouraged at the thought of fighting their way through marshes and flooded country to the headquarters of Sheikh Thamer. After three days, therefore, the Matamet retired to Shuster, taking Mehemet Taki Khan with him.

The road to the hills was now open and there was no longer any reason for the Bakhtiyari families to remain in the unhealthy swamps. Malaria was endemic; most of the tribe were sick, and the children, who had not known trachoma in their highland home, had sore, festering eyes. Layard's stock of quinine and other medicines was almost used up. Sick himself, he found the heat difficult to bear; it was above a hundred and twenty degrees by day and almost as bad in the tents by night. Mehemet Taki Khan's family were nearly penniless, and were dependent on Sheikh Thamer's charity for their very bread. The Khatun thought it would be less humiliating and better for everyone concerned to seek refuge in the mountains among the chiefs whom her husband had befriended in times past.

During the usual delays before departure, Sheikh Thamer took Layard to see Muhammera, the port village which he had built up. This visit supplied Layard with geographical and political information which was to be of considerable use later. When the Bakhtiyari party set off for the mountains, he was in the vanguard with Shefi'a Khan, three brothers of Mehemet Taki, and a few other horsemen. Most of the men, having lost their horses, were on foot. The women and children, seated on quilts, carpets and cooking utensils, rode the mules. Their only other possessions, their gold and silver ornaments, were hidden under their clothes. The tents were left behind for greater mobility, since the party might have to fight its way through hostile tribes.

The first armed struggle took place only a day's journey from Fellahiyah when an Arab tribe attempted to detain the refugees with the intention of delivering the Khatun and her family into the hands of the Matamet. Here the brother whose counsel had caused much of their bitter trouble showed that he was made of warrior stuff after all. "Ali Naghi Khan, tearing open his dress and exposing his breast, as is the custom of the Bakhtiyari when they wish to show that they are bent upon some desperate enterprise, cried out to his followers: 'They come to seize your wives and your children. They will be given over to the *ser-baz* to be dishonoured. Let us be men! Let us be men!'" Though greatly outnumbered they fought off their attackers and got away. One of Ali Naghi's wives, two other women, and two men were wounded. Next evening, after a terrible day of heat and thirst, two children and a woman died and were hastily buried.

Everywhere the tribes were at each other's throats, or too terrified of the Matamet's vengeance to take in the refugees. A council of war was held, and it was decided to send Au Kerim to ask protection from the Il-Khani of the Khashgoi, who, though unrelated to the Bakhtiyari, had always been friendly to Mehemet Taki Khan's tribesmen. Layard offered to go along. They passed a night at the castle of a kinsman of Mehemet Taki, with whom, although he was a notorious brigand, they should have been safe. As soon as they had removed their arms, the host, drunk and abusive, led them to an inner room and locked them up. Layard knew it would do no good to reveal that he was an Englishman; the throat of an infidel would be slit with all the more enthusiasm. This was another of those nights when he could not sleep. "To be murdered in cold blood by a barbarian, far away from all help or sympathy, the place and cause of one's death to be probably forever unknown, and the author of it to escape with impunity, was a fate which could not be contemplated with indifference," writes this master of the British understatement.

After the chief and his fellow carousers had fallen asleep on their carpets in the usual Persian way (unusual among the mountain tribes), his wife released the prisoners. In the course of their wild escape, Layard was forced to separate from Au Kerim. He knew of the Khatun's plans only vaguely; alone in the mountains without a guide, he had no idea of how to find her and the Khanumi. He headed for Shuster, where he might be able to discover what had happened to his Bakhtiyari friends; the worst that the Matamet would dare to do to an Englishman would be to send him out of the country. The first thing he learned was that Au Kerim had been overtaken by his treacherous host, given into the hands of his brother's greatest rival, and shot.

Layard went at once to the Matamet, and told him that he considered Mehemet Taki Khan had been falsely arrested, that the chieftain had shown himself to be a kind host and a noble character. It was useless. Seeing that nothing he could do would help the chieftain and his family, Layard applied for a permit to continue his journey eastward. The Matamet scolded him roundly for the risks he had taken. "You Englishmen," he said, "are always meddling in matters which do not concern you, and interfering in the affairs of other countries. You attempted to do it in Afghanistan, but all your countrymen there have been put to death; not one of them has escaped."

Shocked, Layard realized that he would have to abandon for good his plan to reach India through the Seistan, or perhaps by any land route. In Baghdad he would be able to find out the true facts and make his plans accordingly. He had collected much political, economic and geographical information about Khuzistan, which should be useful to the British authorities, and he wished to get it down on paper while the details were still fresh in his mind. Being in a hurry to do these things, when the Matamet finally allowed him to leave Shuster he chose the shortest route, which was also the least traveled and most dangerous.

Chapter XI

"WE SHALL NEVER SEE YOU MORE!"
(September 1841–June 1842)

Layard arrived at the gates of Baghdad completely exhausted, having walked barefoot across the burning desert after a final robbery had relieved him even of his shoes. Dr. Ross, out for the daily morning canter with the ladies and gentlemen of the Residency, recognized him in spite of his rags, and rescued him, but it was some time before he could again walk without pain. At the beginning of September he wrote to his uncle from Baghdad: "I was detained until nearly the middle of August, when I fortunately succeeded in leaving the Persian camp and reaching Busrah; but in a curious condition—without a farthing in the world and with scarcely a shirt to my back, having been plundered some half a dozen times and exposed to the vicissitudes of war, etc. I found an English ship at Busrah, the captain of which received me civilly, and, having remained with him two or three days, I started off for Baghdad. I was now in hopes that all my troubles were at an end, but it turned out otherwise. Between Busrah and Baghdad I was plundered by the Arabs three times. And at length, after various escapes, I astonished our worthy Resident here by introducing myself to him in my shirt. But I am now accustomed to these things, and, as I have excellent health and spirits, they pass off as common occurrences." Included in this letter and one to his mother of the same date (September 9) was Layard's decision, after much thought, to return to England if his family approved. "I can live at Baghdad without expense, and I have here the most intellectual society in the family of our Resident, Colonel Taylor; and I intend remaining here until I hear from you," he added.

Colonel Taylor, as well as the Governor of Kerak, told him that the Matamet's story of a massacre of the English in Afghanistan was untrue. "Whatever may be the real inclinations of the Shah and his worthy Wuzir," wrote Colonel Henell to Layard, "they certainly want the means to equip an expedition against Afghanistan." Two months later, in November, the murder of the English in Afghanistan began. The Matamet had merely been premature in announcing that the plans, of which he had been secretly advised, had already been carried out.

While awaiting replies to his letters home, Layard accepted an invitation from Lieutenant Selby, commander of the *Assyria*, one of the East India Company's little steamers, to descend the Tigris to Basrah. He hoped to persuade Selby to continue down the estuary of the Shat el-Arab, where the Tigris and Euphrates unite, to the mouth of the Karun. Although Mehemet Taki Khan could no longer benefit by trade relations with the outside world, Layard still wished to settle the question of whether the Karun was navigable to steamships.[1] Leaving Baghdad in early October, they explored the channels of the estuary and the Karun, but the rains had not yet come and the river was too low to risk its ascent for more than a few miles. They landed at Muhammera and found the population terrified at the approach of the Matamet, who was on his way to punish Sheikh Thamer for having sheltered Mehemet Taki Khan. The Cha'b Arabs and their sheikh had fled to Turkish territory.

On the return voyage to Baghdad, Layard and Lieutenant Selby stopped for the night at the tents of Sheikh Mathkur of the Beni Lam Arabs, on the east bank of the Tigris. A few presents won the Sheikh's promise to give Layard his protection at any time. So, toward the end of October, he returned to the Beni Lam encampment, proposing to travel overland to Khuzistan, where there were still ancient sites to see and geographical questions that needed answers. Most of all he wished to find out what had become of Mehemet Taki Khan and his family. Layard's servant on this trip, Saleh the Lur, gave their suspicious hosts as good a definition of archaeological and anthropological research as one could wish (disregarding the moral purpose he assigned to it). "The kings of Feringistan," said he, "send their subjects to travel in different countries in order that they may inquire into the history of ancient monarchs, ascertain how they lived, and inform themselves of their good and bad actions. They are thus able to regulate their own conduct, and to govern their own countries with justice and wisdom."

The British Museum collection contains a small, burlap-covered notebook of this period. On the flyleaf, in somewhat of a schoolboy hand, is scrawled A. H. *Layard of whom let nothing be said* —an enigmatic and youthful remark which makes one realize with a start that this bearded explorer was then only twenty-four years old. Inside the travel-stained pages are list after list of the tribal and clan divisions of the Beni Lam, sketches, accounts of money spent, studies in language, copies of inscriptions, folk tales gathered from Arabs and Bakhtiyari on his journey up from the plains. He ran a triple set of risks this time: from his Arab hosts, who lived up to their reputation for villainy; in the mountains, among Mehemet Taki Khan's successful rivals; and in Shuster, where the Matamet would not be pleased to learn of the return of one whose sympathies were so well known that he was called by the Persians "Sahib Khan Bakhtiyari" (Sir Lord Bakhtiyari).

Some months later, Layard wrote to his mother (January 24, 1842): "During my last trip I discovered other sculptures and the sites of several ancient cities. I luckily escaped very well, having only been plundered once, although the journey was a very dangerous one, and succeeded in visiting every spot of any interest that, during my former excursions in Khuzistan, I had left unexamined. I visited the great robber Bakhtiyari chief [Jaffer Kuli Khan, an enemy to Mehemet Taki] who received me very civilly in his celebrated mountain stronghold, and, contrary to my expectations, gave me every opportunity of visiting the country. I had the honour of being introduced to all his wives (he has twelve) and of getting well drunk with him on some Shiraz wine. In fact, we were sworn friends, and I only regretted that time would not allow me to join him in a few plundering expeditions, and other parties of pleasure, which he very kindly offered to bring about for my amusement. I also spent a few days with the Wali of Luristan, the celebrated mountain prince of the Faiti, who received me with much kindness and treated me with great hospitality. The only two Englishmen who had ever ventured into this country, Captain Grant and Mr. Fotheringham, had been murdered by the predecessor of the present Wali, and, as Major Rawlinson had strongly warned any Europeans against attempting to enter the country, I was somewhat anxious as to the result of my journey. I am now, however, so well acquainted with this curious people that I had little difficulty in forming a friendship with him . . . The Matamet, the commander of the Persian troops, had also left orders at Shuster to have me arrested; but I dared the Governor to do so, and remained in the town and travelled about the country without noticing his threats or remonstrances."

Shuster and its inhabitants were in a sad state. One of the first things Layard saw on entering the city was the head of an old Bakhtiyari friend rotting on a pole in the bazaar. The Matamet had not limited himself to cutting off the heads of those who could by the furthest stretch of truth be considered his enemies, but had applied his ingenious tortures to all who had the misfortune to be wealthy. The poor suffered equally from the Matamet's soldiers, who, not having been paid in months, helped themselves to whatever they desired in the houses and bazaars. Now the army had left for Muhammera in pursuit of Sheikh Thamer, and Shuster was almost deserted.

Layard was greatly relieved to hear that his friends were alive and in the city. Through an influential Persian, he gained admission to Mehemet Taki Khan's prison.

The great warrior chief, who had so passionately loved freedom, sunlight and the mountains, was locked up in a small dark room in the castle, his hands and feet chained with iron fetters to a heavy iron neck ring. Yet he looked up with a smile of pleasure when Layard entered, and to the expressions of indignation and sympathy, answered only, "Ya Sahib! God is great, and we, His creatures, must humbly submit to His decrees. Yesterday I was great;

today I am fallen. It was his will, and I must submit." His was the
fatalism of the good Moslem, which, alternating with fanatical
violence in the cause of religion, explains a good deal in the history
of the Prophet's followers.

In the midst of his misery, Mehemet Taki Khan was concerned for the little sum of money which Layard had left in the
Khatun's keeping. The chieftain had been robbed of his personal
possessions; his lands had been confiscated, but, he whispered,
there was a certain seyyid of Shuster with whom he had once deposited a few valuable things. He slipped Layard a note ordering
the seyyid to hand over a fine Cashmere shawl in lieu of the money.
Layard tore up the note, telling Mehemet Taki Khan to forget the
whole thing.

The prisoner begged Layard to seek out his wife and son and
give them messages from him. Hussein Kuli, said his father, was
in the charge of a good man who was kind to him and even allowed
him to see his parents occasionally. Next to his family, Mehemet
Taki Khan's chief anxiety was for the tribes. Even in this prison,
word had reached him of dissension, blood feuds, tribal warfare.
Everything he had done had gone for nothing; everything he had
tried to spare them had happened anyway.

He spoke of himself last of all. He no longer had any hope of
"drinking snow" in his beloved mountains ever again. But this he
would accept; willingly would he remain a captive for the rest of
his life if the Khatun-jan and Hussein Kuli could be with him. Nor
did he fear death. There was only one fate he feared—to have his
eyes put out. And this too might come to pass.

Layard left the cell with a heavy heart. As he approached the
ruined house where he had been told the Bakhtiyari ladies were
living, the sound of voices rising and falling in lamentation seemed
to continue without end. There was no need to knock on a door;
the house was open on one side. Within it was bitter cold; there
was no fire; women and children huddled together for body heat
like sheep in a storm. The Khatun, sobbing so that she could not
speak, held out her thin hands to him. In a choked voice, she mur-
mured at last how happy she was to see him alive and well; they

had heard that he had been killed with Au Kerim in the mountains.

He could hardly recognize most of the women, so pale and emaciated were they. Many were sick with fever and dysentery. (What the filth and the stench was like in that ruined house, Layard was too delicate to mention.) No beauty remained, he writes, to Khanumi, whom he had thought so beautiful at Kala Tul. The big eyes and the delicate features in the disease-ravaged face must have torn his heart. Like the others, she was clothed in black rags, in mourning, as far as it could be approximated, for Au Kerim, and for Au Kelb Ali, who had died of illness and exposure. Shefi'a Khan too was dead. When Layard asked after Fatima, the Khatun's mother, and others who were missing, he was answered by wailing and repeated cries of "Wahi! Wahi!" If he had not been a man (and an Englishman) he might easily have joined in the lament.

After Layard and Au Kerim had parted from the others, said the Khatun, they had been attacked on the road by hostile tribes. Many had been killed; the ladies had been robbed of their ornaments and finally even of their mounts. They had continued on foot, exhausted and without food. They had been betrayed to the Matamet finally by a chief with whom they had sought refuge, a chief who had received favors from Mehemet Taki Khan in times past. They had been taken to Shuster, to this house, where they had at first been imprisoned under guard. But now they were left to themselves, for, after all, where could they escape to? What could sick women and children do to harm the Matamet? As far as the Khatun knew, he had forgotten them. They had been a royal family; now they were beggars, dependent for the little they ate on families in Shuster that had been indebted to Mehemet Taki Khan in the days of his prosperity. But the weaker sex did not go in for Moslem resignation. The Khatun had taught Mehemet Taki Khan's youngest son, Riza Kuli, who was hardly more than three, the meaning of revenge. "Give me a sword," he cried to Layard in his baby's voice, "that I may cut off the Matamet's head, and bring back my father!"

During the short time Layard remained in Shuster, he spent hours daily with the unhappy women. Though he thought up one scheme after another, he could find no feasible way to help them. In danger of arrest himself, he could give them nothing but his affection and sympathy. Their gratitude for this poor gift was almost past bearing. When the time came for him to tear himself away, they began once more to wail and beat their breasts. "Ah, Sahib, we shall never see you more," cried the Khatun and the poor young Khanumi to their Englishman. "Wahi! Wahi!"

But he did manage to see them one more time—the last—in March. Letters from England had made it clear that he must give up the idea of going to India through Afghanistan. Except for this last part of the journey, he had accomplished everything he had set out to do. He had written his memoir on Khuzistan and given it to Colonel Taylor to forward to Lord Aberdeen, the Secretary of State for Foreign Affairs. He had settled, to his own satisfaction, the question of the site of ancient Susa after visiting Sus, about thirty miles from Shuster. From the summit of the great mound he made hasty sketches and took compass readings on the Dizful River, which (Major Rawlinson notwithstanding) had been identified as the Ulai. Nearby he found an inscribed slab of the Achaemenid period. He was convinced that Rawlinson's theory concerning the valley of Shushan was mistaken, that the mound at Sus represented (as excavation was to prove) the capital city of Darius and other Achaemenid kings of Persia, "and, consequently, it may be presumed, of Shushan the palace, of the Book of Daniel."[2]

He had located a British merchant of Baghdad, Mr. Alexander Hector, who was interested in the products of the Bakhtiyari and other inhabitants of Khuzistan. The problem of transportation of goods remained. With Colonel Taylor's blessing, he embarked again on the *Assyria*, accompanied by Dr. Ross of the Residency staff, to demonstrate that the Karun was navigable as far as Shuster. Though the ship ran aground a few miles below the town, an accident which Layard, perhaps unfairly, put down to Lieutenant Selby's carelessness, he considered that he had proved his point.

The month's delay before the *Assyria* was floated off again gave him all the more time to do what he had come for: see his Bakhtiyari friends. Selby and Dr. Ross, whom he took with him, were tremendously impressed by Mehemet Taki Khan, by his progressive views on his people, and the courage with which he bore his imprisonment. The chieftain was more optimistic now. He hoped that Ali Naghi, who was in Teheran, might be able to persuade the Shah to allow his brother's return to the mountains.

The ladies of the family were in greater misery than before, almost without food, almost without clothes to cover their emaciated bodies. Several more had died; all were ill; Khanumi seemed to be dying. After Dr. Ross had treated her, she improved rapidly, and Layard felt hopeful. But suddenly orders were received to remove the ladies to Dizful. Layard rushed to the official in charge; argued with him; asked him to delay the journey till Khanumi had recovered her strength. The request was refused, and Khanumi died on the way.

Mehemet Taki Khan died, still in prison, still in chains, in 1851. The Khatun-jan lived to old age. She, Hussein Kuli, and her younger son were sent to Teheran as hostages; the rest of the family, about sixty in number, were allowed to return to the mountains. Hussein Kuli and his young wife died in 1855; the younger brother was put to death in 1882. The son of Jaffer Kuli Khan, the robber baron who had entertained Layard after his stay among the Beni Lam, became supreme chief of the Bakhtiyari.

Today this interesting people still live in their mountains between Isfahan, Shiraz, and Shuster. Many are settled in villages now, and they no longer war upon each other or upon the authorities in Teheran. On the contrary, several Bakhtiyari have played prominent parts in the government and politics of Iran; the Chief of Security a few years ago was General Timour Bakhtiar. One still has to obtain the protection of a chieftain in order to visit the Bakhtiyari, and, within their settlements, they live in much the same fashion as when Layard knew them. Their products, especially their beautiful hand-woven carpets in traditional patterns, are brought to the bazaars of Isfahan and Shiraz by motor truck, and sold also on the world market, as Layard and Mehemet Taki Khan had dreamed they would be.

Layard now prepared to go home. He could not have liked the prospect, but he was two years older than when he had fled from London and his dictatorial uncle. His independent life had given him self-confidence; he believed he could now calmly ask Mr. Austen's advice as one man to another. He had made his Grand Tour of the East, and it was time to think seriously of making a living. He prided himself that he had not wasted his mother's money; in two years, he had spent less than two hundred pounds, including the sums which had been stolen from him in holdups too numerous to count.

The Middle East was again on the verge of war, this time between Turkey and Persia, mostly because the Governor of Isfahan, in pursuit of Sheikh Thamer, had invaded lands claimed by the Sultan, and helped himself to the strategically important town of Muhammera. Even in those pre-oil days, Britain and the British East India Company had interests in the Middle East which would be jeopardized by a war. Since Britain's might was incomparably greater than that of any Eastern power, her mediation and pressure exerted on one side or the other could drastically affect the outcome of a quarrel. ("You Englishmen are always interfering in the affairs of other countries," the Matamet had said.) The center from which this influence (or interference) emanated was Her Majesty's Embassy at Constantinople.

Colonel Taylor felt that Layard's firsthand experience of the events leading up to the Turco-Persian conflict, and his intimate knowledge of the territory in dispute, would be of inestimable value to Sir Stratford Canning, British Ambassador to the Porte. He therefore asked Layard if he would be willing to travel home via Constantinople, bearing dispatches for the Embassy, and at the same time to fill Sir Stratford in on the background of the current crisis. Layard agreed to do so.

He left Baghdad in the company of a *tatar*, as official couriers

were called. The word, which is a version of *tartar*, has in this connection no reference to national origins. Before the days of railways
and regular mails, each foreign embassy in the Turkish dominions
employed several tatars, a special class, known for their great endurance and (rare in the East) incorruptible reliability. This one
was carrying dispatches from the Pasha of Baghdad to the Turkish
authorities in Constantinople. At the forefront of the little company rode the tatar's *sureji*, or groom, leading the baggage horse;
the tatar, in his bright red jacket and tarbush, brought up the rear,
urging the horses on with his heavy whip. Layard, in the middle,
carried his own baggage—mostly notebooks and observation instruments—in his saddlebags. His carpet, and his old ragged cloak,
the sole survivor of his original outfit, had, as he wrote his mother,
encountered all the dangers of St. Paul; he thought they ought to
be preserved as relics. He would have to get a complete set of new
clothes in Constantinople.

Knowing that prompt delivery of his dispatches was essential,
he was more than satisfied to have the tatar set a furious pace,
keeping the horses at a gallop or a fast trot day and night. It was
June, full summer in Mesopotamia; the heat rising from the
scorched plains was a furnace blast, but these three men were
hardened to such things. They changed post horses along the way,
but they themselves took little time to rest. The two hundred and
fifty miles from Baghdad to Mosul were covered in something over
fifty hours, a feat which compared favorably with the equestrian
dashes for which Major Rawlinson had been famous in his youth.

They delayed three days in Mosul while dispatches were made
ready for the tatar to take on. Layard spent his time with Botta,
the newly arrived French Consul. Paul Émile Botta had been
chosen for the post because of very special qualities. After Claudius
Rich's *Memoir* on Babylon had caused such a stir, Julius Mohl,
translator of Firdusi and member of the French Asiatic Society,
had insisted that the English should not be left in possession of
this new (though immeasurably old) field for collecting art treasures. He had seen to it that the French Agent at Mosul was
carefully selected to defend his country's interests in matters an-

tiquarian as well as diplomatic. In his youth, Botta had collected botanical specimens during a trip around the world for the *Jardin des Plantes*, and zoological specimens on an expedition to the Sudan, where he had accompanied Mehemet Ali, Pasha of Egypt, as physician. He had journeyed to remote Yemen, and done consular service in China and at Alexandria. H. J. Ross, British merchant of Mosul (later Layard's close friend), wrote of Botta: "He is quite a Frenchman, as he was educated at Paris for a doctor . . . We are great friends in spite of his violent denunciations of England which entirely depend on how much opium he has taken."[3] Botta, who was a little over forty at this time, was the son of Carlo Botta, a well-known Italian historian who had been exiled for his revolutionary opinions, and had settled in France. Layard had read the elder Botta's books, and had often discussed them with his Italian patriot friends.

The opium habit, which Paul Émile had acquired in China, was apt to make him moody and depressed, though he claimed it was a source of comfort and happiness. Layard was not one who needed artificial stimulation, but he was induced to try a pipeful for the sake of experience. He experienced no comfort or happiness from it; only nausea and a bad headache. Botta could not tempt him to try again.

Between smokes, the Frenchman was a delightful companion, open-minded and generous. Most of Layard's three days at Mosul were occupied with exploring the mounds across the river in Botta's company. Having read in Rich's *Narrative* that sculptures were rumored to have been found at Nebbi Yunus, Botta had first attempted to dig there, but the guardians of the Tomb of Jonah had raised such a to-do (as they had with Rich) that he had been forced to remove his operations to Kuyunjik. So far he had found nothing but a few bricks and bits of inscribed alabaster, and at the time of Layard's visit he was thoroughly discouraged. The young Englishman, enthusiastic as ever, urged him not to give up. He was convinced that treasures of great importance—if not Nineveh itself—lay beneath these mounds. And if you did find anything, the rewards, financially as well as in fame, would be tremendous, for finders were keepers in those days. All that was necessary before you took your discoveries out of the country was a firman, usually from a local pasha, who could be bribed. Layard himself had written to Mr. Stirling, a merchant in England who was the agent of Mr. Hector of Baghdad, to suggest that a small investment in the Mosul mounds would repay the investor in the value of art objects discovered, and that he was ready and willing to look for them. But he had received no answer from Mr. Stirling before leaving Baghdad; evidently he was never to have the opportunities by which Botta was blessed. If he had any jealous twinges, he does not admit them in his written account. He encouraged Botta to continue.

Across Syria and Asia Minor rode Layard and the tatar, at the same smart pace, to Samsun, a port on the Black Sea, where they waited for a ship to Constantinople. For the Englishman, this was the actual end of a special phase in his life, a *hejira* that had begun as the "land-march" to Ceylon with Mitford two years before. When he was well on his way to success and honors, he was to write nostalgically: "I look back with feelings of grateful delight to those happy days when, free and unheeded, we left at dawn the humble cottage or cheerful tent, and, lingering as we listed, unconscious of distance, or of the hour, found ourselves, as the sun went down, under some hoary ruin tenanted by the wandering Arab, or in some crumbling village still bearing a well-known name. No experienced dragoman measured our distances or appointed our stations. We were honoured with no conversations with pashas, nor did we seek any civilities from governors. We neither drew tears nor curses from the villagers by seizing their horses, or searching their houses for provisions; their welcome was sincere; their scanty fare was placed before us; we ate, and came, and went in peace."

As he waited at Samsun for the ship that would take him to Constantinople, Layard could not know that this was another crucial step in his life. Had he sailed for England direct from Beirut, as he had originally intended, his future would have been very different.

Chapter XII

INTERNATIONAL INTRIGUE AND POWER POLITICS

(1842–1843)

Since no European clothes could be bought at Samsun, Layard borrowed what he could from the British Vice-Consul in order to be presentable when he reached the Embassy at Constantinople. Presumbly he shaved his black and shining beard. (A portrait in the costume of the Albanians, to whom Layard undertook a mission not many years later, shows him with an elegant moustache only.) His ship dropped anchor in the Golden Horn on the ninth of July, 1842. Pausing only long enough to engage a room and leave his saddlebags at Roboli's Hotel, where he had been so ill on his first visit to Constantinople, he hired a caïque to row him up the Bosphorus to Buyukderé, where the summer embassy was located.

He was deeply tanned and shabby and probably not too neat after his long journey, but he saw no reason in this to be treated as if he were a tatar instead of an English gentleman. To be asked to cool one's heels in an anteroom, after all the hardships undertaken for the sake of speed, was enough to give a man a fine case of high dudgeon. "At length a fashionably dressed young gentleman appeared, asked me cavalierly for the despatches of which I was the bearer, informed me that the Ambassador was too much occupied to see any one, and turning on his heel left the room without deigning to listen to what I had to say." Layard would have marched out of the Embassy then and there but that he needed a passport before he could embark for England. No one at the Embassy would pay any attention to him on this score either. He applied instead to the British Consul, who promised to send him a passport promptly. He was fully determined to leave Constantinople the minute it came through. To relieve his feelings, he wrote a letter—so angry a letter that he expected it to be ignored—to Sir Stratford Canning. Within a few hours he received an answer expressing the Ambassador's apologies and asking him to call again as soon as possible.

The British Ambassador at Constantinople in the mid-nineteenth century occupied a position of paramount importance. The gigantic Ottoman Empire was falling apart; in the fragmentation process, the European powers were constantly intervening, either to encourage independence or to patch things up—whichever suited their national interests. England was the Porte's oldest and most trusted ally, a trust justified sometimes, but not always, by the positions she took. Sir Stratford Canning, during an earlier term of office (1825–27) had been conspicuously active in the intervention of the powers on the side of Greek independence. Nevertheless he was well liked by the Porte and, on his return to Constantinople in 1841, was more influential than ever because of his friendship with the Turkish Foreign Minister, Reshid Pasha. Called by the Turks the *Buyuk Elchi*, or Great Ambassador, Sir Stratford's name was known and feared the length and breadth of the Turkish dominions.

"Sir Stratford received me immediately," Layard reports of his second call at the Embassy. "I was greatly struck by his appearance. His hair was already white. His tall and spare frame was not altogether erect, as he had the habit of stooping. There was, perhaps, a somewhat too evident assumption of dignity and reserve in his manner, which was intended to impress people with the utmost respect for the Queen's Ambassador, and if the occasion required it, with awe. His earnest grey eyes seemed to penetrate into one's very thoughts. His thin, compressed lips denoted a violent and passionate temper. His complexion was so transparent that the least emotion, whether of pleasure or anger, was at once shown by its varying tints. A broad and massive overhanging brow gave him an air of profound wisdom and sagacity. He was altogether a very formidable-looking personage, and he made upon me the impression which he, no doubt, intended to produce. His manner towards me was, however, kind and considerate."

After renewed apologies for the rudeness of his attaché, Sir Stratford questioned Layard keenly about events in Khuzistan. He thanked the young man for his clear exposition of the geographical data, and said that he believed English mediation of the border dispute was called for. He hoped that Layard would remain in Constantinople long enough so that he could avail himself of more information as soon as he knew whether the services of a mediator would be accepted by the disputing parties.

This was both interesting and flattering to young Layard, but if he ran up hotel bills, he would not have enough money left for his passage home. After waiting around for a while, he sent Sir Stratford a note mentioning the probable date of his departure. He received no answer. Still smarting from the earlier insult, he made arrangements to board a ship for Vienna. He was walking down the hill to the wharf when a cawass overtook him with an invitation from the Ambassador reading, "Instead of going away, come and dine here tomorrow, and I will try to arrange a plan with you." After a moment of hesitation, Layard canceled his passage. He began to hope that he would not have to return to England after all.

Sir Stratford asked Layard if he would be willing, while waiting on the mediation plan, to undertake a delicate task for the Embassy: investigation of a revolutionary situation in Serbia. He would have to go unofficially, and would receive no salary, but his expenses would be paid. Another young man might, after Persia, have had his fill of cloak-and-dagger work. Not Layard. "I left Constantinople in high spirits," he writes. "My taste for travel and adventure had not been satiated, and I was further excited by the idea that I was engaged in an important though secret mission, which, in the event of my discharging it to the satisfaction of the Ambassador, would in all probability lead to my permanent employment in the East, the great object of my ambition."

As a supposed private citizen, he talked with Serbians on both sides of the struggle: the reactionary followers of Milosh, the hereditary prince, and the revolutionaries who had recently deposed him in favor of Alexander Karageorgevitch, son of the peasant chief to whom the Serbians owed their partial independence. Prince Milosh was backed by Imperial Russia. Layard felt that "if England was called upon to take any part in the affairs of Servia, her true policy was to give her support to those who were struggling to obtain liberal institutions, to uphold the independence of their country, and to resist the undue interference of Russia in its government and administration."

To make his report with all possible speed, he engaged in another breakneck ride (from Belgrade to Constantinople) with a tatar—or rather three tatars whom he wore out one after the other. They galloped across country; in the towns, with the *sureji* yelling and cracking his whip, they would dash down the main street, splashing mud on the unwary and on merchandise displayed before the shops. Once Layard's horse stumbled and he flew over its head to land in a circle of tailors seated cross-legged in an open booth. It was a question who was more surprised, Layard or the tailors, but no one was hurt. He reached the gates of Constantinople on the sixth day, after a ride of some six hundred miles—very proud of himself for beating a record made by a courier over the same course, which had been remarkable enough to be mentioned in the House of Commons.

Sir Stratford Canning agreed with Layard's viewpoint and made his recommendations to the Foreign Office accordingly. Lord Aberdeen, frequently accused of being pro-Russian, but essentially pro-peace and noninterventionist, did not agree. Sir Stratford, mortified and angry, stuck to the recognition of the revolutionary party. At any rate the Karageorgevitch dynasty, with some interruptions, remained on the throne until World War II, when young King Peter of Yugoslavia was replaced by Tito—another revolutionary leader risen from the peasant class.

Layard had discharged his mission to the satisfaction of his chief but not of the Foreign Minister, to whom his role in influencing Sir Stratford was known. As in his boyhood, Layard's liberal ideas made trouble for him. He was singularly undiplomatic for one whose main ambition at the time was to join the diplomatic service. He was further discredited by a rumor (which Lord Aberdeen continued to believe) that he had announced himself in Serbia as Britain's official emissary—the very thing he had been careful not to do.

And now a scandalous accusation shook him to his boots. He, who was constantly outraged by Eastern dishonesty, found himself named a swindler. He had been forced to borrow money (when robbed of his cash, usually) in Persia and at Kerak, and had made out drafts on his letter of credit to repay the loans. His London bankers had refused to honor the drafts because of a technicality; Layard, lost somewhere among the Bakhtiyari, could not be reached to verify them. The first he knew of the matter was when Benjamin Austen wrote that his nephew had been sued in court, and that he himself had paid the debts and the legal costs of the case. In the meanwhile Sir Stratford had been advised of the disgrace (by whom we do not know). Poor Layard—he had been called a radical; he had been called rash and unsettled, but dishonest—never! Among other reasons for distress, this ended all chance of a career in diplomacy, whose members must be above suspicion. He wrote in a rage to his bankers: they knew very well that he had sufficient funds on deposit to cover the drafts! At his urgent request, Sir Stratford agreed to suspend judgment pending the answer. His faith in a young man of whom he had not even heard till a short time before is a tribute to them both. Layard waited, in such agony as can be imagined, for the return mail from London, a matter of many months. Once in a while Austen Henry Layard, a restrained writer where his private emotions are concerned, says he was "in despair." This was one of those times. The apology, which eventually arrived from the bankers, admitting that they should have honored the drafts in spite of some small irregularities (none of them their client's fault) was small compensation for the cloud of suspicion beneath which he had suffered.

Now, however, after two and a half years of paying his own way, Layard's few hundred pounds were almost used up. Sir Stratford had recommended him for an attachéship and wished him to remain in Constantinople, but he could pay the young man no salary till an official appointment was confirmed by the Foreign Office in London. Meanwhile Layard did not know how he was to live. Roboli's Hotel did not observe tribal rules of free hospitality. There were bills to pay for clothes also; he could not present himself at the Embassy in Bakhtiyari costume, not even in shabby borrowed European dress. A prospective diplomat had to be as elegant as the young gentleman who had received Layard so rudely.

He decided to go ahead, use up his remaining cash, and not worry about trouble until he met it face to face. This was the sort of decision he had made before and would make again, fortunately for his future. On the recommendation of Longworth, the correspondent for the *Morning Post*, he moved into a small room in the house of an Armenian widow. It was inexpensive; he would have Longworth's companionship, and the widow had three pretty daughters. For his working hours, Layard was assigned a room in the Embassy, which had moved to Pera for the winter.

Pera was on the European side of the Bosphorus, climbing steeply uphill from the Golden Horn, where ships of a dozen nations lay at anchor: tall-masted sailing vessels, a few stove-pipe funneled steamships, and many half-moon-shaped galleys of red, blue, and yellow, with eyes painted on their high prows. In and out among them darted the caïques, rowed by swarthy, heavy-muscled boatmen. On the Asiatic side of the harbor, across the Galata Bridge (then a bridge of boats) was Stambul, the old city, a tangled warren of littered streets, with a huge, sprawling covered bazaar, hundreds of domes, and a forest of minarets from which the Faithful were called to prayer. Through those streets surged a mixed crowd: soldiers in their shabby, half-European uniforms; prosperous Turks in voluminous baggy pants; women veiled in black to the eyes.

Europeans were not allowed in Stambul after dark. Flouting the rule, Layard and Longworth frequently spent the night at the large old-fashioned wooden house which was the home of a young Turkish friend, Ahmed Vefyk. There the Englishmen would sit

cross-legged on a beautiful carpet around a silver tray, dipping
their hands into thirty different kinds of food (in less enlightened
households, the minimum that could be served was forty-two
dishes). The menu consisted of soup, followed by "messes" of
meat, fish, and vegetables, alternating with sweets, eggs, and buffalo cream, winding up with a big pilaff, and a china bowl of sherbet (sugar and water flavored with prunes). For the final dish and
the soup, spoons were provided; for the rest you used the imple-
ments that God gave you. It was rather difficult, Layard remarks, to
convey rice, rich sauces and melted butter to the mouth by hand
with decency and cleanliness. An embroidered napkin, however,
was thrown over your shoulder at the start of the meal for the purpose of wiping off your mouth, fingers and shirt front.

He regularly spent two evenings a week at this house in Stambul
or at Vefyk's summer *yali* on the Bosphorus shore. They studied
languages together, Turkish in exchange for English; and read
aloud the English classics and political writings. The young Turk
particularly liked Dickens, and laughed so heartily over Mr. Pickwick that even guests who did not understand a word of English
giggled too. The seventeen-year-old Ahmed Vefyk was convinced,
like Disraeli, that he would someday be Prime Minister.

The spy fiction which has so often been laid in Constantinople
is easily outdone by the facts. Today the super-American Hilton
crowns Pera's heights, but still, in older hotels descending the hill,
ghosts of secret agents lurk in every shabby Turkish cozy-corner,
under every bead-fringed lamp shade. All wars have seen them
there; in times of peace as well, intrigue has been Constantinople's
chief activity. In Layard's day it was focused on an internal struggle between the forces of reaction and the more liberal statesmen,
represented by Reshid Pasha, the author of the new Turkish constitution. Reshid was an ardent supporter of the reforms introduced by Mahmoud, the former Sultan. Mahmoud's mother had
been Aimée DuBucq de Rivery, a French girl from Martinique
(cousin to Joséphine de Beauharnais) who had been captured by
the Corsairs and presented to the royal harem, to become the
Sultan's favorite, and, eventually, *Sultan Valideh* (mother of the

Sultan). Her son, who adored her, had naturally wished every-thing to be up-to-date and Westernized in Turkey. But the present Sultan, Abdul-Mejid, was a conservative, like most Turks. He was also weak, vacillating, and much under the influence of Reshid's greatest rival, the reactionary Riza Pasha.

Sir Stratford Canning's inclinations were on the side of Reshid and the reform party, for he believed that, unless the corrupt Turkish administration was remodeled along European lines, the Ottoman Empire would fall to pieces, which would be contrary to British interests in the East. (By the time of World War I, with Turkey an enemy instead of an ally, Britain encouraged the Arab Revolt.) Imperial Russia, which had much to gain from the breakup of the Empire, secretly supported Riza Pasha. The British Ambassador's manipulations were also carried on in secrecy. In-fluential though the Great Elchi was, he could not afford to be accused of undue interference in local affairs. What more suitable messenger could there be for confidential communications than his young English friend, who had so swiftly caught on to the Turkish language, Turkish practices and prejudices, and who, if discovered, could truthfully disclaim any official connection with the British Embassy?

The task, though difficult and dangerous, had glamor for one like Layard, by his own admission a romantic. The meetings with Turkish statesmen, whether they were in office or out of it and in apparent disgrace, took place usually at night and always in some out-of-the-way place in the Moslem quarter. The gates to the Ga-lata Bridge were locked at sunset, but a *caiquiji* could be bribed to row the stranger across the Golden Horn. In some obscure street, a back door would open at a prearranged signal, and Layard would be whisked into a harem, where discussions could be held without fear of interruptions or eavesdroppers. He frequently spent the night at Reshid Pasha's house, or left there in the small hours to recross the harbor with an urgent message for the Embassy. He ran constant risk of arrest by the Turkish water police and conse-quent imprisonment in a guardhouse. If that had ever happened, he would have had to take his punishment or get out of the scrape through his own efforts. An appeal to the British Ambassador would have provoked a diplomatic crisis.

All the European powers had their secret agents in Constantinople: Greeks, Armenians, social outcasts who lived on spying, Turks of high position in the palace or government. The largest number and the most efficient were in the pay of the Russian Embassy. The struggle was well underway that was to wind up in the Crimean War of 1854, with Russia on one side and the allied powers of England, France and Turkey on the other. There was at least one difference between Layard and other secret agents: he was unpaid. The cause, he thought, was worth the risks.

But he did not entirely approve of his unofficial chief's way of handling things. Sir Stratford Canning, as Layard had suspected on first sight of those "thin, compressed lips," could not bear to be crossed. The Ambassador completely lost control of himself when he believed an action to be wrong, or his dignity was offended. On bad days, his secretaries kept hold of the handle of the door as they entered his room, so that they would be able to escape in a hurry. Not so Layard; he felt that Sir Stratford's bullying did more harm than good, and told him so. Throughout their relationship, he stood up to the Ambassador and was the more respected for it. He even dared to say that the poetry which Sir Stratford was fond of composing was doggerel—criticism which was accepted with a smile.

Reshid Pasha would have fared better if he had been similarly courageous. Layard several times saw the unfortunate Turk, who had been unable to carry out some demand of the Ambassador's, cowering in a corner of the divan, "frightened out of his wits," while Sir Stratford shook his fist and poured out a storm of invective. The Ambassador continually underestimated difficulties encountered by forward-looking Turkish statesmen in dealing with the Sultan, the Moslem doctors of law, and other powerful figures who were bigoted, ignorant, or motivated by self-interest.

The tactics of the Russian Ambassador, Count Boutanieff, were quite different from those of Sir Stratford Canning. Between the two, a constant battle went on, "the English Ambassador imposing himself upon the Turks, seeking to inspire them with awe, and to drive them into doing his bidding; the Russian endeavoring to obtain his ends by cajolery, and by leading his victims by gentle and persuasive means to their destruction."

Though Layard was critical of Sir Stratford's methods, he was deeply grateful to him for personal kindness, hospitality, and his continued trust. Soon after the Serbian mission, the Ambassador called upon him for additional information on Khuzistan and other work in connection with the Turco-Persian border dispute. A Turkish expedition was preparing to drive out Persian forces under the Matamet, which, in pursuit of Sheikh Thamer, had occupied the port of Muhammera and territory north of it. On the verge of tearing each other to pieces over this bone of contention, Persia and Turkey were forced to accept the mediation of two bigger dogs: England and (at Lord Aberdeen's insistence) Russia.

It is easy to see the strategic and commercial importance of Muhammera. Although it was only a village of reed huts, it commanded both the entrance to the Tigris and Euphrates and their outlet, through the Shat el-Arab, to the sea. The great rivers which flowed for over a thousand miles through Turkish territory could be bottled up if the port was given to a hostile power (Persia). Britain's relations with Persia had always been precarious, while Turkey was an old ally. In case of war, Layard pointed out, Turkey would not object to transportation of British troops down the rivers to the foot of the Persian mountains. The passage to India was no doubt a matter for thought. There was also an economic and socially useful reason for ceding Muhammera to Turkey. Layard had seen at first hand the desert to which Mesopotamia had been reduced by the lawless, raiding Arab tribes. His answer to the problem was similar to the plan he and Mehemet Taki Khan had devised for the lawless Bakhtiyari. The only way to settle the Bedouin and make them into peaceful, tax-paying citizens would be to create a market for their products—and this could be done by developing navigation on the Tigris and Euphrates. Who else but England could supply the necessary capital and enterprise?

But would England undertake this if, at the whim of Persia, the rivers could be blockaded?

Layard's practical recommendations were based on geographical factors: on old maps and his own exploration of the Karun with Lieutenant Selby in the *Assyria*.[1] He proved to Sir Stratford's satisfaction that the Persian frontier had never reached the Shat el-Arab. Nor did Persian commerce need that estuary as an outlet to the Gulf; the Karun, admittedly a Persian river, would serve the purpose with a little dredging of its original mouth, the Bahmehshire, as he had proved by descending it with Selby. Layard proposed that a new boundary line be drawn running to the Persian Gulf halfway between the Shat el-Arab and the Bahmehshire, which would allow Turkey to keep Muhammera and the entrance to the two great rivers. This solution, which, regardless of the political purposes behind it, is eminently fair, was presented through the British Foreign Office to Russia, the other mediating power. Russia not only refused to go along with it but demanded for Persia additional territory which the Shah had not even claimed. Lord Aberdeen instructed the British Ambassador at Constantinople to recommend the Russian scheme to Turkey and Persia.

Layard, summoned to the Ambassador, found Sir Stratford stalking up and down his study, flushed and tight-lipped. He handed the dispatch to Layard without a word. Layard was shocked. He believed that Lord Aberdeen's decision was neither correct nor just, was not in the interests of England, and might have serious consequences. Sir Stratford, in angry agreement, ordered Layard to send a dispatch incorporating these views to the Foreign Minister. Lord Aberdeen, for political reasons (the wooing of Russia), would not yield. The British Ambassador was forced to carry out his instructions, to make recommendations that the weak Turkish Government had to accept. The present boundaries between the states of Iran (Persia) and Iraq (Turkish Mesopotamia) follow those recommendations approximately, with the port of Khoramshahr—on the site of Muhammera, above Abadan—and the east bank of the Shat el-Arab for about sixty miles within Iranian territory.

Sir Stratford recommended that Layard be appointed to the international commission that would lay down the actual frontiers. It is not surprising that Lord Aberdeen refused to approve the appointment, considering that this brash young man's advice, both on the border dispute and in the Serbian affair, had been diametrically opposed to his own position. The logical reasons for his rejection did not make Layard any less disappointed. His future now looked blacker than ever. In the face of the Foreign Minister's prejudice, his ambition for a diplomatic career was completely blocked. He might as well give up the idea and go home.

Once more Sir Stratford easily persuaded him to stay on in Constantinople in the hope that eventually he would receive an attachéship in this part of the world, for which everything except his democratic opinions so eminently fitted him. Meanwhile he had neither status nor pay. The months went by, until his departure had been put off for over a year. He felt his peculiar position at the Embassy to be embarrassing; in fact, humiliating. Once more he admits to being "in despair." His funds were very low, and he could not ask his mother, who had younger children to support, for a loan. He knew better than to ask his uncle for money, even on a temporary basis. Had not Benjamin Austen warned him that he might find himself in this very predicament—far from home without resources?

But he *had* been admitted to the practice of law; his uncle could not deny that. Swallowing his distaste and his pride, he wrote to ask if Uncle Austen would take him back into the office at Gray's Inn.

Benjamin Austen had not grown more sympathetic toward his nephew in the years of separation. His answering letter warned Henry that he would have to buckle down and observe rules and restrictions which his uncle would dictate. Austen seems to have overlooked entirely that Henry was no longer seventeen, but fully grown and with more experiences behind him than most young men of his age. Mr. Austen wrote further that, considering the way in which Henry had flouted his aunt and uncle's advice, he could not expect to be received in their home in the same manner as before. Mrs. Austen felt that her nephew had often intruded upon her. This latter remark upset Layard as much as anything; he believed that he had never entered the Austen home unless specifically invited. His pride was deeply hurt. Nor could he bear the thought of giving up his independent way of life, and of returning, hat in hand, to his uncle's sufference—and "the Sahara Desert of the Law."

Chapter XIII

DIVERSIONS AND PREPARATIONS
(1843–1845)

In times of despair, something always came up—or Layard made it come up. The Constantinople correspondent of the *Morning Chronicle*, who was returning to England, suggested Layard as his successor. The salary offered, £150, was hardly enough on which to eat, even with the buying power of the English pound infinitely higher than it is today, but Layard accepted the offer. Not only because he would have grasped any straw to remain in the East, but because Sir Stratford Canning advised and requested him to do so. The support of the British press was important to the Ambassador; in this young man he could be sure of a reporter in sympathy with his aims and policies. Moreover Layard had many friends among the other foreign correspondents, and would be able to influence their dispatches in the same direction. Layard increased his income by writing pieces for the Malta *Times*, an excellent paper which was widely read in the Levant. His reports were largely responsible for the "chorus of praise" which the British Ambassador subsequently received from journals in England and on the Continent. Watching the results, Layard realized "how much the success and reputation of a diplomatist may depend upon his skill in obtaining the support of newspaper correspondents and their incessant and exaggerated approval of all he does and says." Although he numbered his friends among the newspaper fraternity, he had little belief in their integrity. He adds a bit ruefully that he was not able to profit by his newspaper experience in later life. He disliked personal publicity, could not cater to its practitioners, and (to use a

term not yet invented) was a bad public relations counsel for himself. As a boy he had tried his hand at writing romances; as a young
man in London he had contributed to magazines; he wrote extremely well, as anyone who reads his long-neglected works will
see, but he did not think of his job on the *Chronicle* as the start of
a new career. It was just a job, a stopgap. He (and Sir Stratford)
still hoped for a diplomatic appointment.

With his financial problems more or less taken care of, he enjoyed the normal recreations of a young man in an exotic city—a
particularly gay and friendly young man who, writing in his old
age, looked back on the days of his youth with unalloyed pleasure.
His small newspaper stipend had to be carefully distributed; he
and his friend Longworth therefore moved from Pera to lodgings
in Candili, a village on the Asiatic side of the Bosphorus. Besides
being cheap, it had the advantage of being within easy reach of
members of the diplomatic corps and Turkish statesmen, who
spent the summer in their country houses along the shore.

After the day's work was done, Layard and Longworth usually
went for a walk over the hills, talking casually of this and that, and
enjoying the view. One could see almost all the way from the Sea
of Marmora to the Black Sea, and the blue Bosphorus sweeping in
between, flecked with sails and bordered by palaces and *yalis*, half
marble, half wood, with latticed windows overhanging the water.
On Fridays the young men regularly visited the "Sweet Waters of
Asia," which was a short walk from Candili. Hardly a visitor to
Constantinople in those days did not dwell lovingly on the charms
of this favorite spot for excursions, where a small stream mean-
dered under shady ash trees through a green and flowery little
valley. Here the Greek and Turkish ladies, with their children and
slaves, all in brilliant national costumes, would gather to gossip,
eat sweets, smoke their *narguilés*. Sometimes, with attendants
posted to keep the curious male at a distance, the Moslem ladies
even lowered their veils. Gypsy women, jugglers, and musicians
with dancing monkeys wandered from group to group. On the outskirts, gayly painted and gilded wagons hitched to white oxen, and
a few European carriages, waited till their passengers were ready

to return. No wonder the two young Englishmen rarely missed a Friday at the "Sweet Waters of Asia."

Excursions farther afield were part of summertime too. Layard chuckled over a holiday trip to Brusa, the old Ottoman capital at the foot of Mount Olympus in Asia Minor. His companions were the Prussian Minister, his brother and his aristocratic elderly mother. The journey from the port of Mudanya was made on horseback, a matter of seven or eight hours. On arrival, hot and thirsty, they were offered the local "Vin d'Olympe." Supposing it to be weak, since it was a pale wine, the parched tourists gulped down several glasses. "The English Consul, a staid solemn Scotchman, impervious to fun or joke, had in the meanwhile been informed of the arrival of the distinguished visitors, and thought it necessary to wait upon them in full uniform. He found them, to his surprise and horror, stretched upon the divan apparently in a hopeless state of drunkenness. I remembered afterwards a dim vision of something resplendent with silver and gold passing before my eyes. It was the only knowledge I had of the honour paid us by the Consul. The result of this involuntary intoxication was two days intense headache, accompanied by fever, from which all the party suffered. We afterwards carefully eschewed 'Vin d'Olympe.' "

In the autumn of 1843, Layard embarked on the sort of holiday still enjoyed by some lucky travelers: an Aegean cruise in a chartered Greek sailing yacht, "which, like most Greek vessels, was called the *Panaiyah* 'The Virgin.' " His host was Lord Eastnor, a shy, gifted, lovable man somewhat younger than himself. They coasted along the eastern shores of the Sea of Marmora, landing, exploring, and trying to identify numerous mounds, ruined temples and deserted tombs. Passing through the Dardanelles, they spent two days exploring the plains of Troy, some thirty years before Heinrich Schliemann excavated the city mound at Hissarlik. They landed on the beautiful, forest-clad island of Samothrace, where the famous Winged Victory, now in the Louvre, was discovered some twenty years later. The islanders took them for pirates and ran off to their village high on the mountain. They captured one too old to escape, reassured him, and obtained pro-

visions and a guide. Here again they stole a march on later archaeologists (including the twentieth-century team from New York
University, headed by Karl Lehmann) by discovering "a Cyclopean
wall and gateway, and many fragments of Greek sculpture, marble
bas-reliefs and statues." North they sailed across the wine-dark
sea to the pine woods and lovely ruined theater of Thasos; and
from there to the still rarely-visited monasteries of Mount Athos
perched on high rocks above the water. While Lord Eastnor
sketched (as all cultivated Englishmen did in those pre-snapshot
days) Layard interviewed the monks, examined the Byzantine wall
paintings, icons and illuminated manuscripts. Among the stories
he collected was one which explained why the cats of Mount Athos
had no tails. The cats were accustomed to squatting around the
low stools from which the monks ate, and quite often would sweep
off the food and wine glasses with their tails. The monks removed
the tails instead of the cats.

Layard and Eastnor landed at Mytilene (Lesbos) "where burning Sappho loved and sung"; and explored the Greek ruins of
Assos. At Smyrna Layard had to leave the *Panaiyah* and return by
steamer to Constantinople.

In his old age, Layard remembered many lovely ladies; it has
even been said that his reputation with the ladies was no help to
his career when, in later life, he entered politics. One romantic encounter in Constantinople was shared with his friend Charles Alison, chief interpreter and afterward Oriental Secretary to the
British Embassy. From Alison's caïque one day, they stopped to
watch several Turkish ladies in brilliant cloaks, which covered them
from top to toe, standing on the marble steps of an imperial kiosk,
about to embark in a gorgeously gilded and be-cushioned caïque of
eight oars. The ladies, understandably, returned the stare; one of
the young Englishmen was stalwart and handsome, with Byronic
locks waving in the breeze; the other (Alison) had, to say the least,
an interesting appearance: "his fine brow and highly intellectual
countenance were disfigured by a bushy, dishevelled head of hair
and a capacious beard, which he had the habit of pushing upwards
so as to conceal his face." As the ladies stepped into their boat, the

most richly dressed among them slightly lowered her veil and subtly signaled for the young men to follow her. Their boatman, however, was reluctant to obey this order. When his caïque struck against a floating object, and a dead body bobbed up from under the prow, he refused to follow the glittering barge any further, saying the carcass was an ill omen—though it was a common enough occurrence.

The young men were annoyed at the missed opportunity, for, even in the brief moment of unveiling, they had seen that the lady was lovely to look upon. Next day a closely veiled older woman appeared at Alison's lodging with an invitation. The gentlemen were to go at a certain hour to a garden gate in a certain street in Stambul, where they would be admitted to the presence of a certain person. At the appointed hour, Layard and Alison, having obeyed the instructions, were ushered into a large hall, ornately and splendidly decorated. "On a low divan at the further end of this hall was seated a lady, whom we recognized. She was young and singularly beautiful, with the large, almond-shaped eyes, the delicate and regular features, and the clear, brilliant complexion, somewhat too pale perhaps for perfect beauty, peculiar to Turkish ladies of Circassian descent. She was splendidly clad in the dress then worn by wealthy Turkish ladies. Round about her stood a number of girls, all richly clad, and for the most part exceedingly pretty, who were evidently her attendants."

The hostess had an advantage over her guests; she knew who they were. For a Turkish lady she was remarkably well informed. She asked them numerous intelligent questions about politics. Narguilés, coffee, and sweetmeats were served. Alison, who spoke fluent Turkish, told jokes; the ladies giggled appreciatively in their high, tinkling voices. When the hostess considered there had been sufficient polite conversation, she ordered her ladies-in-waiting to entertain the guests with music and dancing. This "degenerated into a kind of romp in which all the girls took part—pelting each other with comfits, and tumbling over each other on the floor and divans amidst shouts of laughter, to the great amusement of their mistress, who encouraged them in their somewhat boisterous play."

Only too soon it was time to leave the fascinating lady. The young men promised to come again. They were bursting with curiosity; she had given no hint of who she was, but her house, her costume, and her manners pointed to a lady of the aristocracy. An elderly female sleuth was set on the trail, only to discover that the object of their charming flirtation was, alas, no less a personage than the sister of the Sultan. Though they were invited again and again, and received messages of reproach for their nonappearance, they dared not continue the game. The stakes were too high. One false move and they might lose their heads. And she, if discovered consorting with members of the opposite sex (infidels too), might end up in the Bosphorus as a corpse. Which would be a pity for one so lovely.

The princess later became notorious for showing herself in public without a veil, and otherwise challenging the conventions and restraints from which Moslem women suffered. She deliberately set an example for those less highly placed to follow. Such rampant feminism in the Seraglio more than a century ago explains why the new Turkey, after World War I, was able to do away with the veil with the minimum of protest.

During the winter of 1843–44, Layard spent most of his time at the Embassy working for Sir Stratford, writing for the newspapers, and studying Eastern languages, both ancient and modern. He was helpful to Lady Canning, whose favorite project was the establishment of schools in Constantinople for poor Christian and Jewish children. Layard greatly admired the work of the American Board of Missions, whose representatives opened schools, translated standard works into Eastern languages, taught the elements of science and the principles of political freedom to Turks of all faiths. "Braving the climate, amid the persecution and ill-treatment to which they were not infrequently subjected, they established themselves in the most remote and least frequented parts of the Turkish Empire, where they lived with their families—not forgetting the comforts of their native land, especially rocking-chairs and pumpkin pie." Layard remarks that many students of Robert College (still in existence) became leaders in the modernization

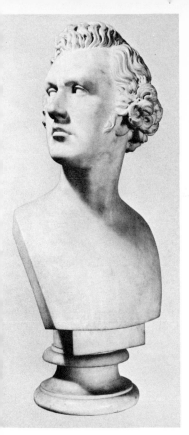

Plate 1   Sir Austen Henry Layard.

Plate 2   Winged Lion from the Palace of Ashurnasirpal II (Nimrud).

Plate 3   The Rock of Behistun.   From Rawlinson, *The Persian Inscription at Behistun*

Plate 4   View of Kala Tul.   From Layard, *Early Adventures*

Plate 5 The Siege of a City (Nimrud). From Layard, *The Monuments of Nineveh*

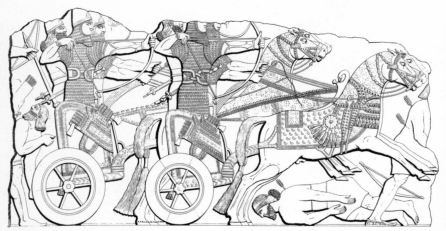

From Layard, *The Monuments of Nineveh*

Plate 6 Assyrian Warriors Fighting in Chariots (Nimrud).

Plate 7 Statue of Ashurnasirpal II, from the small temple at Nimrud.

Plate 8 Ashurnasirpal II being annointed by a magical figure (Nimrud).

Plate 9 The Black Obelisk of Shalmaneser III (Nimrud).

Courtesy of the Trustees of the British Museum

Plate 10 A panel from the Black Obelisk: Jehu, king of Israel, doing homage to Shalmaneser III, king of Assyria.

Courtesy of the Trustees of the British Museum

From Layard, *Nineveh and Babylon*

Plate 11   The Hall of Archives (Kuyunjik).

From Layard, *A Popular Account of Discoveries at Nineveh*

Plate 12   Layard's workers moving a winged bull (Nimrud).

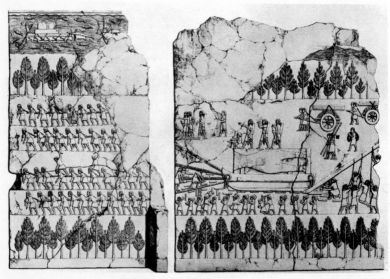

From Layard, *A Second Series of the Monuments of Nineveh*

Plate 13   Assyrians moving a winged bull (Kuyunjik).

of Turkey and in the Balkan struggle for independence from the Turkish yoke.

Though he had plenty of interests and amusements, Layard's real ambitions were as unrealized as ever, and his future as uncertain. Meanwhile his friend Paul Émile Botta had scored a triumph. In the early summer of 1842, when Layard had passed through Mosul, Botta, growing progressively discouraged, had been scratching around on the surface of Kuyunjik. Layard had urged him by mail to continue, and had called his attention to the possibilities of Nimrud. Botta replied that Nimrud was too far from Mosul to be practical for excavation. Months later an Arab from Khorsabad, fourteen miles north of Mosul, had asked Botta's workmen at Kuyunjik why they were being paid for digging up rubbish. When told that they had been ordered to look for carvings, he advised them to try his village; he and his neighbors often came upon that sort of thing in digging new foundations for houses. A dyer by trade, he had built his furnace entirely from old bricks like those at Kuyunjik. Botta, skeptical because he had heard such tales before, waited three months before he sent to Khorsabad an agent who dug a trial trench and came to the top of a wall covered with sculptured slabs.

Botta immediately transferred his workmen to Khorsabad. In a few days he had opened up several rooms lined with marvelous bas-reliefs. The building had been destroyed by fire, and the slabs were almost reduced to lime, but before they crumbled away Botta saw enough to excite him. The obvious antiquity of the walls, the cuneiform inscriptions, the location near the fabled mounds of Mosul—all convinced him that this must be an Assyrian ruin. He sent a message to Julius Mohl and the French Academy of Fine Arts: "I believe myself to be the first who has discovered sculptures which with some reason can be referred to the period when Nineveh was flourishing."

The message caused a sensation. The French Government promptly responded with ample funds for further excavations, and the famous artist Flandin (whom Layard had met in Persia) was sent to Khorsabad to copy the sculptures. This was fortunate, for the bas-reliefs, which had endured for twenty-five hundred years underground, fell to pieces when exposed, and could hardly be held together until they were sketched. Everything disappeared almost as quickly as it was dug up. Botta, knowing of Layard's interest, wrote to him of the great discovery, and kept him up to date thereafter through detailed letters and by allowing him to see the sketches, copies of inscriptions, and official reports of work in progress as they were forwarded to France through Monsieur de Cadalvène, head of the French post office in Constantinople. More than a hundred rooms were quickly excavated. They were lined with powerful bas-reliefs of battle scenes and ceremonials. There were many inscriptions. On either side of the main doorways were enormous winged bulls or lions with human heads, a pair of which Botta hoped to ship to France. Such a huge, richly ornamented building could only be a palace. It was, though neither Botta, Layard, nor anyone at the time could read the name, the palace of Sargon II, king of Assyria in the eighth century B.C. Few Europeans—Botta was not among them—had any knowledge of Arab literature, so he had not heard the legend which described Khorsabad as a village on the site of an ancient city called Saraun or Saraghoun, names not too different from its true name: Dur Sharrukin, or Sargon's Town. It was not Nineveh, though its splendor led Botta to think so.

Layard, in his capacity as a foreign correspondent, was proud to be the first to announce to the press what he considered the greatest Eastern discovery of all time. In three letters to the Malta *Times,* he speculated on the date of the palace at Khorsabad and its connection with Nineveh and the Assyrian Empire. It should again be pointed out how little was known of the Assyrians before Botta's find. According to Scripture, they were powerful, rapacious, and wicked. The Assyrian king Shalmaneser had taken Samaria, capital of the Northern Kingdom of Israel, and carried off the Ten Tribes into captivity. A later king, Sennacherib, had besieged Jerusalem, but the Lord saved His city by smiting the Assyrian camp with mysterious death (probably the plague). "So Sennacherib king of Assyria departed, and went, and returned, and dwelt at

Nineveh." These, and a few other passages concerning the Assyrians and their kings, were taken, along with earlier Bible fables, as literal truth by religious fundamentalists: a matter of faith, not of scientific proof. On the opposite side of the fence were those who claimed all Bible history to be legend with no foundation in fact. Only those with a special interest in ancient history, like Layard, knew the accounts of Diodorus the Sicilian and other early writers, with their exaggerations, mis-statements, and pure fantasies. What had the Assyrians looked like—or, for that matter, the ancient Hebrews? What sort of clothes and armor had they worn, what weapons had been used to besiege Samaria and Jerusalem?

Flandin, having finished his drawings, passed through Constantinople on his way back to France in 1844, and showed Layard his portfolio. In this, far more clearly than in Botta's rough sketches, Layard saw, as the European public was soon to see, the graphic representation of a people they had hitherto known only through the Bible. The Assyrians had powerful, heavy-muscled bodies; their noses were curved and fleshy; some wore tightly curled beards and some were beardless (the Assyrians, like the Turks and Persians, made eunuchs of their attendants). They wore fringed and embroidered garments, many jewels. They were not a pretty race, but they had been fine craftsmen, as these sculptures proved.

The excitement and enthusiasm aroused by the Khorsabad discoveries was immense, in England as well as on the Continent. How did Layard feel about it? In all his Persian and Turkish adventures, he had not forgotten his emotions on first sight of the mounds near Mosul: "Were the traveller to cross the Euphrates to seek such ruins in Mesopotamia and Chaldea as he left behind in Asia Minor or Syria, his search would be in vain. He is now at a loss to give any form to the rude heaps upon which he is gazing. Those of whose works they are the remains, unlike the Roman and the Greek, have left no visible traces of their civilization or of their arts: their influence has long since passed away. The more he conjectures, the more vague the results appear. The scene around is worthy of the ruin he is contemplating; desolation meets desolation: a feeling of awe succeeds to wonder; for there is nothing to relieve the mind, to lead to hope, or tell of what has gone by. These huge mounds of Assyria made a deeper impression upon me, gave rise to more serious thought and more earnest reflection, than the temples of Baalbec or the theatres of Ionia."

Layard must have been remembering this as he examined Flandin's portfolio. Here were the first examples of the form beneath the rude heaps, the first traces of the forgotten civilization. There was so much more to be learned! He had determined that someday, somehow, he would return to Mosul, to explore the mounds, to look for Nineveh. Had Botta beaten him to it? Was Khorsabad Nineveh? Botta now thought it was. Layard disagreed, for logical reasons, not out of the envy which would have been only human but from which he seems to have been singularly free. Khorsabad, he thought, was too far away from the Tigris. There must be other palaces as vast and magnificent closer to the river— at Kuyunjik, for instance, which was the largest of the mounds and the one most often associated in tradition with the great city. Although Botta had worked for months at Kuyunjik without finding any evidence of buildings beneath the surface, the possibility of their existence was not ruled out yet. And, some miles south along the river, was there not the great mound of Nimrud, which had so piqued Layard's curiosity? The discoveries at Khorsabad only served to whet his appetite.

But he did not have the financial backing necessary to satisfy it. He had never had an answer to the letter he had sent from Baghdad to Sterling, the British merchant, suggesting such an investment. If only he could be appointed consul or vice-consul at Mosul so that he could combine official duties with digging, like Botta! He would even have been glad to accept a vice-consulate at Shuster (for which his connections with tribal chiefs and his interest in the trade of the area well qualified him). Though Khuzistan was not Assyrian ground, it was full of interesting ruins. Sir Stratford Canning preached patience, which was not one of Layard's foremost characteristics, although he had shown an amazing amount of it during his connection with the Embassy. When the spring of 1844 came with still no appointment, Layard was discouraged and

sick at heart. He had even given up his newspaper work because
friends advised him that it might be standing in the way of a
diplomatic appointment. The money he had left was hardly enough
to live on even in poor quarters, eating native food and very little
of that.

He was glad therefore to undertake a mission for Sir Stratford in
Albania. He was fed up with the frustrations of Constantinople,
and he would at least be able to eat. The British Ambassador was
the acknowledged champion of the rights of Christians in the
East, and reports had reached him of atrocities perpetrated upon
Albanian Christians by a rebellious mountain tribe. Layard was to
investigate the situation. He found the reports greatly exaggerated;
he tried to forward peace negotiations between the rebels and the
Turkish authorities but accomplished little. It was marvelously
refreshing, however, to ride off again into the mountains, to confer
with bold, proud mountain men of the type he admired, to watch
wild native dances, and sleep on the ground under an oak tree in
the forest.

On his return to Constantinople, Layard was invited to live at
the Embassy, and, since he now did all the work of an attaché as
well as the confidential errands for Sir Stratford, he was paid at
the rate of a hundred pounds yearly. In the summer of 1845, the
Ambassador informed him that he expected to return to England
on leave. He would personally speak to Lord Aberdeen, and believed that the long-promised official appointment would then no
longer be withheld. Layard, in his anomalous position at the Embassy, preferred not to remain in Constantinople during the Ambassador's absence. Turning over in his mind what he could do till
Sir Stratford returned, it occurred to him that now, if ever, was the
time to explore the mounds. Botta had closed the excavations at
Khorsabad and was on his way back to France to write up his
discoveries. Layard suggested to his chief that he might continue
the work where Botta had left off, but at a different location. Sir
Stratford approved the idea and volunteered to put up sixty pounds
toward expenses. Layard figured that this together with a like sum
he had saved from his little salary—one hundred and twenty

pounds in all—"would, if employed with the strictest economy, meet the expenses of my journey to Mosul, and of experimental researches amongst the ruins." It would have to be stretched with the strictest economy indeed to cover steamship fare, horse hire, board and lodging at Mosul, the purchase of a few tools and the pay of workmen on the dig. He would only be able to sink a few trial trenches, but he felt sure that, if he found anything, it would arouse enough interest, as Botta's discovery had, to receive official backing for full-scale excavations. There was an additional motive for archaeological exploration in those days: international rivalry. Instead of the unknown future of mankind and outer space, it was then the almost equally unknown ancient past which was the object of competition, for the sake of prestige and for trophies to be lodged in national museums. England and France were the chief rivals in the Mesopotamian field. Botta had always been most generous in sharing the knowledge of his discoveries, but with his successors it was different. The British Ambassador thought it best for Layard not to admit the purpose of his trip to Mosul. He was not provided with a special permit to excavate but would take with him merely the usual documents furnished by the Porte to ordinary travelers recommended by the Embassy, and the usual letter of introduction to the Pasha of Mosul.

Since summer was no season to work in the Assyrian plains, Layard put off departure till October (Sir Stratford did not actually go to England till the following summer). Once more, as when he had been planning the "land march," Layard prepared himself methodically for the task ahead. Earlier on, even before the scheme had crystallized, and when his exploration of the Assyrian mounds was merely a hope or a dream, Layard had sent to England for books on Hebrew, Chaldean, and Syriac. His remarkable intuition told him that the unknown language represented by Assyrian cuneiform might be related to one of these. Monsieur Cadalvène lent him more books and helped him in the study of Sassanian history and Pahlevi (the Persian of the Zoroastrian books, written in a Semitic script). During the summer before leaving, he took lessons in mapping, the use of the theodolite and other instruments required to make accurate surveys and architectural plans. After his travels in Persia, Turkey, Asia Minor, Syria, and the Greek Islands, he had a considerable knowledge of ancient architecture. During these self-directed field trips he had measured and sketched and copied ancient inscriptions, often without knowing their meaning. Many an academic archaeologist has had less training in these matters than Austen Henry Layard. He was toughened to a hard climate and primitive living conditions. He was fluent in Arabic, Persian, and Turkish. It remained for him to discover whether he had that most unpredictable of assets: luck with the spade.

Part Two

EXCAVATIONS

Chapter XIV

BURIED TREASURE

(October–December 1845)

Layard arrived in Mosul in late October. He had galloped from
Samsun over mountain, steppe, and baking plain in twelve days.
Christian Rassam, now a "portly influential British Vice-consul,"
put him up till a house was found for rent at one pound per
month: a splendid house with a courtyard, a stable, and a terrace
from which he could look down upon the doings of the town, and
out across the roof tops to the mounds, and, beyond them, the
mountains of Kurdistan, already dusted with snow. Five years had
passed since he had first dreamed of solving the riddle of Nineveh.
Now that the opportunity was at hand, he was in rare spirits, as his
letters to his family demonstrate. His humor was so good, apparently, that he even forgave his aunt her unkindness, for several of
his most entertaining letters are addressed to her. Everything
amused him: the intrigues, brawls, and murders to which the
Mosulis were addicted—and the thousand and one stories about
them. The population of Arabs, Kurds, and assorted native Christians were always at each other's throats, and all at the mercy of
the Turkish governor.

Two days after his arrival, Layard presented his letter of introduction to Mohammed Pasha, known as Keritli Oglu (son of the
Cretan) upon whose good will so much depended. A typical
example of the semi-independent pashas appointed by the Porte,
Keritli Oglu's power was limited only by the obligation to forward
a small share of the taxes which he collected to Constantinople,
where they bought immunity for him. "No Arabian Nights' hero

could have been a more appropriate governor than our Pasha," writes Layard to Mrs. Austen. "On his arrival here a year ago, he installed himself by strangling the three principal men of the town on principle, and appropriated their cash and tangible property." It would be hard to imagine an uglier old gentleman than this one, pitted with smallpox and minus an eye and an ear. A single one of each was all he needed for successful interrogations, but his most pointed questions and piercing stares did not ferret out the purpose of *this* Frank's presence in Mosul.

Layard confided it instead to H. J. Ross, Christian Rassam's new commercial partner. Ross as painted in a miniature of the period, in black cloak, satin tie, dagger-pointed mustachios and a monocle on a long black ribbon, resembles a melancholy poet rather than the amiable gentleman, the formidable hunter and horseman, that he was. The only two Englishmen in town were of a like age and had similar tastes. "Layard is such a nice fellow—very clever and amusing," writes Ross to his sister Mary. When Ross had to leave Mosul a few years later, he ceded to his friend Layard the horse that he had bought as a bag of bones and had nursed back to health. Merjan was "a direct descendant of one of the famous horses of the Prophet; a noble horse, as gentle as he is spirited and with paces as easy as a rocking chair." Ross was proud to be known in Mosul not by his own name but as the master of the famous red horse.

Layard and he agreed that it would be rash to attack the mounds right across the Tigris, which were directly under the Pasha's Cyclopean eye, and that it would be better to start digging at Nimrud, twenty miles south. Giving out the story that they were going down river to hunt wild boar, they sent horses and greyhounds ahead, and on November 8 boarded a raft with two servants and an Arab stonecutter. A few spades and pickaxes were hidden among their spears and guns. The autumn rains had not yet replenished the river and the current was slow; it was almost dark by the time they heard the crying waters of the ancient dam, and landed near a cluster of deserted huts. A faint glow guided them to the shelter where a miserable Arab family crouched around their tiny brush fire. Awad, the father, was a sheikh of the Jehesh, one of the many village tribes ruined by Keritli Oglu's taxes. Though half starved, he appeared intelligent. Layard told him that he desired to dig for old stones, and if there were such at Nimrud, Awad should be foreman over the diggers.

There might well be stones, said Awad, because beneath the mound was a palace built by Athur, lieutenant of Nimrod. It was told that, when the holy Abraham broke the stone gods of Nimrod, the Mighty Hunter angrily sought to slay him. The Patriarch prayed to God for deliverance, and when God asked how he should punish Nimrod, who boasted himself to be lord of all beings, Abraham replied, "To Thee armies and the power of men are as nothing. Before the smallest of thy creatures will they perish." So God, pleased at the prophet's faith, sent a gnat, which vexed Nimrod day and night. Nimrod built a glass room in the palace to keep it out, but it got inside anyway, and passed through his ear into his brain, where it tortured him for four hundred years till he died.

Such a tale, a mixture of Bible, Koran, and legend, is typical of many which have served as signposts to archaeological sites; the clues in this one are the name Athur (Ashur) and the rumor of a buried palace. Layard and Ross, remembering the cities which Ashur, according to Scripture, had built—Nineveh, Rehoboth, Calah, and Resen—wondered which of them lay beneath the mound now swallowed up by darkness. They thought it might be Resen; Nimrud, big as it was for a *tel*, did not seem big enough for the term "great city," which the Bible applied to it as well as to Nineveh.

While Awad went off to recruit workers at Selamiyah, a village three miles distant, the Englishmen lay down on the floor to rest. Layard, accustomed as he was to the discomforts of a native hut shared with women, children, dogs, and fleas, could not get to sleep. "Hopes, long cherished, were now to be realized, or were to end in disappointment. Visions of palaces underground, of gigantic monsters, of sculptured figures, and endless inscriptions, floated before me. After forming plan after plan for removing the earth, and extricating these treasures, I fancied myself wandering in a maze of chambers from which I could find no outlet. Then again, all was reburied, and I was standing on the grass-covered mound." A few minutes after he finally managed to doze off, Awad returned with six men ready to work. Outside in the cold November dawn, the plain was empty of life; only a column of dust—the cloud-pillar guide of the Bible—whirled across it toward the dark mountain of Nimrud, a mile away.

Ross writes they "coursed a hare or two" that morning, which sounds unlikely, for Layard was interested solely in the potsherds and brick fragments which littered the mound, plainly visible now in autumn when the grass was gone. The puzzled, eager Arabs brought him handfuls of the stuff. A single crumbling bit of carved stone which resembled the burned gypsum of the Khorsabad reliefs was the first evidence that sculptured walls might be found at Nimrud. Where to begin? One could not excavate a whole mountain with six workmen. Awad pointed out a yellowish stone sticking up in the northwest corner of the mound. No amount of pushing or pulling would budge it. Out came the pickaxes, making hardly a dent at first in earth packed hard by the long dry summer. It was cruel labor for men so weakened by hunger as these village Arabs. Layard and Ross seized picks as well, hacking away with hands that grew blistered and raw, until at last the upper part of an alabaster slab emerged from the clods. Attached to this was a second slab. They worked till they were exhausted; they could not stop. Following a line of upper edges, they cleared the tops of ten slabs forming a square, with one missing at the corner. It could be nothing else but a room with a door: the first room in Athur's palace—the first palace of Nineveh?

An archaeologist today would approach a discovery of this sort with hand-tools, brushing away each fleck of dirt with meticulous care. Not so in the middle of the nineteenth century: Layard and his contemporaries were treasure hunters, after antiquities, preferably sculptured. Time and money were short, international rivalry keen. He ordered his men to "dig down the faces of the slabs." Inscriptions—next best after sculptures—were quickly revealed, and in perfect condition, unlike the slabs at Khorsabad. Therefore sculptures that could be removed whole might well exist in some other part of the mound. Half the workmen were delegated to clear out the first chamber while Layard led the others to the southwest corner. Almost immediately a pick rang against stone. These slabs, when cleared, proved to be inscribed also, but cracked all over from exposure to a devastating fire which had swept through the halls that had once stood here. Nineveh, Layard remembered, had perished in flames.

All continued to dig with enthusiasm till it was too dark to see. Layard labeled his finds the "Northwest and Southwest Palaces," since buildings of alabaster could not be less than royal. He was "well-satisfied"—surely an understatement for the sensations of a young man who on his first day of digging had made such a discovery. Was it Nineveh? In spite of Botta's belief in Khorsabad, in spite of the traditions about Kuyunjik and Nebbi Yunus, Layard felt in his heart that this was it, that Nimrud was his dream come true. Sitting in the Arab hut that night, he must have been awed at the thought that he, Henry Layard, had actually dug up the great city, the center of luxury and the sink of corruption, the long-lost capital of the long-lost Assyrians. Being the character that he was, he would be especially gratified that he had discovered it for England!

Awad was pleased because his boss was pleased, though he did not understand what this Frank could be after unless, like others of his kind, he was on the track of gold. In the morning, five more hungry Arabs trotted in from Selamiyah, and were put to work on clearing out the first chamber, which proved to be of mud brick faced with alabaster to the height of eight feet. Layard was horrified, however, to find carved on the back of a fallen slab the not-so-ancient name of a Turkish pasha. Fortunately for his peace of mind, a workman remembered that Nimrud had been quarried for building material thirty years earlier.

Mixed with the rubble on the floor were bits of brittle whitish stone or porcelain with traces of gilding: part of a tiny sphinx, a small robed figure carrying the Egyptian symbol of life, and fragments of beautifully carved flowers. Awad drew Layard aside. "Wallah, O Bey! Your books are right, and the Franks know what is hid from the True Believer. Here is the treasure, sure enough, and please God, we shall find it all in a few days. Only do not say anything about it to those Arabs, for they are asses and cannot hold their tongues, and the matter will come to the ears of the Pasha." Making sure that no one could see him, he carefully unwrapped a few flakes of gold leaf from a dingy bit of paper. He was more perplexed than ever when Layard told him to keep his gold, and any more of the same he might find.

Layard and Ross puzzled over the carvings in the hut at night, twisting and turning them to discover the material of which they were made, till the light of the candle fell on a splinter in Ross's hand and he recognized the texture for what it was. The odd little fragments—dried out, discolored, falling apart at a touch—were the first of the now famous Nimrud Ivories.

On the third day of digging, Layard investigated the volcano-like cone or "pyramid" which Xenophon and other early travelers had described. It was Nimrud's most distinctive feature at a distance, and must surely cover a large building of some importance. Disappointingly it appeared to be a mass of solid brick, similar to the structure at Khorsabad which Botta had labeled the "Observatory." It was, of course, a *ziggurat*, the staged tower typical of Mesopotamian temple compounds. Neither the term, which means "Hill of Heaven," nor its religious significance was yet known, and though Layard found the brick pile interesting, it did not promise anything in the way of sculpture. The chamber in the northwest corner of the mound, which he had perhaps too hastily dubbed a palace, was isolated, a dead end, so he withdrew his workmen, to concentrate them in the southwest, where there seemed to be walls leading off in several directions, indicating something more complex. Though a large accumulation of charcoal repeated the story of destruction by fire, a few sculptures might have escaped. Five days of excavation yielded the maze of chambers, the inscribed walls, of which he had dreamed, but no sculptures, damaged or undamaged. And the time had come when he must confess the doings at Nimrud to the Pasha before wild rumors made extra trouble for him.

He found Mosul in more than its usual uproar. Keritli Oglu had played one of his tricks. After retiring to his private rooms, he had given out the story first that he was ill, then that he was dead. As soon as the festival of thanksgiving for this happy event was in full flower, the Pasha had reappeared, and, to punish his disloyal citizens, had fined the rich a fat amount and thrown most of the poor into jail. Layard with difficulty kept a straight face while congratulating Keritli Oglu upon his recovered health. He made his report on Nimrud, to which the Pasha listened as if he had never heard a word about it before. Having failed to catch the Frank in any lies, Keritli Oglu suddenly confronted him with a speck of gold leaf lying in the desk tray; Daoud Agha, captain of the mercenaries at Selamiyah, had brought it in. Layard remarked calmly that he would welcome Daoud Agha, or any officer whom the Pasha might appoint, to take care of precious metals found at Nimrud.

The Pasha was pacified, but the rumors of gold had already set tongues to wagging in the bazaars, at an inauspicious moment when the fanatic element was aroused to the point of attacking the British Consulate because, according to their Moslem judge ("his reverence, the Cadi"), the Franks intended to buy up all Turkey— as was proved by the storage warehouse recently purchased by the Consul. Within a day or two of Layard's arrival from Constantinople, he had been denounced by the Cadi for playing farthing-point whist with the Rassams. The learned judge declared that such gambling had never before been seen in town, was counter to the Koran, and should be punished, in the case of an unbeliever, with the loss of the nose and both ears. Layard did not yet realize that some of his difficulties with the authorities were fomented by Rouet, Botta's successor, who regarded the English as unfair competition in the field of antiquity hunting. But he did know that he would have to move fast if he was to accomplish anything before there was real trouble. He therefore hired native agents to explore as many as possible of the small mounds near Mosul for signs of sculpture. Their reports came to nothing when followed up; Layard regretted the time and money spent on them. But he did collect a few inscribed bricks and fragments to take home, including some from Bashiqah (now known as Tell Billah, where an American expedition later excavated a city a thousand years older than the oldest ruin so far uncovered at Nimrud).

He took on more workmen, mostly Chaldean Nestorians from the Tiyari Mountains of Kurdistan: big men, better able to swing a pick than the lightly built Arabs. The picture at Nimrud, the ground plan of the Southwest Palace, instead of making sense, grew ever more peculiar and confusing. The trenches sunk at right angles did not fetch up against walls as they should; the walls already found continued on and on without turning a corner. One could not tell whether the exposed surface was the outside or the inside of a chamber. But one thing was clear: the inscriptions were mutilated; the slabs had been trimmed to make them fit the space where they now stood; one was even upside down. On examining the inscriptions carefully, Layard recognized them as identical with those on the slabs in the northwest corner of the mound; it was from there that the materials for the construction of the Southwest Palace had been taken.

On occasions like this he would send a message to Ross, who could not leave his business in Mosul for long, but would come out for a visit, and they would sit far into the night trying to piece together broken bits of inscription. Layard had moved to a hut at Selamiyah, which was less exposed to Bedouin raids than the deserted village nearer the mound, though hardly more comfortable. The rains had begun, and the mud walls would keep their dampness like an all-enveloping wet blanket till the spring. On bad days the mud-plastered brush roof let in the downpour and Layard had to take shelter on his carpet in a corner of the hut under a sort of wooden table he had built, surrounded by gutters dug in the dirt floor to carry off the water. Under the same roof, separated only by a half-partition, were the Arab owner's cows and bullocks; and just outside huddled his sheep and goats, which coughed and bleated all night till they were milked at dawn. Before then Layard had ridden off to the mound. He did not return till after dark. Fortunately there was fine weather as well as foul; on all but the stormiest days the men continued to work, fighting sticky mud instead of hard-packed earth. Except for a cornerstone with scroll-work and flowers (which apparently did not count), no sculptures had been found. Layard ordered a trench to be dug from a large entrance near the edge of the mound toward its center, presuming that an entrance must lead into a chamber, whose opposite wall would ultimately be struck. After removing an immense amount of earth, charcoal, and rubble, the workmen came up against a line of slabs. Layard told them to clear both sides. The near sides were plain, but the first pick stroke on the reverse uncovered a figure in relief.

Though it was raining heavily, the excited workmen swung their picks and dug away with their spades till they had cleared two whole slabs. Just before dark on November 28, scarcely three weeks after he had begun to excavate, Layard was able to see what the builders of his palace had looked like. It was a moment of high suspense. As the dust of ages fell away, the Assyrians of Scripture took shape—fit citizens of bloody Nineveh, in scaley armor and pointed helmets, striking the enemy down with the sword and the bow; pursuing him with chariots; trampling his body under the hoofs of their high-spirited horses. The second slab disclosed an attack upon a city with catapults and flame throwers; from the battlements a warrior fell headlong, and a lady threw up her arms, begging for mercy. The design was sophisticated, the craftsman-ship superb; a number of details proved that the figures and land-scape, though stylized, were based on keen observation. Who had been capable of executing such excellent work? Whose deeds did it celebrate? Layard was no closer than before to knowing what king had built the Southwest Palace. A band of cuneiform separated upper and lower bas-reliefs on each slab. Like those with inscrip-tions only, these must originally have been used in an older palace, for they had been cut down without regard to subject matter, and one was reversed. They were far too badly damaged to move.

At such a moment, hovering on the verge of great discoveries, Layard was informed that operations at Nimrud must cease. Daoud Agha, appointed watchdog over Layard, had become his friend, ally, and hunting guide instead, but on this occasion, he explained ruefully, he was forced to act as the servant of the Pasha, who was again the slave of the Sultan—what could servants do but obey their masters?

Layard galloped up to Mosul to have it out with Keritli Oglu. If he failed he would have to send a protest all the way to Constantinople and twiddle his thumbs till the answer came. The Pasha, polite as always to an Englishman, said he had regretfully learned that the mound of Nimrud was covered with Moslem graves, which it was against the law to disturb. If the desecration continued, the Cadi would invoke a religious riot. Layard answered that there were no Moslem graves at Nimrud and the Pasha knew it. And was not the Pasha a big enough man to deal with the Cadi?

"No, I cannot allow you to proceed," said Keritli Oglu; "you are my dearest and most intimate friend; if anything happens to you, what grief should I not suffer; your life is more valuable than old stones; besides, the responsibility would fall upon my head."

Layard fumed, but since the Pasha was adamant, he pretended to yield, asking only that he be permitted to sketch the sculptures and copy the inscriptions already discovered. The Pasha could send his own *cawass* to watch over everything he did. Back at Nimrud, he persuaded the cawass to allow a few workers to serve as watchmen; these quietly went on digging under Layard's direction. Daoud Agha considered that the presence of the cawass removed his own responsibility to the Pasha, and confessed that for two nights his troops had been bringing gravestones from distant villages to plant at Nimrud. "We have destroyed more real tombs of True Believers in making sham ones," said he, "than you could have defiled between the Zab and Selamiyah. We have killed our horses and ourselves in carrying those accursed stones."

Many more sculptures were turning up now, but in a sorry state. Near the western rim of the mound were the nether parts of several giant figures which had been sawn in half for building material; in the center, a pair of bulls, headless; in the southwest, the smashed bas-relief of a nine-foot figure bearing a flowering branch. Nearly six weeks had passed since the opening of the excavations, six weeks during which Layard had not rested or spared himself during the worst of the winter weather, under the most uncomfortable living conditions. He had found his treasure cache, but if he was to exploit it for England, he positively had to have a permit which the local authorities were bound to respect. He wrote to Sir Stratford Canning, reporting the discovery of sculptures, and in the same letter urgently requested an Imperial Firman from the Porte.

For the present he covered his sculptures with earth as protection from the weather and local idol-smashers, and rode back to his splendid house in Mosul. He found the town celebrating, with proper cause this time. The Pasha's crimes had finally caught up with him; the Porte had dismissed him and appointed a new governor. With the old Pasha on his way out and the new one not yet arrived, the country districts were in so lawless a state that the workmen were afraid to live at Nimrud. The excavations would have to remain closed till the new governor was installed. Layard decided that in the meanwhile he would go to Baghdad to arrange for the shipment of sculptures—when there should be any fit to ship. He would spend Christmas at the Residency with Major Henry Rawlinson, who had taken over Colonel Taylor's position two years previously, and whom he was eager to meet.

It was a good time to leave Mosul as well; the town was minus any form of law enforcement. Keritli Oglu was relegated to a wretched back room with a leaking roof, where he sat transacting his last bits of business before he sneaked out of town. "Thus it is with God's creatures," he told Rassam's dragoman. "Yesterday all those dogs were kissing my feet; today everyone and everything falls upon me, even the rain."

Chapter XV

HUNTERS, OF ONE KIND AND ANOTHER
(Christmas 1845–March 1846)

Layard had read Major Henry Creswicke Rawlinson's papers, published in scientific journals, as preparation for his own travels, and had carried one of them, *Notes on a March from Zohab*, with him as a guide to Persia. He had investigated the sites mentioned in this, and had much to tell Rawlinson about them. These two men, both on the threshold of international renown, were both still young: Layard was twenty-eight, Rawlinson thirty-five. Their backgrounds were similar: upper middle-class English families with Church and Army in their ancestry and literary figures among their friends. Of the two, Rawlinson's childhood and education had the more conventional elements: horses at home and classics at school. He was a normal product of his environment, normally ignorant of the oriental world, when, like many a well-born youngster with no specialized interests or training, he received a cadetship in the East India Company. Even then, in the words of his brother and biographer, Canon George Rawlinson, "The feelings of an English gentleman were as strongly marked in the boy of seventeen who sailed for India in 1827 as they were in the Resident at Baghdad."[1]

By good fortune, young Rawlinson had as fellow passenger on the four-month voyage out Sir John Malcolm, Governor of Bombay, historian of Persia, and a great raconteur. As a result, Lieutenant Rawlinson, posted to Poona with the First Grenadiers, took up the study of the Persian language. He did not allow it to interfere with other recreations, for he was, as he admits himself, "distinguished in all athletic amusements." He was always willing to bet that he could outride, outjump, outshoot, and outwit his fellow subalterns in games of chance—and he was as proud of winning a wager that he could ride seventy-two miles in under four hours as he was of being appointed interpreter to his regiment in Indian languages. He was to exercise mind and body in this fashion all his life; at seventy he still rode daily in Rotten Row, shot partridge almost till the day he died, and, whenever he traveled, carried his cuneiform notebooks with him for mental relaxation.

In 1833 Rawlinson was sent with other officers of the Indian Army to reorganize the Shah's troops at Teheran; en route he detoured to see Persepolis, the ruined palace of Darius the Great. A year and a half later, stationed as military advisor at Kermanshah, he frequently rode to the Rock of Behistun, twenty-two miles away—a mere romp for such a horseman. The big trilingual inscription four hundred feet above the ground was beyond reach of the human eye—as Layard had found—actually beyond anyone's reach in any fashion. Flandin and Coste had been specifically instructed to copy the Behistun inscriptions, but gave it up as impossible after many attempts to climb the rock. Eventually Rawlinson was to use ropes and ladders, but at first, with no aids other than his talent for athletic amusements, he struggled up the rear face of the rocky height, and lowered himself to a narrow ledge beneath the sculptured panel, where he clung and copied as much as he could see of the Old Persian. The other inscriptions were still too far away to be clear. Back in quarters, Rawlinson studied his copies, devised a system for deciphering them, and by 1837 had interpreted the first two paragraphs as follows:

I am Darius, the Great King, the King of Kings, the King of Persia, the King of provinces, the son of Hystaspes, the grandson of Arsames, the Achaemenian.

Says Darius the king:—My father was Hystaspes; of Hystaspes the father was Arsames; of Arsames the father was Ariyaramnes; of Ariyaramnes the father was Teispes; of Teispes the father was Achaemenes.[2]

Genealogies are hardly exciting as literature, but the very repetitiveness makes their translation easier. The King of Kings had inscribed his proclamation at Behistun in the three national languages of his empire: Old Persian, Babylonian and Elamite, rendered in the cuneiform character. Cuneiform developed from the picture writing of earliest Sumerian times (about 3000 B.C.) incised on soft clay tablets at first with a reed, later with a metal instrument which produced wedge-shaped marks. Each symbol consisted of several wedges in combination and soon no longer resembled the original pictograph. The characters, as they appeared on the clay tablets, were copied in stone on monuments. This method of writing prevailed in most of Western Asia until the Persian Empire fell before Alexander. The trilingual inscription on the Rock of Behistun was the chief key to cuneiform, as the Rosetta Stone was the key to Egyptian hieroglyphs.

Rawlinson's claim to the title of Father of Cuneiform is based on his first two *Memoirs* on this inscription. He was not working in a total void, however. As early as 1802, the German scholar Grotefend had deciphered the names of Cyrus, Xerxes, Darius, and Hystaspes on copies of the Persepolis inscriptions made by Karsten Niebuhr in the eighteenth century. The names were historical, and the title *Great King, King of Kings* was used by later Persian monarchs, and was known. These were the clues from which Grotefend derived nearly a third of the cuneiform alphabet of Old Persian. Younger scholars published further studies, particularly Eugène Burnouf, who based his on two tablets from Hamadan. (A little more than ten years later, Layard was to discuss his own discoveries with Monsieur Burnouf.)

Rawlinson, because of his isolation at Kermanshah, could not get a copy of Grotefend's alphabet when he began his attempts to decipher Persian cuneiform, but, applying the same reasoning and method, he achieved far more satisfactory results. He had the advantage of knowing dialects still spoken in remote parts of Persia (the Bakhtiyari dialect, for instance) which were akin to the old language. He had not only his own copies of the Behistun inscription to study, but had seen at firsthand the Hamadan tablets and the Persepolis material. In 1842 he resigned from the Army after active duty on the Afghan front, and moved to Baghdad to continue his investigations. From the Behistun inscriptions he hoped some day to be able to decode the cuneiform symbols on the bricks and stones of Mesopotamia in whatever languages had been spoken there. In the summer of 1844 he returned to Behistun, climbed the rock, and in a week copied the whole of the Persian and Elamite (then called Median) columns, and some detached lines of the Babylonian. The great Babylonian inscription, it seemed, would be out of reach forever, as Darius had planned the entire monument to be.

Rawlinson worked on the copies which he had brought back from this excursion during every minute that he could spare from the official duties he had now undertaken as Resident. It was a considerable sacrifice, writes Canon Rawlinson, for his brother, who was a sportsman accustomed to fresh air and exercise, to stick to his desk throughout a Baghdad summer, which often boasted a temperature of 120 degrees. Sitting in a kiosk at the foot of the Residency garden, by the river, where a water wheel poured a continuous stream over the roof and kept the temperature inside down to a reasonable 90, Rawlinson rewrote his memoir on the Persian inscriptions—five hundred and forty-one pages. A lion kitten, found in the rushes of the Tigris, habitually lay under his chair as he wrote. He had tamed this pet by giving strict orders to his household that none but he should feed it; he told a servant to pretend sometimes to remove its food; then he would scold the servant, knock him down, chase him from the room, and himself bring the food back to the lion. It ate out of his hand, followed him about house and garden like a dog, and died one day quietly under the desk chair. Since Rawlinson did not allow himself time to hunt, he had trained various other wild animals to regard the Residency as home; among them was a leopard named Fahad, ultimately presented to the London Zoo, where Rawlinson frequently visited him in later years, and a mongoose, very useful for killing snakes.

In his official capacity, his manner could be abrupt and imperious, but he was more than generous when he had once accepted someone as a friend. The Residency was run in the style of Claudius Rich and Colonel Taylor, only more so. "He has a sepoy guard commanded by a native officer; when he goes out drums are beaten and arms presented as to a general," H. J. Ross reports. During his second term as Resident, Rawlinson's prestige in Baghdad was so great that if he had put his English hat on his dog and sent him out, all the people in the bazaar would have made way for the animal, and bowed to him, and the soldiers would have stood still and presented arms as he passed.[3] As host to visiting Britishers and the European colony, he was apt to keep guests at a distance till he decided whom he liked, but he did not allow this to dampen the conviviality. "He had a Bombay Portuguese Indian cook—very good he was—and everything was done according to the Indian custom," writes Ross, regaling his sister with the details of his first dinner at the Residency. After the sweets, cheese and ale, guests were invited to the tea room; the gentlemen then returned to the dining room, where the table had been cleared of fruit and wine and in their place was a tureen of hot punch, with deviled herrings and turkey legs scattered about. Toast after toast was given; so many that Ross felt quite queasy next morning. Rawlinson, pleading a broken collarbone from a fall while pig-sticking, had excused himself from the latter part of the evening, leaving Captain Felix Jones of the East India Company steamer *Nicrotis* in charge.

Such was the hospitality which Layard was to enjoy at Christmastime 1845. It was also the start of a fruitful partnership and a lifelong friendship between two men who liked and respected one another even when their opinions differed. Canon Rawlinson remarks on the good fortune which brought them together: "Layard the excavator, the effective task-master, the hard-working and judicious gatherer of materials; Rawlinson the classical scholar, the man at once of wide reading and keen insight, the cool, dispassionate investigator and weigher of evidence." The Canon rather underestimates his brother's colleague. Dispassionate, Layard certainly was not, but some of his wildest guesses turned out to be correct; he did not have Rawlinson's classical training, as he himself was the first to deplore, but he could hold his own in history and living languages. No cuneiform expert, he learned from Rawlinson to decipher a good deal of it, and the copies he made, even before he understood the sound or meaning of a single character, were amazingly accurate. From this time on, he sent a steady stream of copies and papier-mâché impressions to Rawlinson for study, as well as most sculptures destined for England, which Rawlinson took charge of and examined before shipping. The mass of Assyrian material inspired Rawlinson to make his final, successful attack on the Rock of Behistun two years later.

Layard returned to Mosul in January, fortified with the Resident's promise to send the *Nicrotis* up the Tigris to take on a load of sculpture at Nimrud as soon as required. Ismail Pasha, the new governor, had no objection to Layard's reopening the excavations. The whole atmosphere of Mosul and the surrounding country had changed for the better; even the weather had cheered up. It was spring already in Mesopotamia. When Layard rode out to Nimrud, he rode over a plain sprouting new green grass and the first tiny flowers; barley shoots softened the harsh contours of the mound itself. Encouraged by the Pasha's reputation for levying reasonable taxes, the village Arabs had returned to their homes, and since Bedouin raids were now to be strictly punished, it was safe for Layard to move from Selamiyah to the more convenient settlement at the foot of the mound. He again employed Nestorians and Arabs, and enrolled Hormuzd Rassam, brother of the British Vice-consul, as his assistant. Rassam, a native-born Mosul Christian, spoke the local Arab dialect perfectly, understood the workmen, and proved invaluable in dealing with them.

Layard's optimism was short-lived. Keritli Oglu was finished, but there was still the Cadi. His Reverence's current theme was that Layard was digging for inscriptions which would prove that the Franks had once owned the entire country, had a right to take it over again, and to kill all True Believers. Ismail Pasha requested

Layard to stop work till the excitement in the bazaars died down. Did some atavistic memory of the Crusaders inspire the Cadi's fantastic statements? Or the highhanded ways of the Grand Elchi and the Resident at Baghdad? Layard was only aware that the Cadi's nonsense made for maddening interruptions to the work of a man who could barely sleep at night for curiosity about what he would turn up next.

He was never one to sit out frustrations in idleness. So one morning he rode over to settle some minor irritations with his new neighbors, the Abou Salman Bedouin, whose herds and black tents were scattered over the plain of Nimrud. Shortly before Christmas, the warriors of this tribe had been intercepted by Daoud Agha's troops in the act of raiding Layard's own quarters. They were not vicious, only mischievous as monkeys, seeming to steal for the fun of it. Layard hoped that the tactful present of a silk robe to their sheikh, Abd-ur-rahman, would at least ensure the return of a few stray articles in the future. At the encampment, after coffee had been drunk, compliments exchanged, and the gift accepted, Layard said: "*Inshallah*, we are now friends—though it is scarcely a month ago you came over the Zab on purpose to appropriate the little property I am accustomed to carry about me."

Abd-ur-rahman replied that yes, by God, they were now friends, and if, in the past, he had planned a *ghazou* against the Frank, it was out of necessity. "Look at these white hairs," he said, lifting up his *keffiyeh*. "They turned white when Keritli Oglu threw me, an Arab of the tribe that fought with the Prophet, into a damp cell for forty days. I was released at last; but how did I return to my tribe? A beggar, unable to kill a sheep for my guests. He took my mares, my flocks, and my camels, as the price of my liberty. Now tell me, O Bey, in the name of God, if the Osmanli have eaten from me and my guests, shall I not eat from them and theirs?"

Thenceforth Abd-ur-rahman made no more attempts to eat from the Englishman, except by invitation. He and his tribe became an enthusiastic cheering section and occasional participants in the doings at Nimrud. By mid-February, the Mosul fanatics had sufficiently lost interest in Layard for him to resume digging on an inconspicuous scale. In the Southwest Palace, more walls, inscriptions, and shattered sculptures were coming to light in rapid succession. Some were not charred but worn almost smooth by weather, an indication that this building had been only partly gutted by fire; much of it, deserted and half ruined, had gradually sunk into decay. Hardly a day passed that did not add some new bit to the story which Layard was piecing together. A bas-relief, often to be repeated thereafter, disclosed three imposing, over-life-sized figures: a central one, in tiara and robes, attended by a eunuch with a fan, or fly whisk, and a second gentleman whom Layard dubbed the Vizier. He wrote to his mother: "I have now found the king who constructed the building. He is evidently of the same race as the kings who constructed the Palace of Khorsabad. This, perhaps, may have been really the Palace of Sardanapalus, rebuilt under the second Assyrian Dynasty. However, it is no use speculating at present; as I work on, I hope for many interesting results. I have just discovered two beautiful lions, but unfortunately they have lost their heads, which appear to have been human, like those of the two great bulls already uncovered; also like them they have wings. The two lions form a gateway or entrance on the west. These extraordinary animals are sculptured in very high relief upon a solid block of marble, 14 feet long and 16 or 17 feet high! Unfortunately the two I have now discovered are much damaged. Should I discover one sufficiently preserved to deserve removal, I shall have a pretty work to move it. Those of Khorsabad, which were much smaller, could scarcely be dragged along by 500 men. Mechanical power in these countries is unknown. How the Assyrians moved these immense blocks, I cannot conceive. There are no marble quarries, that I know of, within seven or eight miles."

The problem of moving sculptures was still academic, since he had not found any in good condition, though almost four months had passed since the start of the excavations. It was possible that all Nimrud had been ruthlessly destroyed, and he would never find what he was searching for. He decided to have a second look at the northwest corner of the mound, where, in an isolated chamber, the slabs (inscribed, not sculptured) had been in excellent condition. The winter rains had worn a ravine deep into the core of the mound, and there he ordered a trench to be dug. Clod by clod the picks tore away the soil from a row of slabs: uncracked, uncharred, and covered with carvings. The first showed two large human figures with wings, standing back to back; one bore a branch with five flowers, the other a bucket and what appeared to be a fircone. Layard thought them gods of the seasons, but he did not know what to make of a similar pair of figures which had eagles' heads. Between the two pairs was the tree of life, made up of flowers and scrolls, which he compared to the network of pomegranates that had decorated King Solomon's Temple.

Current scholarship interprets the winged figures, whether human or eagle-headed, as genii—supernatural beings that were the early models for the Jinns of whom Layard had read in the *Arabian Nights*, and in whom the Arabs still believed. The griffin-headed figure is always represented in an action beneficial to man. Here, with a date spathe and a bucket probably filled with pollen, he is fertilizing the sacred date palm, which is twined about with life-giving irrigation canals.

These slabs seemed to be in their original positions, forming the interior walls of a large hall. They were in the same style and workmanship as those which had been moved and cut to fit the walls in the Southwest Palace. Layard believed them older, and considered them finer than those at Khorsabad, an aesthetic judgment with which today's critics agree. Every detail of fringed and embroidered robes, of jeweled bracelet, sword hilt, and sandal, every curl in hair and beard, was clearly cut and precise. The design was ornate but not cluttered; the bones and muscles accurately drawn though somewhat overemphasized (especially the structure of the knee and the bulging calf of the leg). It has been suggested that captives flayed alive—as we know from other bas-reliefs that they were—served as anatomy models for the Assyrian sculptors.

Every day brought fresh discoveries. Layard was immensely busy drawing the sculptures and copying inscriptions. Now that he had found these, he knew that there would be many more, for only the smallest part of the mound had yet been explored. His experiment had succeeded beyond his wildest dreams, but his dreams were expanding, and he was impatient for the official backing which would make possible full-scale excavation instead of pecking here and there with a few workmen. All he needed now was an Imperial Firman, and money to do the work properly. So far he had neither. But he had treasure hunter's luck. On the day after the appearance of the benevolent Jinns, on his way back from Abd-ur-rahman's encampment, he met two of the tribesmen coming from the direction of the mound. They pulled up short in a cloud of dust. "Hasten, O Bey—hasten to the diggers," they cried, "for they have found Nimrod himself! Wallah! it is wonderful, but it is true. We have seen him with our own eyes. There is no God but God!" So saying they galloped off to bring the news to their own tents.

Layard hastened, and found the diggers gathered by a fresh trench out of which, like a supernatural being slowly ascending from the lower depths, rose a huge, blanched stone head. He recognized it at once as the human head of a lion or bull colossus like the broken ones he had already found. Even at this moment of excitement, his practiced eye noted that its headdress, instead of being high and flat-topped like those of the bulls at Khorsabad, was a rounded turban twined with triple horns.

The Abou Salman, arriving in full force and at full speed, stopped dead in their tracks at the sight. "There is no God but God and Mohammed is His prophet!" cried the terrified warriors. Layard induced Abd-ur-rahman to climb into the trench to see for himself that this was no god or demon but an image of stone. Even so, said the sheikh, it was not the work of men's hands, but of those infidel giants whom the Prophet had described as taller than the tallest date tree. "This is one of the idols which Noah, peace be with him! cursed before the flood."

From the discoveries at Khorsabad, and the broken figures which he himself had found, Layard knew that these colossi were usually in pairs, forming a gateway or entrance. He paced off a probable distance and ordered the men to dig a trench to the south, where, twelve feet from the first, they came upon a second giant head. Since it was now almost dark, the workers and tribesmen retired to the village, where Layard purchased a sheep to be butchered, and engaged a band of musicians. Nimrod's appearance was celebrated with feasting and dancing till dawn.

Unfortunately, at the first sight of the giant, a workman had thrown down his basket and scurried off to Mosul as fast as he could run. Layard tried to stop him, but he paid no heed to the shouts. Arriving breathless in the bazaar, the man gasped to everyone he met that Nimrod himself had risen from the ruins of his old palace. The story soon reached the ears of the Cadi; the Cadi took it to the Moslem doctors of law, the *Ulema*; the Ulema plus the Cadi and all good Moslems of Mosul marched to the Pasha to protest the desecration—or whatever it was; the Cadi was not sure whether the bones of the Mighty Hunter had been dug up, or merely his image. The Pasha could not remember whether Nimrod had been an infidel or a True Believer; to be on the safe side he sent Layard a jumbled message that he was to treat the remains with respect—and suspend digging immediately. It would have been funny if it had not been so frustrating. Since Layard had no permit to dig, there was nothing he could do but obey—more or less, as usual. Two workers in the familiar guise of watchmen, continued to burrow along the walls. By March they had located a second pair of colossi, forming a second entrance to the same hall. The first pair was completely dug out and proved to be magnificent winged lions, about twelve feet tall, in perfect condition. The head and forepart of each animal was in the round, the remainder in high relief. An odd artistic convention was that the animal had five legs, so the observer saw it from the front, standing; from the side, walking. Between the legs were long cuneiform inscriptions. "I have been very busy lately with this strange character, and I am happy to say, not without results," Layard wrote to his mother in April. "For instance, I have got at the proper names, the names of cities (without being yet able to decipher them), the ends of words, etc.; and with the assistance of the materials furnished by the joint stock of Major Rawlinson and myself, I hope very shortly to have the alphabet; we have already many letters." (They were in for a disappointment: Assyrio-Babylonian cuneiform is not written alphabetically.) "Then for the language; is it Chaldean, in the common acceptation of the term, and plain sailing? Or is it some dialect, long forgotten, of one of the existing family of languages, and to be made out by persevering comparisons and research? Or is it some unknown language, which will have to be reconstructed?"

He spent hours looking at his winged lions, and meditating on their history and purpose. He thought them fit guardians for the portal of a temple. What better image of a Supreme Being could a pre-Christian people have chosen than a creature that had a human head for wisdom, an eagle's wings for swiftness, a lion's body for power? The currently accepted explanation differs only slightly from Layard's poetic musings. As far back as Sumerian times, temples had been adorned with lions and bulls to guard them from evil. In Assyria they also guarded palaces, since the dwelling of an Assyrian king, who represented God on earth, had almost the same significance as the temple. The multiple animals represent man, the lord of creation; the eagle, monarch of the skies; the lion, king of beasts; the bull, fecundator of the herds. The horned headdress signifies the creature's divinity; the girdle, a leash used on hunting dogs, indicates its readiness to pounce upon intruders.[4]

Like most Englishmen of his day, Layard was well versed in Scripture, and he was moved to wonder and awe by the way in which his discoveries seemed to illustrate Bible history. Though he had shocked his Church of England family by attending the Unitarian Chapel, he was in a true sense deeply religious. As he sat and contemplated his wonderful stone beasts, he was reminded of the vision which came out of the whirlwind to Ezekiel on the banks of the Chebar—probably, he thought, the Khabur, a branch of the Euphrates—while the prophet was among the captive children of Israel there:

And everyone had four faces, and everyone had four wings . . .
As for the likeness of their faces, they four had the face of a man
and the face of a lion, on the right side; and they four had the
face of an ox on the left side; they four also had the face of an
eagle.

The extravagant imagery was explained if one realized that
Ezekiel had seen the Assyrian palaces, ruined in his day, but still
above ground.

Layard found it hard to understand why his achievements were
receiving so little recognition at home. "Nothing so beautiful as
these lions was discovered by the French," he writes to his mother
with pardonable pride. Botta, he had learned, had been allotted
sixty thousand francs to carry on his excavations and other work
in connection with the discoveries at Khorsabad, but the British
Museum Trustees had greeted with remarkable indifference Sir
Stratford Canning's suggestion that Layard be similarly supported.
He wrote to Sir Stratford again, asking advice on what to do, for
he had spent the major part of the sum which he and the Ambassador had put up. If it had not been for his mother, who sent him
what she could spare out of her small income, he could not have
continued. He had cut his own living expenses to the bone; unless
he soon received official recognition and financial aid, he would
have to abandon the field to his French competitors, which, he
felt, would be a disgrace after such a fine start. In one of his rare
moods of depression, he wrote to his aunt that his life was monotonous; that he lived in a mud hut in a deserted village with no
companionship; he was rapidly forgetting how to speak English. As
long as he continued to expose himself recklessly to the extremes
of a merciless climate, he would have to put up with bouts of fever.
Perhaps he was squandering health and money to no purpose.

In spite of this, he was supremely happy much of the time. How
he loved this country, how he would hate to leave it! Seated before
his tent of an evening, he would watch the sun go down into the
desert, and the last rosy glow reflected on the snow-topped mountains to the east. The scene before him never lost its fascination:

"The bleating of sheep and lowing of cattle, at first faint, became louder as the flocks returned from their pastures, and wandered among the tents. Girls hurried over the greensward to seek their fathers' cattle, or crouched down to milk those which had returned alone to their well-remembered folds. Some were coming from the river bearing the replenished pitcher on their heads or shoulders; others, no less graceful in their form, and erect in their carriage, were carrying the heavy load of long grass which they had cut in the meadows. Sometimes a party of horsemen might have been seen in the distance slowly crossing the plain, the tufts of ostrich feathers which topped their long spears showing darkly against the evening sky. They would ride up to my tent, and give me the usual salutation, 'Peace be with you, O Bey,' or, 'Allah Aienak, God help you.' Then driving the end of their lances into the ground, they would spring from their mares, and fasten their halters to the still quivering weapons. Seating themselves on the grass, they related deeds of war and plunder until the moon rose, when they vaulted into their saddles and took the way of the desert."

Chapter XVI

PLEASURES AND PALACES
(April–July 1846)

Since for lack of a permit and money, work at Nimrud had come to a virtual standstill, Layard joined an excursion to Hatra. Six years earlier, on a similar trip, he had enjoyed his first dramatic view of the mound of Nimrud. That had been a rough camping trip, and he a passing traveler; this time he rode out in grand style, with H. J. Ross, Mr. and Mrs. Rassam, and "a cheerful party of Christian and Mohammedan ladies and gentlemen from Mosul," plus a whole retinue of cawasses and attendants. Twelve camels and numerous donkeys were needed to carry the baggage—for in those days one brought one's linen and silver and delicacies and servants, when camping out. Two barrels of raki, emitting a pungent odor, were provided for the refreshment of the saddle-weary. Circumstances had changed for Layard, but Bedouin custom had not, and must be considered. Lawrence of Arabia writes: "Men have looked upon the Desert as barren land, the free holding of whoever chose; but in fact each hill and valley in it had a man who was its acknowledged owner and would quickly assert the right of his family or clan to it against aggression . . . The desert was held in a crazed communism by which nature and the elements were for the free use of every known friendly person for his own purposes and no more. Logical outcomes were the reduction of this license to privilege by the men of the desert, and their hardness to strangers unprovided with introduction or guarantee."[1]

Unprovided, Layard and his friends on the earlier visit had been in some danger from a minor sheikh of the great Shammar tribe, within whose lands Hatra and the neighboring oasis of Al Hadhar lay. This time, by arrangement and accompanied by a Shammar guide, the party was to call upon Sofuk, the paramount Shammar sheikh, who was known to be tenting at Al Hadhar. Layard had a triple purpose: to see Hatra again; to buy a horse; and to gain the friendship of Sofuk, whose plundering talents were notorious, and who was likely to be raiding in the neighborhood of Nimrud during the coming summer.

Gertrude Bell, still another intrepid British traveler in the desert, tells of seeing a group of Shammar on their way north from a clan gathering at Hatra. "They were moving camp when I came up to them and the whole world was alive with their camels. Now the Shammar are *Bedu;* only the Shammar and Anazeh are real Bedawin, the others are just Arabs. Akh-el 'bair we call the Bedu, the people of the Camel. They never cultivate the soil or stay more than a night or two in one place, but wander ceaselessly over the inner desert."[2]

Layard's party also caught up with the main body of the Shammar on the march. Round about the flocks and camels ranged the warriors on fast mares or dromedaries, carrying their tall, ostrich-tufted spears. Donkeys and bullocks were laden down with tents, carpets, caldrons, supplies. Mothers billowed along belly first, carrying on their shoulders the children too young to walk; infants peeped, with black button eyes, out of saddlebags. The high-born ladies rode in wide-winged, gay-colored camel howdahs; elder members of lesser standing were tied on top of the baggage loads. There was a terrible confusion of dust and noise: dogs barked, babies cried, herders shouted, flocks bleated. The beat of a thousand hoofs rippled over the flinty floor of the desert with the sound of a stream.

Sofuk (called by Ross "that old fox Sfoog") received the party with the usual Bedouin coffee and hospitality. Mrs. Rassam was so embarrassed by the stares from all around the tent that she asked to retire to the harem. Being the daughter of a regimental schoolmaster and the sister of a clergyman, she was, in Layard's words "over-nice." She committed a *faux pas* by refusing the refreshment offered by the sheikh's ladies: *eau sucré* mixed by a black and dirty slave who stirred it with his fingers and licked them between mixings. Fortunately Amshah, Sofuk's chief wife, was gracious enough to excuse the breach of manners in a woman who obviously did not know how a lady should behave.

Sofuk had two other more or less permanent wives, and in addition, as a status symbol, took a new one each month whom he would divorce and marry off to one of his retinue after thirty days— a more amiable habit than that of Scheherazade's spouse. But no matter how many wives Sofuk had, Amshah was queen of the household, and her throne, which stood in the middle of her enormous tent, was a heap of sacks containing all the household supplies. At request she had only to lift a corner of her carpet, untie the mouth of a sack, and dip out rice, corn, coffee, or whatever was needed. Meanwhile, to show her superior position, she called her handmaidens names which Layard begged to be excused from translating. "It may not perhaps be known," he writes, "that the fair inmate of the harem, whom we picture to ourselves conversing with her lover in language too delicate and refined to be expressed by anything else but flowers, uses ordinarily words which would shock the most depraved amongst us."

After the refreshments, and the presentation to Sofuk of a silk coat of many colors more beautiful than Joseph's, the party, provided with one of Sofuk's men as guide and sponsor, moved on to Hatra. Blue-black clouds were boiling up out of the desert; a few shafts of sunlight touched the old stones of Hatra with purest gold. Then the storm broke; lightning played among the tumbled buildings, thunder echoed in the deserted halls. A stinging hail compelled the travelers to rein up their horses and turn their backs. They camped for three days in the great courtyard of a palace of hewn blocks decorated with masks and other sculptured motifs. Layard thought it older than Sassanian, though it was a type of building sometimes constructed in Sassanian times. He sketched and drew plans of it, but, as he wrote jokingly to Mitford, he was no longer really interested in anything "which did not come under the immediate cognisance of Noah or his sons."

Nevertheless Hatra had the charm of mystery: a Western bastion of the little known Parthian kings who had warred constantly with Rome and fallen before the Sassanians in the third century. Recently the government of Iraq has excavated at Hatra, and though much has been learned, it is still a strange place. Its temples show the influence of Greece, Rome, and perhaps even India, and its deities are curious compounds: the sun-god Shamash and Zeus; Assyrian Ashur-bel in the costume of a Roman Emperor.

Layard was refreshed by the trip into the desert, and on his return found that still another governor—the third within six months—had been installed at Mosul. Tahyar Pasha, who seemed a reasonable man, gave Layard official permission to reopen the Nimrud excavations under the eye of an official cawass, Ibrahim Agha. Like Daoud Agha, this man soon became more of an ally than a spy. But Layard could not, without the Imperial Firman, be sure how long his luck would last. At any time the present Pasha might be replaced by a Keritli Oglu. And there was always the Cadi, ready to rabble-rouse at the least excuse.

In order to stretch his funds as much as possible, Layard picked only a few workmen, the strongest and most skilled, and set them to work on the Northwest Palace. One night in early summer, he was asleep in Abd-ur-rahman's tent before going to hunt gazelle with the sheikh at dawn, when he was awakened by an Arab messenger with dispatches from Mosul. "And I read by the light of a small camel-dung fire, the documents which secured to the British nation the records of Nineveh, and a collection of the earliest monuments of Assyrian art." The Sultan, in recognition of the Great Elchi's friendship, made a personal gift to Sir Stratford Canning of such antiquities as Layard should find.

With the Vizierial letter in hand, Layard now dared to send a small work party to explore Kuyunjik, which, with Nebbi Yunus, had so long been identified with the name of Nineveh. No sculptures had been found at Kuyunjik either by Botta or by Rouet, his successor as French Consul at Mosul. Layard firmly believed sculptures did exist somewhere in the heart of the great pile. That was the trouble; it was so big—half a mile long and a quarter of a mile wide. A palace, if there was a palace at Kuyunjik, could lie buried in any part of it. There was no corner of a slab conveniently poking up, as at Nimrud, to promise quick success and act as a signpost for excavators. Rouet claimed the whole mound as French property because of Botta's brief explorations; when Layard sent his men to work there, an international clash was avoided only by the size of the area and the fact that neither his nor the Frenchman's work party found anything but loose bricks and fragments. Layard realized that the same name appeared on many of the bricks, but he could not, of course, read it.

Rich's *Narrative* had mentioned a large bas-relief which had been discovered, not on the mound itself, but near one of the low, dirt-covered ramparts to the north of it. A Turkish officer had told Rich that the sculpture had been a figure on horseback followed by foot soldiers. It was higher than a man could reach and of great thickness; so remarkable was it that all Mosul came out to see it. After the Pasha and the town notables had examined it, it was broken up by the orders of the Ulema. Layard was particularly eager to find the fragments of this bas-relief, but again the question was, where? There was more than one rampart north of Kuyunjik; his work-men tore up the ground for days without uncovering any indication of sculpture—not even one tiny alabaster fragment. Then an aged stonecutter, who claimed that he had been employed to smash that very idol, came to Layard, saying he could point out the spot where it was buried. Though Layard had little faith in the story, it was worth investigating. For the first time the trail grew hot; frag-ments of alabaster appeared one by one like the pieces of a puzzle. Sorted out, cleaned, and assembled, they formed not a bas-relief, but the largest pair of winged beasts yet discovered. Layard thought they might have guarded the portal to a gatehouse or watchtower on the ruined ramparts whose bricks were piled nearby. Every brick bore the same name as the fragments from Kuyunjik.

During this period, when success might (or might not) be im-minent, an incident occurred which could have ended Layard's career forever. Because it was spring and the river was high, the bridge of boats was not in use; Layard crossed the Tigris to and from the mounds by boat. Late one night when the ferry had stopped running, he hired the only available boatman to take himself, a few workmen, and two Albanian mercenaries who would otherwise have been stranded, back to Mosul. The boat had already moved out into the stream when it was hailed from shore by someone asking to be taken across the river. Layard recognized the voice of the Cadi—no friend of his—but the hour was late and boats scarce, so he told the boatman to turn back. The Cadi and several followers climbed in amidships; Layard remained on the high poop deck beside the helm. Halfway across, the Cadi began to shout and curse, crying out, "Shall the dogs occupy the high places while the True Believers have to stand below?" adding a string of typical Arab terms for Christians: "sons of dogs, sons of filthy dogs, misbegotten sons of shameless mothers, sons of mules and asses, offspring of Lot—Allah damn their fathers, Allah blacken their faces!"

Layard, as hot-tempered where his honor was concerned as when he had been a boy, silenced the Cadi's insults by hitting His Reverence over the head with a heavy camel stick he was in the habit of carrying. Immediately the blood began to run from under the Cadi's turban and down his face. At this his followers drew their swords and pistols; the Albanians and Layard's workmen drew theirs in answer. A full-fledged battle was about to take place when Layard jumped into the waist of the boat, seized the Cadi by the throat, and threatened to throw him overboard if his followers made a single move. On reaching shore, he let the Cadi go, and go he did as fast as possible to show his bloody face in the bazaars, crying Wallah! Billah! Tillah! that he had been attacked by an infidel; that the Prophet and the Faith had been insulted. Layard knew such an outcry could easily be turned into a holy war against the Christians of Mosul. He went immediately to the Governor with the real story, pointing out that Tahyar Pasha would be held responsible by the Great Elchi and the British Government if harm came to one who held the Imperial Firman.

The Pasha was quite willing to denounce the Cadi, with whom he was having a personal feud, but he begged Layard to remain secluded in the Governor's Palace till the hotheads among the populace calmed down. Layard refused, and refused also Rawlinson's invitation to come to Baghdad till the affair blew over. He did not do this out of bravado. He knew that if he appeared frightened, and seemed to doubt whether the Pasha was able to protect him, he would never again be safe in Mosul. He returned to his own house and to his usual routine, crossing the Tigris daily to the mounds and riding alone through the streets apparently oblivious of the black looks he received. The Pasha's police prevented an open attack—but a more sinister revenge was being plotted by a group which gathered nightly at the Cadi's house. The infidel who had dared to lay a finger on His Reverence was to be quietly wiped out.

Luckily, Layard was warned of the assassination plot. "I had, by singular chance, made the acquaintance of the daughter of the Cadi himself, who frequently came to see me, notwithstanding the great risk she ran," he writes some fifty years after the event. "As she knew all that was passing in her father's house, she kept me fully informed of what was going on against me." Layard passed the information on to the Pasha, who jailed the plotters— all but the Cadi, who was untouchable.

It is an intriguing story, left hanging in mid-air by Layard's reticence. By what "singular chance" had the young Englishman met the daughter of the greatest fanatic in town? How did she dare to call upon him, not once but "frequently"? Orthodox Moslem maidens of Mosul were not permitted to go out unattended. Even heavily veiled, she might have been recognized by a passerby as she slipped into Layard's house. The risk of discovery by her father was great indeed, and the Cadi would not have hesitated to "send floating to Baghdad" a daughter who not only consorted with an infidel dog but was disloyal to her father. Disappearance into the river was a common fate of ladies too fond of roaming.

We shall never know what the relationship was between Layard and the Cadi's daughter. "I did not refer to it in the published narrative of my first expedition to Nineveh for obvious reasons," he writes. The story waited on publication till he was old and she presumably safe from a father's wrath. One thing is sure: she saved his life.

Sir Stratford Canning, advised of the quarrel, privately sent word that, though the Cadi deserved what he got, he hoped Layard would be more cautious in future. And since the Cadi, corrupt and overbearing, was disliked among all but the most rigid True Believers, his denunciation of the popular young Englishman was soon forgotten.

Layard was popular not only because of the charm which he obviously possessed, but because he was well aware that the good will of neighbors, workmen and officials, so necessary for his project, could be helped along by tactful gifts and occasional entertainments. On his return to Nimrud, he gave a great party for the leading Christian and Moslem families of Mosul, and for all the Arabs in the vicinity. It was such a success that the Abou Salman sheikh invited the company to continue the festivities in his tents. Pulling Layard along with him, he led off a dance in which some five hundred warriors and Arab women took part. During a pause for breath, Abd-ur-rahman sat in a corner of the tent staring at a French lady who had come with Layard. "Wallah," he whispered, "she is the sister of the Sun! What would you more beautiful than that? Had I a thousand purses, I would give them all for such a wife. See! Her eyes are like the eyes of my mare, her hair is as bitumen, and her complexion resembles the finest Busrah dates. Anyone would die for a Houri like that."

The feasting and dancing went on for three days and accomplished just what Layard had hoped. The Arabs talked about it endlessly, and his reputation for generosity spread to the far corners of the desert. Thereafter he knew that he could count on Arab friends whenever he needed them, which proved how much "a little show of kindness to these ill-used people" could mean. After the party, his own workmen at Nimrud went back to the excavation with renewed vigor.

Wonderful bas-reliefs had been coming to light in the Northwest Palace almost every day. There were scenes of the chase, in which the chariot horses, the lions and wild bulls were executed with the greatest spirit and skill; Layard considered the sculpture of the lion hunt "probably the finest specimen of Assyrian art in existence."[3] The siege of a castle on a river showed warriors swimming on inflated skins in the same fashion as the Mosuli Arabs still did. There were processions of captives bearing vases, monkeys, elephant tusks. The costumes of the captives were differentiated; some wore boots with turned up toes like those still worn in Turkey and Persia; the figure with the monkeys was perhaps a Negro.

There were many representations of the king. Some showed him going forth to war or the chase; in others he was engaged in a magical ceremony, adorned with the horned cap and a necklace of sun, moon, and stars while two eagle-headed winged figures stood on either side of him. One of them might be anointing him with the date spathe, or fir cone, with a mystic substance contained in the bucket. He was seen sometimes in duplicate; sometimes seated on his throne quaffing a cup of wine while a eunuch stood by with a towel over his shoulder to be presented for the king to wipe his lips after drinking. The king ordinarily wore a long, fringed and embroidered robe and a broad girdle, a fez-like cap, earrings, armlets and bracelets; his weapons were two daggers, a sword, and a bow. His waved and curled hair swept out to the back; his square-cut beard was set in waves and tight little curls, forming a design. A curious feature of these bas-reliefs was that all the human faces, whether of the king, his attendants, or the genii, whether bearded or not, were the same fleshy face, with large, slightly slanted staring eyes, a strong-nostriled curved nose, thin sneering lips. It was not a handsome face such as one finds idealized on classic Greek sculptures. It was a portrait, repeated on every figure, of a real person—and that person was the king who had built the Northwest Palace at Nimrud.

Above the king's head there was often the device of an archer with the wings and tail of a bird, enclosed in a circle, similar to the god of the Persians, which was carved on the bas-reliefs of Persepolis. In Assyrian art, the sun disk (which is not always an archer) signifies Ashur, god of might and procreative power. The wings and tail form the masculine symbol T; the circle is feminine; the whole symbolizes the life force, and, when placed over the head of the king, reminds the beholder that the monarch is the god's representative on earth.

In these sculptures everything was covered with ornamentation: minute designs upon the accouterments and harness; eagles' beaks holding the bow strings; figures of men and animals upon the quivers. There were bas-reliefs within the bas-reliefs, scenes within the scenes. Engraved upon the buckets carried by the genii, and embroidered upon the robes of the king were a variety of mythological figures similar to those on the cylinder seals of Assyria and Babylon. Traces of color remained: black on the hair and beard, red on the headdress and sandals of the king. Again Layard thought of passages from the Book of Ezekiel:

She doted upon the Assyrians her neighbors, captains and rulers clothed most gorgeously, horsemen riding upon horses, all of them desirable young men . . . She saw men portrayed upon the wall, the images of the Chaldeans portrayed with vermillion, girded with girdles upon their loins, exceeding in dyed attire upon their heads, all of them princes to look to.

The most impressive chamber in the Northwest Palace was a great hall, 154 feet long and only 33 feet wide. Its walls, faced with alabaster, stood to a height of twelve feet. Flecks of brilliantly painted plaster still clung to bricks that had fallen from above the slabs. Blackened ashes pointed to the location of wooden beams, which had upheld the roof. Bit by bit Layard was beginning to put together what an Assyrian palace had looked like. The principal rooms had been long and narrow because it was difficult to roof-over a wide space; roofs were presumably of mud-plastered matting laid on wooden beams, as in ordinary Arab huts today. At the upper end of the Great Hall was an immense stone dais for a throne; behind this was a larger than life bas-relief of the king. The walls of the throne room and other public chambers were lined with alabaster slabs, carved with a double row of bas-reliefs divided by a band of inscription—the same text repeated many times over around and around the room. The sculptures portrayed the king's triumphs in war and the chase; above them were brightly colored frescoes telling more of the story. Floors were paved with inscribed slabs, or were of brick bearing short inscriptions and set in sand and bitumen for insulation. Some of the floors at least were probably covered with carpets. Vertical drains in the walls carried off the rain from the roofs in winter; floor drains carried off sewage and probably water that was thrown over the floors to cool them in summer. The walls were tremendously thick to keep out extremes of weather in both seasons. Awnings may have been used in the courtyards. Doorways formed by giant figures led into other apartments and courtyards, which again led into other halls. The private apartments were furnished with chests, divans and chairs of wood ornamented with carved ivory like those of Solomon's house described in Scripture. Of the royal entourage that passed through these rooms there remained only a few beads, bracelets, and hairpins found in a grave of a court lady whose skeleton, briefly visible to the diggers, fell into dust almost immediately.[4]

The workmen at Nimrud cried out in wonder at every sculptured figure they uncovered. If it was a bearded man, they said it was a Jinn and spat upon it; if a eunuch, they thought it a beautiful woman, patted its cheek, and kissed it. Now that Layard had his permit and before the Cadi should again make trouble, he was eager to send off a load of these sculptures to Sir Stratford Canning in England. Though several more pairs of bulls and lions had been dug up, these were too heavy and big to move; even the bas-reliefs presented innumerable problems, for no ropes strong enough to bear such a weight could be found, no hoisting machinery of any kind. By digging out the mud-brick walls behind the slabs, they could be moved with wooden levers into the center of the trenches where Behnan, the Arab stonecutter, sawed the double reliefs in two and chiseled as much as possible from the backs.

Before the sculptures were shipped away, Tahyar Pasha came to view them and the other curiosities of Nimrud. "Although I have a great respect for him," Layard wrote to Mrs. Austen, "I wished him at the ——, for, with his attendants and hangers-on—about two hundred in all—he completely devoured the provisions intended for six months consumption, and which an excess of frugality and economy had led me to lay up."

The Pasha's attendants were no less puzzled by the human-headed winged beasts than the Arabs had been, and, likewise, cried out to God upon the first sight of them. One Turk, claiming more knowledge than the rest, said these were the gods of the infidels. "I saw many such when I was in Italia with Reshid Pasha, the Ambassador. Wallah! They have them in all the churches, and the *pappas* kneel and burn candles before them."

"No, my lamb," said another. "I have seen the images of the infidels in their churches; they are dressed in many colors, and although some of them have wings, none have a dog's body and a tail; these are the works of the Jinn, whom the holy Solomon, peace be upon him! reduced to obedience and imprisoned under his seal."

"There is no infidel living who would make any thing like that," said an engineer, who was looked upon as an authority. "They are the work of the Magi and are to be sent to England to form a gateway to the palace of the queen."

The final word came from the Cadi's deputy: "May God curse all infidels and their works! What comes from their hands is of Satan."

For almost three weeks Layard sweated over moving alabaster blocks covered with delicate carving and very fragile, some of them nine-feet square and a foot thick even after cutting. Day after day he stood in the cruel sun, shouting orders till he was hoarse, while the workmen operated according to their own ideas, in ways that seemed calculated to produce only broken sculptures and broken toes. When, finally, twelve cases had been packed and moved to the riverbank "in carts which in England would scarcely be used for carrying hay," the steamer *Nicrotis*, sent from Baghdad to take them on, could not get past the dam at Tekrit. After a long delay, Layard was forced to send his cases by raft to Rawlinson, who would send them on to Basrah, where they would await transshipment. A French naval vessel was already in port loading Botta's antiquities, but there was still a chance that an English ship would overtake it in the race to bring the Assyrian finds before the European public. Layard was exhausted, and could only hope that the Nimrud sculptures would reach England promptly, and once there, would arouse the interest of the British Museum's phlegmatic Trustees. His discoveries were beginning to be talked about in England and the Continent; every mail now brought him inquiries and offers of help—scientific, but not financial.

Chapter XVII

"HOW PEOPLE LIVE"
(July–December 1846)

Full summer had come to Nimrud in May. The Abou Salman left their black tents for reed huts along the river, and Layard moved to a little recess cut in the bank and screened with boughs. Unfortunately other creatures enjoyed this shelter too: yellow scorpions and the invisible but vicious sand flies and gnats, which made Nimrod's tortures by these tiniest of God's subjects agonizingly clear. Shrimp-pink locusts, with green wings, had eaten each blade and leaf not scorched crisp by the sun. A suffocating wind from the desert covered everything with dust, and sometimes a full-fledged sandstorm made the sky as dark as night. With burning eyes and lungs, Layard would crouch under a toppled lion portal, while the workmen huddled together in the trenches, covering their faces with their *keffiyehs*. Even on the best days it was no joke to copy intricate inscriptions with the thermometer at 117 in the shade. In July, after the cases of sculpture had been safely shipped off (as he thought) on their way to England, he indulged himself in a short stay in Mosul, where he could spend the noon hours in the underground *sordaub* of his house.

Even with occasional work at Kuyunjik, this was too inactive for him; his way of resting was to get up two hours before dawn to hunt wild boar. "I find the exercise and excitement keep me in good health," he writes to Mrs. Austen. "I had the most desperate encounter two days ago, in which Mr. Ross, my only fellow-countryman here, got very nearly 'settled.' His horse threw him upon being gored, and the boar, a most ferocious animal, was rushing upon him when stunned on the ground. I had but time to place myself between them, and received the animal upon my spear, which unfortunately struck him between the eyes and glanced off. He caught me on the sole of my boot, and then ripped my horse in the belly. He recovered himself and made a second charge, and although my spear entered above a foot into his shoulder, he succeeded in shaking it out and goring my horse a second time. He then 'took up a position,' charging furiously whenever I approached. We faced each other in this way for about half-an-hour, when at length he made a desperate plunge at me, leaping several feet from the ground. My horse, notwithstanding his wounds, stood admirably, and I received him upon my spear, which passed completely through his neck and laid him dead at my feet." Ross himself reports that he was shot five feet up from his saddle, pitched on his head, a bunch of hair was cut off, an eyelid bruised, and he thought he had broken his neck. Thus did young Englishmen distract themselves from the heat of a Mosul summer.

Layard returned to Nimrud with his workmen in August. Though bas-reliefs were turning up everywhere, he finally had to admit that one could not fight the Mesopotamian summer in the airless trenches of a dig. Even the Arabs, accustomed to the climate, were collapsing one by one. He himself was suffering constantly from the malarial infection which he had never been able to shake off and which attacked him virulently when the weather was hot and his vitality low. As a rule he refused to let the bouts interfere with his activity unless he was completely knocked out. He took it for granted that he might be struck by a chill while in the saddle; when this occurred he simply rode on, shivering and shaking till the chill turned to fever and dizzyness, which forced him to dismount and lie on the ground wherever he happened to be. He knew that eventually he would break into a sweat, which ended the attack. Then, so weak he could barely keep his seat, he would climb back on his horse and continue the journey.

By now, in August, he had suffered so many attacks in succession that he had a feeling of utter lassitude, both mental and physical. The best cure was mountain air. He closed down the excavations and took off for the kind of holiday which was to become a regular habit: traveling among the wild tribes and odd sects—or, as he rationalized it, "the people who are now found within the limits of the kingdom of Assyria." Anthropology, the study of Man and his Works (or, informally "how people live") did not yet exist as a science. Layard, without knowing the term, was an excellent anthropologist. He had a great curiosity about people and their ways; he observed, investigated, asked intelligent questions, and meticulously took notes on everything he found out. His immediate purpose, in the summer of 1846, was to visit the villages in the Tiyari Mountains of Kurdistan from which came his hardiest pickmen, the so-called Nestorian Chaldeans. With him went Hormuzd Rassam, Ibrahim Agha, a couple of servants, and soldiers—the latter only for part of the way. He carried a letter of introduction from Mar Shamoun, the Nestorian patriarch in Mosul, to the priests and village chiefs.

The air, the green shade of oaks and oleander, the running brooks were all good medicine, but as the party traveled north through the mountains, they met depressing sights: dozens of ruined villages and thousands of skeletons of Nestorians slaughtered (their women had been sold as slaves) by a Kurdish chieftain, Bedr Khan Bey. In the villages that survived, or had been rebuilt, Mar Shamoun's letter (and the presence of Hormuzd Rassam) produced a warm welcome. "Before we entered the first gardens of the village, a party of girls, bearing baskets of fruit, advanced to meet us," Layard writes. "Their hair, neatly platted and adorned with flowers, fell down their backs. On their heads they wore coloured handkerchiefs loosely tied, or an embroidered cap. Many were pretty, and the prettiest was Aslani, a liberated slave, who had been for some time under the protection of Mrs. Rassam; she led the party, and welcomed me to Zaweetha. My hand having been kissed by all, they simultaneously threw themselves upon my companion, and saluted him vehemently on both cheeks; such a mode of salutation, in the case of a person of my rank and distinction, not being, unfortunately, considered either respectful or decorous."

Layard lived in the Nestorian homes and interviewed many of the priests and leaders of this sect, which split off from the main body of the Eastern Church in the fifth century. It was an isolated group whose doctrine had actually little to do with the Nestorian heresy, but retained the form of early Christianity without numerous superstitions added later. Layard called the Nestorians "the Protestants of the East." In earlier times its missionaries had spread their faith all across Asia as far as China, where the fabulous Prester John, King of Tartary, was a convert. By the nineteenth century, only a few mountain communities, persecuted by Moslems and fellow Christians alike, survived in Kurdistan. Some, the "Catholic Chaldeans," had been forcibly converted by Rome, and were none the better for it, as Layard discovered in one unhappy village. Racially he believed that the Chaldeans of both persuasions were the descendants—probably the sole descendants—of the ancient Assyrians. Today some live in Iran (and some in the United States) and call themselves Assyrians and members of the Church of the East.

In October he visited the Yezidis, a sect which combined certain Moslem doctrines with the belief that Satan was a fallen angel, and must be propitiated. These poor people were much misunderstood, and bitterly oppressed as Devil-worshipers. Layard thought he had never seen a more interesting sight than six thousand Yezidis gathered in a wild-wooded valley in the Kurdish foothills, "a family under every tree," for the annual festival at the shrine of their prophet, Sheikh Adi. Layard was allowed to witness all the curious and impressive ceremonies at night—everything but the worship of King Peacock, which was Satan. He wrote to Mrs. Austen that he was so impressed with the kindness, good humor, and quiet enjoyment of the Yezidis that he was half tempted to turn Devil-worshiper himself. A few weeks later he was unwilling witness to a bloody massacre by the Pasha's army of Yezidi communities in the Sinjar Hills.

Good news awaited him on his return to Mosul, the news for

which he had been hoping for a year. As a result of Sir Stratford Canning's representations to the Prime Minister, Sir Robert Peel, the British Museum, backed by Treasury funds, had agreed to finance Layard's excavations. The Trustees were eagerly expecting the first shipment of sculptures (supposed to be already on the way), which Sir Stratford had made over to them. At last, Layard felt, he would be able to excavate properly instead of in the unscientific fashion made necessary by the small sum he had raised on his own. It had only been intended to cover the cost of a few trial trenches; it had been stretched to the utmost, and it had more than fulfilled its purpose. Now the procedure would be different.

But as he read further, his spirits plunged as low as they had soared high. And he grew angry. The amount of the grant from the Treasury for the great things still to be done in Assyria was far less than the French Government had allowed Botta for his short-lived and unfinished work at Khorsabad! It would simply not be possible, on this miserable sum, to fulfill the expectations aroused by the first discoveries at Nimrud. The amount was intended to cover everything: all the costs of excavation, personal expenses, even the unusual outlays necessary in the East, such as bakhshish for diggers and silk cloaks for sheikhs. But Layard was both a stubborn and a conscientious man. He pulled in his belt and determined that somehow, even with those few pounds, he would make a fine collection of antiquities for England.

The first step was to organize the most efficient work crew for the smallest amount of cash. Layard's solution was to employ the Jeburs, a semi-nomad tribe which, driven by the Bedouin from its traditional pastures along the Khabur, now pitched tents near Nimrud. A Jebur encampment at the mound would act as a barrier to Bedouin raids, and by paying one man from each family as a worker, Layard would have the free services of all his male relatives as watchmen. The Jeburs and the Arabs from neighboring villages would carry off the rubbish, while fifty Chaldeans, some of whom had worked for Layard before, would do the heavy digging.

Layard himself was a very busy fellow. He had to carry on all the functions that, in a better financed expedition, would have been distributed among specialists. He spent an irritating amount of time dealing with the current Pasha and other Turkish authorities. In the course of one day, he had to speak the Turkish, Arabic, Kurdish and Chaldean dialects. He planned and supervised the day's work, often digging out a delicate find himself. He directed the moving and packing of sculptures. He copied and took paper molds of inscriptions. He was his own artist. He felt that he had neither the experience nor the skill for this, but it was the only way to make a record of nonmovable antiquities because the Trustees had not seen fit to provide the professional artist he had requested. His schedule would have broken a less energetic man, but Layard knew that if he tried to hire an expert for each job, the subsidy would be used up before the digging had half started.

On an ordinary day he rose at dawn, had a quick breakfast, and rode to the mound. As he approached he would see long lines of wild-looking creatures, with disheveled hair and shirt-tails flapping above bare brown legs, who hurried back and forth jumping and capering and screeching like madmen as they dumped baskets of dirt over the edge of the mound. In the excavations there was even more noise and confusion. Arabs were running through the narrow passages with baskets of earth and water jars; Nestorians, in their striped gowns and odd, peaked caps, were heaving away with picks and raising a cloud of dust at every stroke. In a corner somewhere a Kurdish musician would squat, piping strange minor wails which somehow encouraged his fellows, while the Jeburs, in quite a different key, chanted their war songs and swung their empty baskets as if they were swords.

Layard would remain at the diggings till dark, ride back to the village and work late into the night, planning the next day's operations, finishing up sketches, comparing copies of inscriptions with molds. His headquarters, shared with Hormuzd Rassam, was a mud-brick hut of two rooms and a courtyard which served as reception hall. The bricks had been made with straw from the threshing floor, and when the rains came before the roof was on, the walls of his room sprouted long white festoons of barley.

The Arab encampment at the mound grew more swollen daily as relatives arrived to share the bread of the fortunate. The Jeburs had taken to bringing their quarrels to Layard for settlement. It was a strange position for a foreigner and a Christian who knew little of Moslem law, but he hoped he was just in his verdicts, and he knew he was cheaper than the Cadi. When in doubt, he consulted Hormuzd Rassam. If a culprit had to be forcibly removed from the court room, Ibrahim Agha and a new member of the staff known as the Bairakdar (the standard bearer, his military rank) stood ready. Usually the judgments were promptly carried out. Since the chief cause of trouble was woman, Layard raised the price of a respectable female to twenty sheep, which acted as a check to the almost daily "Helen and Paris cases." A husband commonly showed disapproval of his wife's housekeeping by beating her with a tent pole—which practice Layard tried to discourage. "May God reward you!" cried the poor wives. "Have we not eaten wheaten bread, and even meat and butter, since we have been under your shadow? Is there one of us that has not now a coloured handkerchief for her head, bracelets, and ankle-rings, and a striped cloak? But what shall we do when you leave us, which God forbid you should ever do? Our husbands will then have their turn, and there will be nobody to save us."

The men were glad to be eating well but sometimes felt the work beneath their dignity. Once when he was riding back from the mound, Layard saw the Jeburs driving a flock of village sheep before them, drowning the shepherd's indignation with war cries. "It is not for a man to carry dirt about in baskets, and to use a spade all his life; he should be with his sword and his mare in the desert," they explained. "We are sad as we think of the days when we plundered the Anazeh, and we must have excitement, or our hearts would break. Let us believe that these are the sheep we have taken from the enemy, and that we are driving them to our tents."

The Nestorians lived, with their women and children, in a house which Layard had built for them on the top of the mound. Watching them kneel bareheaded on the Sabbath in the very shadow of the great bulls, he was deeply moved; the gods of the Babylonians had long since disappeared, but the God of Moses, whose temple the king of Babylon overthrew, was still worshiped the world over.

Full-scale excavation was begun on the first of November. Work was carried on in the Northwest Palace, the Southwest Palace, in the center of the mound, in the southeast, and other spots not previously examined. For economy's sake, trenches were carried along the walls, leaving the central core untouched. Small finds were bound to be missed through this method, but Layard had no choice. You did not sift the soil when your objectives were bas-reliefs and bulls. Acting on instructions, he filled up each chamber, after he had examined and sketched it, with earth from the next one in order to bury the buildings before he left them. If he found no movable art treasures, he felt bound, against his own inclinations, to abandon that part of the mound. In spite of these meas-ures, the six weeks that followed the Museum grant were the most fruitful in Layard's archaeological career; hardly a day went by without an important discovery. Before Christmas, eight chambers in the Northwest Palace were explored, all of them lined with fine bas-reliefs. In the Southwest Palace, one whole room was paneled with slabs brought from the Northwest Palace, placed with their sculptured faces against the brick walls and with their backs smoothed preparatory to being recarved with the records of another king, who, so far, had only inscribed his name upon them.

In the center of the mound, where up to now not even a single wall had been found, there came to light one of the greatest treas-ures of the British Museum today—a black marble obelisk, flat on top and about seven feet high. It was carved with twenty small reliefs of vanquished kings bringing tribute: elephants, dromedar-ies, monkeys, a rhinoceros—exotic gifts from far places, perhaps as far away as India. Long inscriptions encircled top and base. Layard quickly copied these, sketched the reliefs, and had the obelisk care-fully packed for shipping. On Christmas Day, 1846, a raft bearing twenty-three cases, in one of which was the obelisk, went floating down the river to Baghdad. Layard watched with pride and joy till his art treasures were out of sight, "and then galloped into

Mosul to celebrate the festivities of the season with the few Europeans whom duty or business had collected in this remote corner of the globe."

In the next three months, he opened twenty-eight rooms in the Northwest Palace, a few of which were not sculptured but plastered and painted. In a small inner suite he found a hoard of ivory plaques, and spent hours on his knees extracting them from the earth with a penknife. Behind the broken bulls, near the center of the mound, there was a storehouse of slabs neatly stacked in rows, ready to be reused. It was clear to him that the buildings at Nimrud had been constructed at different periods by different personages. He could not read the names in the inscriptions, but he could figure out their relationship to each other from the repeated cuneiform signs for "son" and "king," which by now Rawlinson and others had deciphered. Certain symbols, representing royal names, were combined with these to make up genealogies (similar to those on the Persian monuments) at the beginning of inscriptions on bas-reliefs, bulls, and pavement slabs. Some of the genealogies went back six generations, and overlapping genealogies gave an even longer list of king-names. Studying them, Layard realized that the king represented on the Black Obelisk was the son of the builder of the Northwest Palace. To give the reader the benefit of modern scholarship, the Northwest Palace was built by Ashurnasirpal II (883–859 B.C.); the Black Obelisk king was his son, Shalmaneser III (858–824 B.C.). Esarhaddon, who came along almost two hundred years later, robbed the two earlier structures for his own pretentious but unfinished palace in the southwest corner of the mound.

Layard, whose thoughts turned so often to Scripture as he dug up the remains of the ancient Assyrians, did not find out till later that he had discovered the first demonstrable link between the two: the Black Obelisk, which records, among other tribute, a gift of gold and silver, a golden bowl, a golden vase with a pointed bottom, golden tumblers, golden buckets, tin, a scepter, and some unidentified objects of wood, from Jehu, King of Israel—who is pictured in one of the bas-reliefs, a pathetic little figure kneeling before the Assyrian tyrant.[1]

GENERAL PLAN
of
NIMRUD

VAULTED CHAMBER

DEEP TRENCH

DEEP TRENCH

TOMBS

SOUTH EAST EDIFICE

PALACE OF TIGLATH-PILESER III

PALACE OF SHALMANESER III

PALACE OF ESARHADDON

SOUTH WEST PALACE

UPPER CHAMBERS

PALACES OF ASHURNASIRPAL II AND SARGON II

NORTH WEST PALACE

SMALL TEMPLES

THE HIGH PYRAMIDAL MOUND

SCALE OF YARDS

From Layard, Nineveh and Its Remains

General View of Nineveh

Chapter XVIII

MOVING DAY
(February–June 1847)

Both the firman and the Museum grant specified excavations at Nimrud "and other sites." One of the sites Layard wished to explore was Kala Sherghat, the huge mound on the banks of the Tigris to the south, which he had glimpsed on the first expedition to Hatra. The place was a notorious rendezvous for Bedouin plundering parties; nevertheless, the rumor that a carved black stone had appeared at Kala Sherghat was too tempting to resist. Layard arranged for a desert sheikh to sponsor him and to supply such extra workers as might be needed, sent his foreman Mansur ahead, and followed a few days later with Hormuzd Rassam, the Bairak-dar, and a few well-armed Jeburs. By the time he arrived, Mansur had already found the mysterious stone: a life-sized figure in basalt, headless and handless, and, unlike other sculpture so far discovered, carved in the round. It was seated on a block inscribed with a recognizable genealogy. (Ross, on Layard's orders, later shipped this statue of Shalmaneser III to London.) The mound itself bore some similarities to Nimrud: the tall cone rising above it (the ziggurat) and the low ramparts enclosing the land around it. Layard judged it to be a very old city, perhaps Calah, or Ur, the city of Abraham. Neither he nor his workmen had the skill to trace the brick walls of Ashur, earliest capital of Assyria. There were no signs of slabs or any sculpture other than the black statue. Mansur reported that the Bedu were stealing everything in sight; if he and his workers were not killed first, they would soon starve to death. In light of this and the few finds, Layard remained only two days and removed the workmen shortly thereafter.

So far thirteen pairs of giant human-headed bulls and lions had been dug up at Nimrud. The Museum Trustees had directed Layard to cover them before leaving, for it did not seem possible to move anything so heavy without mutilating it. Botta had sawed his sculptures from Khorsabad into eight pieces; even so one "French bull" had bogged down and was still where it had been abandoned, halfway between the ruins and the river. But Layard refused to give up, without a try, the idea of shipping a bull to England. If it was to be attempted at all, it would have to be done by March, before the Shammar and others of the Desert Brethren took to riding on *ghazou*. Since the October rains, which had sprouted the barley on Layard's walls, not a drop had fallen; no seeds had sprouted at all in the fields, and famine was in the offing. The nomad tribes, unable to obtain grain from the village Arabs by barter, would seize it by force, and with the arrival of spring no one would be safe outside the walls of Mosul.

Layard had given the mechanics of removal a great deal of thought. His workmen, the Pasha, and everyone whom he knew, had made suggestions on how to get the blocks down from the mound and all the way to the river; each step in the process was a problem, because the most simple and essential materials were not to be had. One look at the ropes ordered from Aleppo was enough to know that they would never support the weight of a solid piece of marble ten feet square. Layard ordered additional cables, made of twisted palm fiber, from Baghdad, and, reluctantly, sawed away part of the backs of the sculptures. A carpenter was sent to the mountains to hunt for hardwood trees to be made into planks, levers, and cart wheels a foot thick. The iron axles from the cart Botta had used were surreptitiously bought from the dragoman of the French Consulate. While the cart was being constructed in the courtyard of Christian Rassam's house, it was the wonder of all Mosul, and when it was finished, the whole population closed up shop and turned out to see if the heavy vehicle would get across the frail bridge of boats. Layard had selected one of the smallest human-headed bulls and a lion of similar size, both in excellent condition. A trench, or road, was cut from the base of the sculptures to the foot of the mound, where the cart waited. All was ready on March 18. Volunteers from neighboring villages plus a large number of the Abou Salman joined the regular labor force for the event. Sheikh Abd-ur-rahman and the women had come to cheer on their men. The first specimen, which was the bull, had been wrapped in protective covering, and the earth had been dug out from under it, leaving it supported on wooden beams, securely wedged. It was to be tipped over and lowered on ropes to greased rollers in the cutting twenty feet below, its progress checked by wooden props held by the strongest of the mountain men. Layard, standing on a heap of earth above, shouted for the wedges to be struck. The bull did not move. "A rope having been passed round it, six or seven men easily tilted it over. The thick, ill-made cable stretched with the strain, and almost buried itself in the earth round which it was coiled. The ropes held well. The mass descended gradually, the Chaldeans propping it up firmly with the beams. It was a moment of great anxiety. The drums, and shrill pipes of the Kurdish musicians, increased the din and confusion caused by the war-cry of the Arabs, who were half frantic with excitement. They had thrown off nearly all their garments; their long hair floated in the wind; and they indulged in the wildest postures and gesticulations as they clung to the ropes. The women had congregated on the sides of the trenches, and by their incessant screams, and by the ear-piercing tahlehl, added to the enthusiasm of the men. It was no longer possible to obtain a hearing. The loudest cries I could produce were buried in a heap of discordant sounds. Neither the hippopotamus hide whips of the Cawasses, nor the bricks and clods of earth with which I endeavored to draw attention, were of any avail. Away went the bull, steady as long as supported by the props behind, but as it came nearer to the rollers, the beams could no longer be used. The cables and ropes stretched more and more. Dry from the climate, they creaked and threw out dust. Water was thrown over them, but in vain, for they all broke together when the sculpture was within four or five feet of the rollers. The bull was precipitated to the ground. Those who held the ropes, thus suddenly released, were rolling one over the other in the dust. A sudden silence succeeded to the clamour. I rushed into the trenches, prepared to find the bull in many pieces. It would be difficult to describe my satisfaction when I saw it lying precisely where I had wished to place it, and uninjured!"

What a triumph! The Arabs scrambled to their feet, seized the hands of the watching women, and yelling louder than ever, began a wild dance. Abd-ur-rahman flung aside his cloak to lead them off in the *debkë*, the most violent of Arab dances. Layard, after so much anxiety, horror, and relief in rapid succession, kept his English dignity and did not dance on this occasion, but he did not try to stop the workers because he knew it would be no use till they had danced themselves out. At such a pace, this did not take too long. The bull was then moved on sleepers and rollers to the edge of the mound. As the sun was going down, Layard called an end to the great day's work. The workers put on their clothes, and, chanting war-songs, flourishing swords, and throwing lances into the air, marched to the village. Layard rode back with Abd-ur-rahman and an honor guard of tribal horsemen.

"Wonderful! Wonderful! There is surely no God but God, and Mohammed is his prophet," the sheikh reflected. "In the name of the Most High, tell me, O Bey, what you are going to do with those stones. So many thousands of purses spent upon such things! Can it be, as you say, that your people learn wisdom from them? These figures will not teach you to make better knives, or scissors, or chintzes; and it is in the making of these things that the English show their wisdom. But God is great! God is great! Here are stones which have been buried ever since the time of the holy Noah— peace be with him! Perhaps they were under ground before the deluge. I have lived in these lands for years. My father, and the father of my father pitched their tents here before me; but they never heard of these figures. But lo! here comes a Frank from many days' journey off, and he walks up to the very place, and he takes a stick, and makes a line here, and makes a line there. Here, says he, is the palace; there, says he, is the gate; and he shows us what has been all our lives beneath our feet, without our knowing anything about it. Wonderful! Wonderful! Is it by books, is it by magic, is it by your prophets, that you have learned these things? Speak, O Bey; tell me the secret of wisdom."

Layard gave Abd-ur-rahman a short lecture on the advantages of civilization, since the more he could impress the Arabs with the wisdom and power of the Franks, the safer his property would be. To himself he was thinking, meanwhile, that the modern West owed the foundations of its knowledge to the ancient East. Giving it back again to the present inhabitants was but the repayment of a debt.

That night Abd-ur-rahman and his brother plied Western knives and forks in Layard's house—a great honor, else they would have far preferred to be outside with the workers, dipping hands into immense platters of boiled sheep. The feasting, dancing and singing continued till dawn. When Layard suggested that, in the light of the past day's exertions, and the work which still lay ahead, sleep might be advisable, he was assured that his men could dance all night and move a stone bull too. Besides, how else could a guest show his appreciation of a feast? At sunrise everyone and his wife set out for the mound, still capering and chanting. The buffalo team, in less good humor, balked completely at the weight of the load, and had to be removed. Three hundred men, "all screaming at the top of their lungs," attached themselves to the cart; the women ran beside them, screaming too. There was more trouble to come: two wheels of the cart sank into an abandoned storage pit, so that when the sun went down on the second day, the Nimrud bull, like its French competitor, was stuck fast. Men were left to watch it, while the rest retired to the village. In the morning the watchmen reported a scrimmage with a Bedouin party which had a craving for the mats and quilts in which the bull was wrapped. The scar of a bullet is plainly to be seen on the hide of the stone bull as it stands today in the British Museum.

The cart was dragged out of the pit on the following morning; it stuck again in soft sand a few hundred yards from the river. Finally, after the greatest effort and all sorts of tricks, the bull colossus reached the platform prepared for it on the riverbank. A few days later the lion was brought down with similar effort, and similar celebration. The next problem was how to get the great blocks of stone to the seaport of Basrah, for the riverboats which ordinarily took sculptures on from Baghdad would be swamped by these two. The only way to send them would be by raft, a feat declared impossible by all who should know. Layard persuaded a raftsman who was threatened with debtor's prison and whose sole assets were skins, that he had nothing to lose by undertaking a dangerous but well-paid job. By April 22, the river was high enough to float two loaded-down super-keleks of six hundred skins each. Layard presented two sheep to be sacrificed before the sailing, and a third to be immolated at the tomb of a certain Moslem saint who would interfere with navigation unless propitiated. The raftsman kissed Layard's hand, hawsers were cast off, and the bull and the lion floated away toward the Persian Gulf. There a British ship would take them aboard, together with seventy bas-reliefs, a large number of inscriptions, and almost 250 drawings—the fruits of the last months of excavation.

By mid-May it was summer again; the drought and famine had brought on the expected epidemic of robberies, and it was impossible to keep the workmen together in a place so exposed to desert raids as Nimrud. After a brief, unsuccessful stab at the ziggurat, which he now thought the tomb of a king, Layard ordered the men to bring back all the earth and rubble that they had so painfully taken out, throw it into the excavated chambers and over the sculptures, and thus bury the palaces once more. Then he set out for Mosul.

Halfway to the city there was a hill with a view in both directions: on the one side toward the high cone of Nimrud; on the other toward the river lazily winding through the dry yellow plain toward the dark patch in the distance that was Mosul, and the barren mounds across from it on the eastern riverbank. Layard reined in his horse and tried to picture how this desolate, empty stretch of land had looked when it had been filled from Nimrud to Mosul with houses and gardens. The mud-brick homes of the commoners had long since melted away, as Arab houses still did when neglected. The bright-flowered gardens had vanished too; only the palaces, lined with stone and raised up on solid brick platforms, had resisted flood, fire and the devastation of war, to persist in the form of mounds.

During the first months of excavating, the richness of the finds had led him to believe (as Botta had believed of Khorsabad, for the same reason) that Nimrud was Nineveh. How could such enormous and lavishly decorated buildings have existed unless this was the royal city, or at least a part of it? The question plagued him constantly. By now he had come to the conclusion that each mound represented a different quarter and had been built at a different period, yet all were part of the same metropolis—just as there were different sections of London. How else could one explain the statement in the Book of Jonah, "An exceeding great city of three days' journey"? In the East, a day's journey was no figure of speech, but a linear measure—as far as the average caravan could travel between sunup and sundown, or approximately twenty miles. The sixty miles that could be covered in three days was exactly the outside measurement of a rectangle drawn with the mounds of Nimrud, Kuyunjik, Khorsabad, and Karamles at its four corners. The space occupied by Kuyunjik, Nebbi Yunus and their attendant ramparts was just not big enough; it was no more than eight miles around, and could scarcely have supported a population of the size described by the Lord to Jonah: "More than sixscore thousand persons that cannot discern between their right hand and their left hand; and also much cattle."

Such was Layard's thinking, but he could not be certain that it was correct. He had spent a little more than three thousand pounds of the Museum grant; with the small sum that remained, he would make a third attack on the Mosul mounds. These presented problems from which Nimrud had been fortunately free. Nebbi Yunus was sacrosanct because of Jonah's tomb; neither Rich nor Botta had been permitted to explore it. Kuyunjik had been mined for building material for years; investigated for months by Botta, and more recently by Rouet and by his own workmen. Layard believed that all this digging and delving had merely scratched the surface

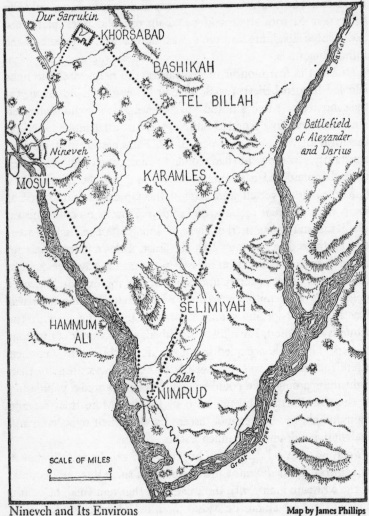

Ninevch and Its Environs   **Map by James Phillips**

of the mound; the prizes must lie deeper. By now he knew enough
of the principles of Assyrian architecture to go about the search
systematically.

He ordered his pickmen first of all to probe for a brick platform.
They struck it at twenty feet below the surface. He then sank

trenches at right angles to each other. But Kuyunjik appeared to be a solid mountain of rubble, as if anything which had existed there had been ground up in a giant meat grinder, or smashed to bits by a giant hammer. He was still at home one morning when two Arab women arrived at his door, dripping, to claim the bakhshish due to whoever was the first to announce an important new discovery. They had swum across the Tigris on their inflated sheepskins to tell Layard that sculptures had been found at Kuyunjik! A few moments later Toma Shishman—Toma the Fat, the foreman at the mound—panted in, having run across the bridge with the same good news.

The workmen had dug out a portal and part of a wall-relief, so badly damaged that one could scarcely make out the figures upon it. Like the Southwest Palace at Nimrud, this building had been destroyed by fire. It had been set aflame when the armies of the Medes and Babylonians burst open the gates of Nineveh to take their revenge on the cruel city. Again Layard had found a palace where others had found nothing, where there had been legend but no proof.

He ordered his men to dig along the line of the wall; a chamber opened up, and another and another. In a month nine chambers were gouged out, some so charred that a white dust was the only remaining trace of the alabaster slabs. A few reliefs were sufficiently undamaged to sketch, though not to remove and ship. The first room of the series led through a narrow entrance formed by the biggest bulls discovered yet, almost seventeen feet square, into a great hall, narrow and long like that at Nimrud. On first glance, Layard thought the sculptures technically not as good as those in the Northwest Palace. The subject matter was similar: a glorification of the king and his deeds.

Four pairs of bulls were found, with tall, elaborate headdresses of the same type as those in the Southwest Palace, and like them, with four legs instead of five. The style of the sculptures also resembled those at Khorsabad more than the bas-reliefs in the Northwest Palace. It would therefore appear that Khorsabad, the Southwest Palace, and this palace were more or less of the same period, while the Northwest Palace was older. The inscriptions here were few, and in the form of short epigraphs, explanations, or titles, above the bas-reliefs. There were longer inscriptions, however, which began and ended with the name of a king, between the legs of the bulls. These were so badly worn and broken that Layard could hardly copy more than a few characters from each bull, but since they were all identical, he hoped to get a fair copy by piecing the good bits together. Who was this Kuyunjik king? There were a few hints here and there. Layard had seen the group of characters which represented his name in the genealogies at Nimrud. He was the son of the king who had built the palace at Khorsabad, and the father of the builder of the Southwest Palace, which was the most recent of the Nimrud palaces. So much for placing his period, but what was his name? Had he been one of the Assyrian kings mentioned in the Old Testament? There was one interesting piece of evidence: a slab depicting the fall of a city on a rocky seacoast reminiscent of Syria or Asia Minor. The refugees were fleeing the city in ships which resembled the Phoenician galleys one saw on old coins. Perhaps the Kuyunjik king was Shalmaneser, who, according to Josephus, had besieged and taken Tyre. On the other hand Sennacherib, later in history, had defeated the Greeks (who also used galleys) off the Silician coast. Layard's own opinion was that the builder of the Kuyunjik palace was the great and ruthless Sennacherib—though so far he had no real proof of it.

And he had neither time nor money left in which to find out. The Museum grant was almost used up; his work in Assyria would have to end. The great works of art which he had discovered were at Basrah, ready for shipment to England. The inscriptions, from which he hoped the history of Assyria would one day be learned, had been faithfully copied. In two years of unrelenting effort he had dug up eight palaces, at least four of them associated with kings mentioned in the Old Testament: Shalmaneser, Tiglath-Pileser (the Biblical Pul), Sennacherib, and Esarhaddon. Entirely on his own initiative, he had discovered something new under the sun—or rather something old and long lost. He was proud to consider his excavations "convincing evidence of that magnificence, and power which made Nineveh the wonder of the ancient world, and her fall the theme of the prophets . . . without them we might have doubted that the great Nineveh ever existed, so completely had she become 'a desolation and a waste.'"

With the small amount remaining from the Museum grant, Toma Shishman, under Ross's direction, would carry on minor excavation at Kuyunjik, mostly in order to make sure that the French did not take over. Layard gave a last feast for all who had helped him. He spoke of his satisfaction with his workers and asked any who had been wronged to come forward and say so, in order that the wrong might be set right if possible. A sheikh of the Jebur answered for the rest: "We have lived under your shadow, O Bey, and, God be praised, no one had cause to complain. Now that you are leaving, we shall leave also, and seek the distant banks of the Khabur. All we desire is each man a note, to certify that he has been in your service. This will be not only protection to him, but he will show it to his children, and tell them of the days passed at Nimrud. Please God, you may return to the Jebur, and live in tents with them on their old pasture lands, where there are as many ruins as at Nimrud."

On June 24, 1847, Layard and Hormuzd Rassam left Mosul for Constantinople. H. J. Ross, Christian Rassam and his wife, and other friends rode with them to the outskirts of the town. At the foot of the bridge stood the Mosul ladies who had come to tell him a sad good-by, and behind them the wives and daughters of the workmen, who ran to kiss his hand, cling to his horse, and weep at his going. He bade them all farewell, and started on the first lap of the long journey home—wiser perhaps, but no richer than when he had left England eight years before. Nor was the question of his future career any more settled. There was much still to be done in the Land between the Rivers, and much more to be learned, but whether he himself would have any part in it, Layard did not know.

Chapter XIX

INTERLUDE

(June 1847–October 1849)

On arriving at Constantinople late in July, Layard learned that an attachéship was his at last; Lord Palmerston, the current Foreign Minister, had immediately granted Sir Stratford's request for his appointment. Now, of course, Layard no longer wanted it, being anxious only to get home to show his drawings and copies of inscriptions to the Museum Trustees, and to tell the story of his discoveries. He wrote to Sir Stratford in London, asking for a leave of absence; there was no answer, which left him in as uncomfortable and undecided a state as before he had gone to Assyria. After he had suffered a severe malarial attack, an Embassy doctor solved the problem by ordering him to leave the climate of the East at once.

He stopped off in Italy to "crawl," in spite of a fever, to Pompeii and Cumae, to show his drawings to archaeologists in Rome, and renew old friendships in Florence. In Paris, he looked up Botta, who, declaring with characteristic generosity that the discoveries at Nimrud and Kuyunjik were far more important than his own, rushed off to announce Layard's arrival to the *Académie d'Inscriptions et Belles Lettres*. As a result Layard was invited to lecture before the Academicians. He wrote to Mrs. Austen that he spoke for one hour in French with a fluency which he put down to a high fever "with consequent audacity and excitement of the brain. From all sides poured questions and compliments . . . M. Lagard, in ecstacies, convinced me by frequent, as I thought at the time very unnecessary, digs in the ribs, that I had established fully to his satisfaction theories which, in spite of the sneers of the learned, he had been building up for nearly half a century. Had I not remembered that I was on the banks of the Seine, I might have left the *Académie* very well satisfied with myself, and fully convinced that I had bestowed on some fifty most intelligent Frenchmen the happiest day of their lives! In fact, if the results of the Nimrud excavations create half so favorable an impression in London as they have done in Paris, I may hope that something may be done towards publishing them."

Botta was just completing the text for the beautiful five-volume collection of Flandin's drawings from Khorsabad, entitled *Monument de Ninive*, which had been commissioned by the French Government. Burnouf, the eminent scholar of cuneiform, urged Layard to publish his own drawings and copies of inscriptions as soon as possible and suggested that he use the typefaces made for Botta's work. Layard could make no promises till he found out whether his own Trustees would back him; it was, however, good to know that international rivalry was not as bitter on the academic level as it was in the field.

Botta's finds from Khorsabad had arrived in France in 1846 and were installed in a *Salle de Ninive*, where Layard went to see them. Except for a few specimens, he was not much impressed, but he admired the skill with which the segmented bulls had been put together again. He dined with Botta and his friends, discussed politics, and learned of the general discontent in France and the King's unpopularity. In December 1847, all Europe was on the verge of revolution; two months later Louis Phillipe had lost his throne. The Second Republic sent Botta to a minor consular post in Tripoli, where he seems to have had no opportunity for archaeological explorations. He died in France in 1870.

Layard reached London on December 22, 1847, no longer the unknown young man who had left it, but not very famous yet either. It must have pleased him, who had been denied a university education, to receive the honorary degree of D.C.L. from Oxford in July 1848. Privately a good deal of fuss was made over him, but government recognition was singularly absent. The barricades

were up across the Channel; no one knew what would happen
next, but a financial panic was expected. The Treasury greeted
with silence the British Museum's request for four thousand pounds
to publish Layard's discoveries.

Ross kept Layard informed by mail of affairs at Mosul. Even
while he was on his way home, more slabs, mostly smashed, had
been dug up at Kuyunjik. The whole mound seemed to have been
covered with alabaster buildings, many of them destroyed wantonly, when not burned. In December Ross went to Bavian, north
of Mosul, to look at rock carvings that had been discovered by
Monsieur Rouet. Ross thought the caves in the cliffside similar
to the tombs of Darius and other Achaemenian kings at Naqsh-i-
Rustam, near Persepolis. He was not sufficiently familiar with the
cuneiform symbols to be able to copy the inscriptions as he was
sure Layard could have done. The French Consulate had denounced some of the Jebur workmen as thieves, for the purpose of
sabotaging the work at Kuyunjik, Ross thought. In January, results
were better, but the excavations would soon have to be called off
for lack of funds. A few weeks later Ross reported that fine inscriptions and bas-reliefs were coming up in the southwest corner of
Kuyunjik but he could afford to employ so few workmen that the
work went slowly. It was clear that palaces had stood in all four
quarters of the mound. "I am at the last gasp for funds," he wrote
at the end of January. "However I shall not stop with such good
indications before me. If I did, Guillois [the current French
Consul] would certainly carry my unfinished trench on, and if it
did lead to anything, it would be vexatious. Therefore I shall if
necessary advance 500 piastres upon the chance of its being
allowed."

Layard wrote back from Canford Manor, the country home of his
rediscovered first cousin, Lady Charlotte Guest, née Lady Charlotte Bertie, daughter of the 9th Earl of Lindsey. Her husband,
Sir John Guest, was a wealthy ironmaster, one of the new aristocracy; Lady Charlotte was one of the old, and an accomplished
scholar of Welsh literature. She had welcomed Layard warmly on
his return to England, and called him "the Ninevite." He now

frequently stayed with Sir John and Lady Guest, but neither in this letter to Ross nor in others from Canford, does he mention the small daughter of the house whom he was to marry more than two decades later.

Layard wrote that the Museum Trustees wished the excavations to continue but could not allow more than ten pounds (fifty dollars) per month for the present. Ross's letters began to mention the probability of his leaving Mosul. Layard directed him that, in this case, he should place the excavations under the direction of Christian Rassam, the British Vice-consul, who was to employ a few men, rather to keep possession of the site and prevent interference from others (the French) than to carry on extensive operations. A financial crisis in England and events on the Continent had driven all interest in Nineveh out of people's heads, Layard wrote. The Treasury had rejected the British Museum's request for the expenses of his publication. He would have to see what could be done by subscription or out of his own pocket. But he did not expect to remain in England long enough to be able to accomplish much.

Ross, who had closed the excavations for lack of funds, now acted on Layard's instructions by reopening them with Fat Toma and six men. In May he wrote: "I have just come from Kuyunjik, where the excavations are regular catacombs . . . There are chariots and palm trees by dozens, one or two castles assaulted by the king in the act of drawing his bow, scaling ladders, men and headless corpses falling to the ground. In fact, just like the Nimrud ones, but completely charred . . . I have been to Nimrud; the slabs you buried and which have begun to appear, I directed to be well covered again. Some of those you left exposed have been wantonly injured . . . I did not like to take it upon myself to have the whole covered up as the expense would be considerable. If you wish it done write to Rassam, as I shall have left Mosul before this reaches you."

Fortunately a private publisher, John Murray, had the foresight to back *Monuments of Nineveh*, a beautiful folio of one hundred engravings "by the best artists," from Layard's sketches. His friends

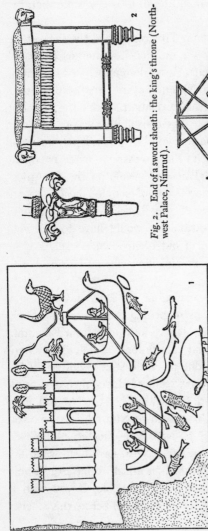

Fig. 2. End of a sword sheath: the king's throne (North-west Palace, Nimrud).

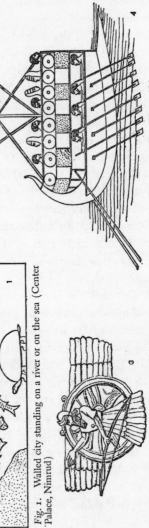

Fig. 1. Walled city standing on a river or on the sea (Center Palace, Nimrud)

Fig. 3. Emblem of the Deity (Northwest Palace, Nimrud).

Fig. 4. A galley (Kuyunjik).

From Layard, Nineveh and Its Remains

urged him to write the story of his discoveries, so, in spite of fever bouts, a busy social life, and his sense of so little time, he delivered to Murray at the end of 1848 the two volumes of *Nineveh and Its Remains*. After telling of his excavations and travels among the tribes, he discussed in Volume II the history of the Assyrians as it was so far known, citing the evidence of the sculptures and genealogies against a background of Bible and pseudohistory drawn from classical sources. His king lists still included Ninus, legendary founder of Nineveh, the fabulous Queen Semiramis; and Sardanapalus, the last king of Nineveh, said to have immolated himself in his burning palace as the city fell. Byron's tragedy, *Sardanapalus*,[1] written almost thirty years earlier, had focused the interest of English scholars and literati upon this lurid character; throughout their writings Layard and Rawlinson constantly either stated or speculated on which historical Assyrian king he could be. Layard also related with gusto the legends of Semiramis, said by some to have changed into a dove and a goddess, while according to Pliny she burned herself up because of the death of a favorite horse—"although Mr. Birch suggests that the correct reading of the Latin might be *regno* instead of *equo*."

Comparing, in a more serious vein, methods used to obtain king names and dates, Layard pointed out that the information was very incomplete, since only three sites (Khorsabad, Kuyunjik, Nimrud) had been explored, and those superficially. More accurate data would be available when the inscriptions were deciphered— which was no longer so remote a possibility. Even without this a great deal had been learned of the architecture, arts, household equipment, dress, and methods of warfare of the ancient Assyrians. "The records are now before us," Layard concluded. "From them we may hope to fill up a part of the great blank in the history of the world."

The deciphering of Babylonian-Assyrian cuneiform was well on the way since Rawlinson's final, successful attack on Behistun in 1847. With the help of slings, ladders, and a Kurdish boy who could climb like a monkey, he had obtained a papier-mâché mold (a "squeeze," nowadays done with rubber latex) of the great Babylonian inscription. Several scholars, including Rawlinson himself, were busily engaged in trying to decipher it. This was infinitely more difficult than Persian cuneiform. The characters were not alphabetical letters, but forty thousand or so symbols for an unknown language. The language eventually proved to be a dialect of the great Semitic group, related to Hebrew and Syriac, the very languages which Layard, with his remarkable intuition, had studied before embarking upon his excavations—and before anything had been learned of Assyrian cuneiform. Now, however, he would leave the actual decoding of cuneiform to others with more time and erudition at their disposal. His reasoning on the Kuyunjik king proved to be correct. In June 1849, after *Nineveh and Its Remains* had been out for several months, Dr. Edward Hincks, using Rawlinson's method, read the name of Sennacherib at the beginning and end of the bull inscriptions and almost all the other texts Layard had copied at Kuyunjik.

Layard was an impatient man, but he had more than enough justification for it at this time. The sculptures that, after so much planning and effort, he had watched float off down the Tigris almost two years previously, arrived in October 1848, having narrowly escaped sinking to the bottom of the Indian Ocean in a storm. Two things they had not escaped: innumerable delays, and the prying of the British community of Bombay. While on the wharf awaiting transshipment to England, the cases had been opened, enthusiastically pawed over, and carelessly repacked. A parson who wished to lecture on the Black Obelisk had taken a squeeze of it. The larger sculptures were in fair shape, but when Layard, with what happy anticipation can be imagined, opened the boxes of small finds in the company of the Keeper of the British Museum, all was shocking confusion and damage. Fragments of inscription, which he and Ross had painfully managed to match up, had been separated, often into two different boxes. The order in which the ivories, copper ornaments, vases and other objects had been placed, with the information on where they had been found, was irrevocably lost. Certain Bombay Britishers had helped themselves to odds and ends which they fancied. Layard raised a scandal about it. This had at least one good result: cases destined for the British Museum thereafter received special handling along the way.

After eighteen months in the bracing air of England, Layard was feeling fit again, and weary of acting the minor lion at tea-parties. Mr. and Mrs. Benjamin Austen and Henry Crabbe Robinson did not know what to make of all the fuss over a young man whom they had regarded, if not as a black sheep, at least as an improvident and reckless boy. He did not wait for the publication of *Nineveh and Its Remains*, but in December returned to the Embassy at Constantinople, having received, once more, an unpaid appointment. He did not know until some time after he reached there that his book was a success.

The London *Times* of February 9, 1849, published a one-column, full-page review, which reads in part: "This is, we think, the most extraordinary work of the present age, whether with reference to the wonderful discoveries it describes, its remarkable verification of our early biblical history, or of the talent, courage and perseverance of its author . . . We question whether a more enlightened or a more enterprising traveler than Mr. Layard is to be met with in the annals of our modern history . . . His strong mind, rapidly developed—the indomitable will—the desire to acquire knowledge, and to use it profitably and for the benefit of his fellow creatures, carried him into lands and through a series of extraordinary adventures, an account of which we trust he will some day give to the world. Certainly no man has had greater experience of life, had more difficulties to contend with, or a nobler aim." After relating a bit about Layard's background, travels, and discoveries, the review went on, "We wish it was in our power to add that the Government has adequately rewarded the man who has thus sacrificed his health, and, with unwearied energy and courage, devoted his high talents to our service, enriching our national museum with such splendid remains of patriarchal times. But we are sorry to be obliged to inform our readers that Mr. Layard has had no reward, and, if we are not misinformed, he has gone back to the Embassy an honorary *attaché* without any remuneration what-

ever, and before his health was re-established." After quoting the
passage which describes the discovery of "Nimrod himself," the
review concludes, "This noble sculpture, with another equally interesting, is now lying, we regret to say, in the mud at Busrah, waiting for a conveyance to this country."

Without planning to do so, Layard had invented a new *genre:*
the book of travel plus archaeology plus adventure, which is still
popular with armchair explorers. And in spite of some passages of
multisyllabic Victorian English which today's reader may consider
purple prose, it is a most entertaining book. Of course, like Botta's
Monuments de Ninive (which concerned Khorsabad), *Nineveh
and Its Remains* had little to do with Nineveh, being actually, till
almost the last pages, about the exploration of Nimrud. The final
identification of Nineveh was still to come. Meanwhile many people were so pleased to be able to point out to skeptics and atheists
this proof that Bible was more than myth, that in the first year
they bought over eight thousand copies—which may not seem
much to us, but in those days placed it, as Layard wrote jokingly
to Mitford, "side by side with Mrs. Rundell's Cookery"—in other
words, on the best-seller list. For several years, Layard's half-share
in the profits of *Nineveh and Its Remains* was to bring him an
annual income of £1500.

Immediately the Austens did a right about-face. Sara Austen,
who knew John Murray, offered to help with corrections of her
nephew's book for future printings. She sent a copy of it to Wordsworth, the aging poet laureate, and received a flatteringly appreciative reply. Benjamin Austen was now lavish with offers to lend his
nephew money, and, after Layard had returned to Nineveh, wrote
him this typically practical advice: "I hope at all events you will
secure on your own account sufficient portable Treasures, for in
excavating such magnificent Ruins, surely there must be a great
deal which must be valuable and precious to an antiquarian and
you are the discoverer." Whether Layard remained fond of his uncle in spite of everything, or whether he was being subtly ironical,
Nineveh and Its Remains was "Affectionately Dedicated" to Benjamin Austen, Esq.

At Constantinople he was slated to serve on a commission which would lay down the frontier between Turkey and Persia as a result of the arbitrations—a position for which his past experience eminently qualified him. He suggested to the Trustees of the British Museum that in the interstices of this work he could continue the excavations in the Mosul neighborhood. He was directed to do so, and in April 1849 was promoted to a paid attachéship by Lord Palmerston. Shortly thereafter he discovered that he was expected to fill a very minor post on the Border Commission while a man whom he considered less qualified received the position which he had expected. This affronted his always touchy pride. It would also have left him no time for directing the excavations. He resigned the diplomatic post, and forwarded to the Trustees an ambitious master plan for obtaining information on the arts, history, and language of Assyria and Babylonia, basing his outline on the survey made by Lepsius in Egypt some ten years earlier. He proposed to share his finds with the Turkish Government, which was interested in setting up a national museum in Constantinople. This new concept—that a country had the right to keep its own treasures of ancient art—was to culminate in Mesopotamia in the Baghdad Museum established by Gertrude Bell in 1923.

Layard estimated that two and a half years would be sufficient for the project he suggested, the expenses of which could be covered by three annual grants of four or five thousand pounds. The Treasury, in reply, granted a total of three thousand pounds, which was to be stretched over two years; the initial payment, fifteen hundred pounds, was to last till May 1850. Shocked and disappointed, Layard wondered if it was worth his while to start at all. He thought it over for some time before writing, August 20, 1849, to Sir Henry Ellis, who represented the British Museum: "I will not fail to meet the wishes of the Trustees as far as it lies in my power, both with regard to any collection of Antiquities that I may be able to make and to archaeological and other information which they desire me to transmit to them. I must however observe that the journey from Constantinople to Mosul is a long and expensive one, and that proper provision must be made for the members of the expedition during their residence in Assyria." There was also the cost of supplies, the wages of the workmen, and the costs of shipping sculptures to Basrah. He would contribute his own salary of one hundred and fifty pounds to the general fund, at least for the present. Even so, "It is hardly prudent on my part to embark in a second expedition with such very limited means at my disposal, but as the Trustees have reckoned upon my services I will not raise difficulties at the last moment. My private resources are far from considerable, but such as they are they shall be devoted to the undertaking, and I can only promise the Trustees that no exertions shall be wanting on my part to ensure the success of the expedition." Though he considered arrangements in England had been "hastily and inadequately made," nothing short of disaster would have kept him away from Nineveh. The artist whose services he had requested, Frederick Charles Cooper, a timid soul who was never in very good health, arrived from England with Hormuzd Rassam, who was again to act as Layard's assistant. The three left Constantinople at the end of August accompanied by Dr. Humphrey Sandwich, an English physician, by Layard's cawass, Mohammed Agha, two other attendants, and Cawal Yusuf, a Yezidi leader, who had been to Constantinople to present the case of his people to the Sultan. Through Layard's introduction to Sir Stratford Canning, and the Grand Elchi's intercession with the Porte, he was bringing back with him an imperial order which gave the Yezidis equal rights with the Moslems.

The party left the Black Sea steamer at Trebizond, and, mounted on seventeen hired horses and mules, took the well-traveled Persian caravan route as far as Erzerum. From here Layard seized the opportunity to see more strange lands and interesting people by branching off through little-known Armenia and Kurdistan. He crossed the Tigris at the spot forded by Xenophon and his Ten Thousand on their way to Trebizond, then a Greek Colony. In the wild Kurdish mountains, where, as seems to have been the case from that day to this, there had just been a rebellion, poor Cooper was frightened to despair by tales of murder and robbery poured into his inexperienced ears. Instead of being killed, as he had been led to expect, the party was royally entertained by a notorious Kurdish chieftain. The Yezidi villagers gave Layard and Cawal Yusuf a hero's welcome, and a party of Yezidi horsemen escorted them till they were out of danger from raiding Bedouins.

While still a day's journey from Mosul, Layard and Hormuzd Rassam stopped to ask for a drink of water at some Arab tents. They were immediately surrounded by men and women wild with joy and excitement—the Jeburs, who had heard that their Bey was again to dig for old stones, and were on their way to join him. A little further along the road, his old foremen, Toma Shishman and Mansur, Behnan the stonecutter, and Hanna the carpenter were waiting for him. Christian Rassam greeted him at the village of Tel Kef, where a feast had been prepared at the home of the Chaldean bishop. Next morning, as he rode toward Mosul, he was welcomed by many others who had come out to meet him: Awad, and the sheikhs of the Jebur, and his groom, holding Merjan, ready for his new master to mount, "the noble animal looking as beautiful, fresh and sleek as when I last saw him, two years ago." Even his greyhounds were on hand. How enchanted he was to be back! "As we ascend an eminence midway, walls, towers, minarets, and domes rise boldly from the margin of the broad river, cheating us into the belief, too soon to be dispelled, that Mosul is still the not unworthy representative of the great Nineveh. As we draw near, the long line of lofty mounds, the only remains of mighty bulwarks and spacious gates, detach themselves from the low undulating hills: now the vast mound of Kuyunjik overtops the surrounding heaps; then above it peers the white cone of the tomb of the prophet Jonah; many other well-remembered spots follow in rapid succession. Hastening over the creaking bridge of boats, we force our way through the crowded bazaars, and alight at the house I left two years ago. Old servants take their places as a matter of course, and, uninvited, pursue their regular occupations as if they had never been interrupted. Indeed it seemed as if we had but returned from a summer's ride . . ."

Chapter XX

FULL SCALE EXCAVATION
(October 1849–March 1850)

In the cool of the early morning next day Layard rode across the bridge of boats to the ruins on the east bank of the Tigris. If one were to look down upon the mounds from the air, one would see low, dirt-covered ramparts enclosing an irregular quadrangle. Within it two large tels, Kuyunjik and Nebbi Yunus, lie along the western ramparts, facing the river. The Tigris has changed its course in the last twenty-five hundred years and no longer washes the foot of the old walls. A small, sluggish branch, the Khosr, or Khausser, which divides the quadrangle from North to South, winds around the southern tip of the pear-shaped mound of Kuyunjik. Layard's workmen had been digging at the south end of the mound, above the Khosr; on the north were the deserted roofless huts of the Arab village of Kuyunjik, a name meaning "many sheep" after the large flocks that grazed on the new grass of the mound in spring.

Layard followed a path which led up to his old trenches, now filled in with rubble. The winter rains had gouged deep ravines in the sides of the mound since he had last seen it, laying bare in places the brick platform on which the palace had stood. At the top, a hundred feet above the plain, one could imagine how the Assyrian tyrants, lolling on the palace terraces, had looked down upon their mighty ramparts and gates, and upon the huts of their six score thousand loyal subjects, never expecting this landscape to change. On the other side of the Khosr, probably dredged then to permit men and supplies to be disembarked at

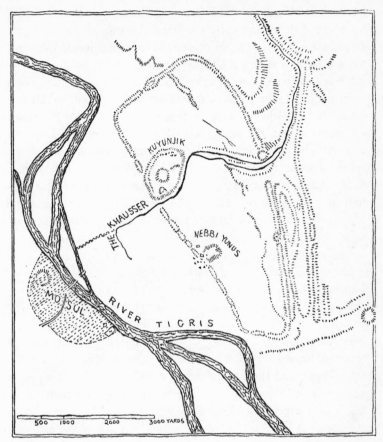

The Mosul Mounds   From Layard, *Nineveh and Babylon*

the foot of the palace, stood a sister palace on the mound now
called Nebbi Yunus. Fifty miles away to the north were the towering Kurdish mountains; closer by and a little to the east was another chain of ribbed and wrinkled mountains near the foot of
which nestled Bashiqah and other villages, and Khorsabad, or
Dûr-Sharrukin, the new city of King Sargon II. To the west, rising
abruptly from the plain, were the Sinjar Hills. Only to the south
was a clear view of undulating ploughland, with the Tigris winding
through it, marked by a green border of groves.

Toma Shishman showed Layard what had been accomplished in his absence. Ross had aptly described the excavations as regular catacombs. In the southern corner the men had found the depth too great and had taken to making underground passages, burrowing along the walls and leaving pillars of earth to uphold the roof, as in a mine. Light and air came through shafts sunk at intervals; Toma had to light a candle so that Layard could see the details of the bas-reliefs. He recognized the style at once and knew this was not a second building as Ross had supposed, but part of the same enormous palace, ravaged by the same fire. The slabs were so badly disfigured that Toma had shifted his men back to the great hall that had been opened up just before his master's departure. Layard ordered the underground tunnels to be carried on in the same fashion (for reasons of economy), with a work crew enlarged to approximately a hundred men.

On October 18, he and Hormuzd Rassam rode out to inspect Nimrud. The earth that had been shoveled over the sculptures had sunk a bit, and several giant heads rose above it, calmly surveying the plain with their stone eyes. Vandals had not done as much harm as expected; a number of bas-reliefs left exposed were untouched. Layard collected his former workmen from the neighboring villages, and the few Jeburs who still lingered nearby, to resume work in the Northwest Palace. He slept that night in his old headquarters, and, rising early next morning, was surprised to see horses picketed on top of the mound. In one of the excavated chambers he found Rawlinson, fast asleep after riding from Baghdad, a trip which usually took eight to twelve days, in seventy-two hours. Unfortunately heat and exhaustion had brought on a bad attack of fever, and though Rawlinson wished to discuss a multitude of matters with Layard during this, their first meeting among the ruins, he was soon forced to seek the shade of a hut in the village. By midnight he was so ill that it seemed wise to ride at once to Mosul, where he could be put to bed in comfort. It was not till the third day, when it was time for him to leave, that he was able to snatch a superficial look at the Kuyunjik excavations before riding off on his way to England and well-deserved fame.

Layard, "the hard-working and judicious gatherer of materials," remained on the job. Archaeology was beginning to develop as a science, with its emphasis no longer so much on art treasures as on ancient life revealed in art, inscriptions, and handicraft. By the end of November, the workers had entirely cleared out the great hall, 124 feet long and 90 feet wide. The bas-reliefs were very different from those at Nimrud. Instead of being divided into upper and lower scenes by a band of cuneiform, these were filled from top to bottom of the slab with hundreds of small figures and masses of realistic detail, forming a continuous series which unrolled around the walls like a comic strip. Places were identified by landscape, and people by their national costume. A campaign in Kurdistan was pictured against a background of rocks and trees, sometimes with birds nesting in the branches to indicate that it was spring. The location of a city was suggested by placing it on a mountain, on the seacoast, or by the side of a river teeming with fish, turtles and decapitated corpses. The missing heads were heaped at the feet of the king, while a scribe stood by making a record of their number. Each group of captives showed national characteristics: the Elamite ladies, for instance, wore their hair in long ringlets, while those from Syria favored pointed caps. Thus the bas-reliefs threw light not only on the Assyrians, but on all the peoples of the ancient Near East who paid them tribute.

On the north wall of the great hall and in a long gallery adjoining was a series which illustrated the building of this very palace. Thus Layard's question—how had the Assyrians moved the huge stone statues—was answered. They had done it exactly in the same way as he had twenty-five hundred years later: by the use of cables, rollers, levers, wedges, and, above all, man power. The finishing touches on the colossal animals had been carved after they had been placed, for one bas-relief showed a block of stone on which a human-headed bull had been roughly chiseled, being dragged to the foot of the palace platform on a sledge. (The peoples of Mesopotamia had known the principle of the wheel for many centuries. But without iron axles, no wheels were strong enough to bear such a burden.) The power was supplied, not by such enthusiastic helpers as the Jeburs and the Abou Salman, but by long lines of slaves, urged on by overseers. The king himself supervised the operation from a movable throne, or throne-chariot. Above his head was a short inscription in which Layard recognized the name of Sennacherib. Dr. Hincks later translated it:

Sennacherib, king of Assyria, the great figures of bulls, which in the land of Bedad, were made for his royal palace at Nineveh, he transported thither.[1]

The next step in identifying the palace and the city in which it stood came in December, when the grand entrance to the building was unearthed: a façade of overpowering splendor, fitting approach to the magnificence within. Towering far higher than a man were ten colossal winged bulls and six enormous figures; two of these, curly-bearded giants casually holding an animal the size of a large dog under one arm, were dubbed by Layard "the Assyrian Hercules strangling a lion." Actually they represent Gilgamesh, hero of the great Sumerian epic inscribed on countless clay tablets which had not yet been discovered (if they had been, no one could as yet have read them). Two years after the grand entrance to the palace had been found, Rawlinson deciphered the long inscriptions between the bulls' legs and announced that he had found in them the annals of six years of Sennacherib's reign. The events described in them agreed in detail with accounts in the Old Testament.

Each year in spring the Assyrian armies marched out to gain new territory for the empire, or to subdue a province that had tried to break away. Among names mentioned in the annals and in Scripture are the Hittites, Moabites, Edomites, the Babylonians and their king, Merodach Baladan. During the third year of Sennacherib's reign, he invaded Syria to defeat the forces of Egypt. During this campaign he punished the king of Judah, as follows:

Hezekiah, king of Judah, who had not submitted to my authority, forty-six of his principal cities, and fortresses and villages depending upon them, of which I took no account, I captured and

*carried away their spoil. I shut himself within Jerusalem, his capital
city. The fortified towns, and the rest of his towns, which I spoiled,
I severed from his country and gave to the kings of Ascalon, Ekron,
and Gaza. On addition to the former tribute imposed, I added a
tribute . . .*

Dr. Hincks, who translated this inscription, found the next passage defaced but could make out that Sennacherib took from
Hezekiah eight hundred talents of silver and thirty talents of gold.
Sennacherib's annals do not admit that his army was smitten by
the Lord at the gates of Jerusalem, and retreated to Nineveh. In
other details, however, it is very similar to the Bible account in the
Second Book of Kings:

*Now in the fourteenth year of king Hezekiah did Sennacherib
king of Assyria come up against all the fenced cities of Judah, and
took them. And Hezekiah king of Judah sent to the king of Assyria
to Lachish, saying, I have offended; return from me: and that which
thou puttest on me will I bear. And the king of Assyria appointed
unto Hezekiah king of Judah three hundred talents of silver and
thirty talents of gold.*

The very amount of gold tribute is identical, though there is a
discrepancy in the silver. Even before the annals of the king had
been made public, proofs were piling up that Assyrian and Biblical
history were two sides of the same coin. Another connecting link
was a series of thirteen bas-reliefs in the Kuyunjik palace, which
Layard points to as "the first actual illustration of a king, a city,
and a people, with whose names we are acquainted, and of an
event described in Holy Writ." It is a representation of the siege of
Lachish, in southern Palestine, the very city to which, according
to the passage above, Hezekiah sent his emissaries. It is both a
beautiful and a horrible series of panels: "In no other sculptures
were so many warriors seen drawn up in array before a besieged
city. In the first rank were the kneeling archers, those in the second

were bending forward, while those in the third discharged their arrows standing upright, and were mingled with spearmen and slingers. A reserve consisted of large bodies of horsemen and charioteers. Against the fortifications had been thrown up as many as ten banks or mounts, compactly built of stones, bricks, earth, and branches of trees, and seven battering-rams had already been rolled up to the walls. Spearmen, archers, and slingers thronged the battlements and towers, showering arrows, javelins, stones, and blazing torches upon the assailants. On the battering-rams were bowmen discharging their arrows, and men with large ladles pouring water upon the flaming brands, which, hurled from above, threatened to destroy the engines. Ladders, probably used for escalade, were falling from the walls. Part of the city had, however, been taken. Beneath its walls were seen Assyrian warriors impaling their prisoners, and from the gateway of an advanced tower, or fort, issued a procession of captives, reaching to the presence of the king, who, gorgeously arrayed, received them seated on his throne. Amongst the spoil were furniture, arms, shields, chariots, vases of metal of various forms, camels, carts drawn by oxen, and laden with women and children, and many objects. The vanquished people were distinguished from the conquerors by their dress. Several prisoners were already in the hands of the torturers. Two were stretched naked on the ground to be flayed alive, others were being slain by the sword before the throne of the king. The haughty monarch was receiving the chiefs of the conquered nation, who crouched and knelt humbly before him. The captives were undoubtedly Jews, their physiognomy was strikingly indicated in the sculptures, but they had been stripped of their ornaments and their fine raiment, and were left barefooted and half-clothed." Over the head of the Assyrian king was this inscription:

Sennacherib, the mighty king, king of the country of Assyria, sitting on the throne of judgement before the city of Lachish, I give permission for its slaughter.

There was no longer any doubt that, deep under the rubble of Kuyunjik, Layard had found the palace in Nineveh of the mighty Sennacherib. In the book which he wrote on these discoveries, *Nineveh and Babylon*, Layard maintained a cool aloofness as he built up his proof, detail after detail, argument by argument. He wished to be known as a scientist. But he could not help himself; his imagination took flight in romantic descriptions, and his heart was filled with religious awe as he paced the tunnels of the palace which had once been the epitome of luxury, pomp, and circumstance.

At Nimrud, his next project was to solve the mystery of the pyramid. After trenching through a mass of earth, pebbles, burned brick, and stone fragments, he was forced to call the whole thing off for fear that a cave-in would bury his workmen. He surmised that the structure had been a square tower, perhaps terminating in one or two setbacks. Deep within it might be the burial chamber of Sardanapalus, whose tomb, according to the Greek writers, stood at the entrance to Nineveh. The state of Assyriology at the time is no better demonstrated than by Layard's explanation of the ziggurat of Nimrud in terms of legend, while he was simultaneously reconstructing genuine history at Kuyunjik.

The spoil of the captured cities turned up in a room in the Northwest Palace at Nimrud; a severely plain room of brick coated with asphalt, which had a single entrance leading to a terrace on the river. In one corner was a well, which, when cleared out, led down to brackish water. On the floor near the well was a pile of copper caldrons and jars filled with bronze bells, hooks, cups, odd ornaments, a wine strainer. Scattered about were hundreds of buttons, studs, and rosettes of ivory, metal, and mother-of-pearl, which resembled the harness ornaments pictured in the bas-reliefs. Lying in a heap behind the caldrons were exquisite bowls of bronze, with incised or embossed patterns, or of iron, bronze-plated —a technique of metallurgy unknown in nineteenth century Europe. Two shallow round vessels nearly six feet in diameter answered the description of the "brazen sea" of Solomon's temple. There were glass bowls iridescent with age; and a rock-crystal lens which could have been used either as a burning glass or for magnifying. Two alabaster vases were inscribed with the name of Sargon. There were swords, daggers, shields, spears, arrow heads, a pick, a double-handled saw, and sledge hammers, made of iron which fell to pieces at a touch and bronze which dissolved into green powder. If only the scientific knowledge and chemicals had existed which enabled twentieth-century archaeologists to resurrect if not preserve such disintegrated artifacts! Layard could not, like Sir Leonard Woolley at Ur some seventy years later, restore missing parts by taking a cast of their impression in the soil. All he could do was to remove the earth with utmost care from around what had been a chair, and note, as it vanished before his eyes, that it had been of wood overlaid with bronze, with ivory feet—almost identical with the throne on which Sennacherib had sat before Lachish when he had given permission for its slaughter, and, presumably, had received Hezekiah's message of submission.

Layard carefully packed up many objects not too badly decayed, and sent them to the British Museum. It amused him to think that the tin ingredient in the bronze bowls now on their way to England had probably been brought from there by Phoenician merchants two and a half millennia before. Rawlinson, when he examined the alabaster jars on their arrival, found traces of preserves in one of them, and on this basis ventured to guess that the room in which they had been found had been a kitchen. Layard thought it was more likely to have been a royal storeroom.

The Museum Trustees now wished him to move and ship to England the two human-headed lions which formed the portal of the great hall in the Northwest Palace. Originally it had been considered impossible to move any as big as these without sawing them up into many pieces, as Botta had done with his bulls from Khorsabad. But Layard was more experienced now, and also better equipped. By the end of January, the lions were ready to start on their way as soon as the river was high enough to float a raft with such a heavy cargo. This pair of beasts were the first that had been found, "Nimrod himself" and his twin, and Layard had a very special feeling for them. Often, when he had been lonely or discouraged during his first season of excavation, he had sat and contemplated the meaning of those majestic creatures. So he rode out to the mound one calm and cloudless night to bid them farewell.

"The moon was at her full, and as we drew nigh to the edge of the deep wall of earth rising around them, her soft light was creeping over the stern features of the human heads, and driving before it the dark shadow which still clothed the lion forms. One by one the limbs of the gigantic sphinxes emerged from the gloom, until the monsters were unveiled before us. I shall never forget that night, or the emotions which those venerable figures caused within me. A few hours more and they were to stand no longer where they had stood unscathed amidst the wreckage of man and his works for ages. It seemed almost a sacrilege to tear them from their old haunts to make them a mere wonder-stock to the busy crowd of a new world. They were better suited to the desolation around them; for they had guarded the palace in its glory, and it was for them to watch over it in its ruin. Sheikh Abd-ur-rahman, who had ridden with us to the mound, was troubled with no such reflections. He gazed listlessly at the grim images, wondered at the folly of the Franks, thought the night was cold, and turned his mare towards his tents."

If one can judge by the trouble they caused, the lions themselves did not wish to leave. Heavy rains had changed the dusty plain into a swamp. Once, when the cart wheels sank in the mud, it was unanimously declared by the grunting, struggling Arabs that the young artist Cooper brought bad luck and must be sent away. When this did not help, a Frank lady who was Layard's guest was asked to sit on the lion to bring *good* luck. But someone with the Evil Eye still lurked among those present. Hormuzd Rassam devised all sorts of tricks to discover him and drive him off. As a last resort, Layard seized a rope in his own hands, and amid shouts of defiance from the different tribes that were competing as teams, and to the deafening *tahlel* of the women, the cart and its burden were dragged down the sticky track. Layard wrote to Sir Henry Ellis February 8, 1850: "I am happy to inform you that I have succeeded in removing the two lions *entire* to the banks of the river. I hope to have them embarked on rafts in the month of April." He had learned through the Bombay papers that the warship *Fury*, a vessel of five hundred horsepower, was being especially dispatched to Basrah to pick up his sculptures. For once, everything seemed to be in good order.

Alas for his optimism! With the melting snows, such a flood swept over the plain as had not been seen since the days of Noah. The river rose so fast that many were drowned, and it was easy to understand the story of the Great Deluge. Christian Rassam, who in Layard's absence was supervising the embarkation of the lions, was forced to take refuge with his wife on the summit of the mound of Nimrud, which had become an island. When the waters subsided, the lions were plastered over with black mud. Some days later, while they were being loaded on rafts, one, which was cracked, fell in two; the other was found to have suffered a broken nose from some unknown assailant during the night. Between Baghdad and Basrah, the river having burst its banks, the shattered lion broke loose and sailed off with the current till it grounded in a swamp about a mile from the main stream. It was given up for lost, but Captain Felix Jones and his little steamer rescued it with two large boats, one for each half of the lion. Layard wrote angrily to Sir Henry: "Had proper means been placed at my command, the Lions would have been embarked under my own superintendence. As it is I have been struggling this winter and spring to make ends meet, and have been obliged to defer from day to day and week to week that which ought to have been done at once."

He had been absent because he was trying to cover the "other sites" specified in the Museum grant, and he could not be in more than one place at once. From Ross's description of Bavian, and the glimpse of it which he had had on his way to Mosul in the autumn, he believed it well worth careful examination. Now it was spring, and the Gomel, swollen from melting snow, foamed through its narrow gorge, bursting over the rocks and the great blocks of sculpture which had fallen down into it from the steep-sided cliffs. A few Kurds whom Layard hired to excavate at the entrance to the ravine found the foundations of a building under the silt brought down by spring floods. Higher up was a delightful spot which might have been a sacred grove: a fountain with a bas-relief of two rampant lions from which clear cold water cascaded into a series of stone basins; along the edge of the stream grew myrtle and pink-flowering wild oleander.

The tombs which Ross had described were late, for they had been gouged out of the cliffs without regard to the sculptures, which consisted of a number of tablets enclosed in recessed frames. Three of the sculptures had cuneiform inscriptions running across them, and all were much eroded, but Layard considered them the most important rock carvings yet found in Assyria. On the principal bas-relief were two figures representing the same king, who resembled in costume and detail the builder of the palace at Kuyunjik. These two kings were adoring two deities who stood upon mythical animals. All but one of the inscriptions were too far away for Layard to copy them from below, but, emulating Rawlinson, he had the Kurds lower him by rope to a six-inch ledge, where, teetering and fuming at the stupidity of his helpers, he copied inscriptions for most of two days.

Monuments such as these, carved upon a rock in an appropriate place, were customarily erected by the Assyrians to commemorate a historic event. The Bavian inscription commemorates Sennacherib's successful campaign against Babylon, from which he brought back images of the Assyrian gods captured by the Babylonians 413 years before. The tablet was the first proof that the Assyrians had kept exact track of time. Layard was excited and delighted by the discovery, which meant that sooner or later chronological tables would be found which would establish definite dates in Assyrian history. He had no idea that by the time Dr. Hincks deciphered the Bavian inscription, he himself would have already found those chronological tables.

Chapter XXI

THE BANKS OF THE KHABUR

(March–May 1850)

Mohammed Emin, a sheikh of the semi-nomad Jebur, sent word to Layard that two idols like those of Nimrud had risen from the earth near his tents on the banks of the Khabur. The Jebur workmen at Nimrud were constantly praising their traditional pasture ground as an earthly paradise, rich in grass, trees, flowers—and ruins. The prospect of a desert excursion was tempting, and here was a valid reason for it: to find out how far west Assyrian influence had extended, and whether the ruins near the Khabur were of the same type as those at Nineveh.

The river, from its source in Kurdistan to its juncture with the Euphrates at ancient Carchemish, ran through country that had never been mapped, for the Shammar, whose territory it was, did not take kindly to strangers. Layard was well known by reputation to the desert tribes, but it was still necessary to secure the friendship of the sheikhs through arrangement, messages, and gifts, all of which took time, and money from Layard's personal pocket. Sofuk, the paramount Shammar sheikh, had been killed in reprisal for his own treachery; Layard got in touch with Suttum, a younger man, who was said to be trustworthy. Suttum agreed to furnish an escort, and animals, and to accompany the party on the expedition till all were safely returned to the walls of Mosul.

With Layard went Hormuzd Rassam, Cooper, Mr. and Mrs. Roland (two English visitors to Mosul), Dr. Sandwich, and Cawal Yusuf, the Yezidi leader, who wished to visit the Yezidi settlements in the Sinjar Hills. Suttum's tribesmen were in charge of twenty-five camels, which, with the same number of horses, would carry people, baggage and supplies for a two-month trip. Several Jebur families, returning to their tribe, twelve Chaldean workmen and fifty of the best village Arabs followed on foot—about one hundred armed men in all.

Watching the complicated arrangements for departure, Layard may have remembered with regret the days when he traveled light, fast and alone. The faithful Bairakdar supervised the loading of tents, blankets, digging tools, rice, flour, sugar, coffee, tea, as well as spices and other luxuries intended, along with silk robes and colored boots, as gifts for sheikhs met along the way. The primitive Bedouin pack-saddles were constantly slipping over the camel's tail or toppling sideways; when a load had finally been balanced, the camel would often fall to its knees, shrugging it off, and the camel driver, throwing up his hands, would cry out that the burden was too cruel for his poor beast. Packing had begun at daybreak, but the muezzins were calling the faithful to midday prayer by the time the caravan plodded through the Sinjar Gate of Mosul. At the head of it, on his cream-white *deloul* (riding dromedary) was Suttum, a striking figure in red-embellished blue cloak and striped keffiya, with scarlet ribbons streaming from his ostrich-feather tufted spear.

Layard was as glad to be quitting the stinking alleys of the town as any true Son of the Desert. He had much in common with Suttum: love of freedom, of adventure, of horses—and a firm belief, no matter what ailed him, that the desert air would cure it. The trip was a welcome break from the disagreeable penny-pinching forced upon him by the terms of the Museum grant. Not that he could or wished to escape completely from the signs of the past. The caravan's line of march lay through a range of man-made mountains (from the summit of one he counted almost two hundred of them). Suttum knew these since his childhood, for his father's tents had been pitched among them twice each year; they were the landmarks which guided the tribe to its summer pastures by the Khabur, and back to the winter encampment near Babylon. Layard rode with him from mound to mound, stopping now and then to pick up and examine a potsherd, or take a compass bearing and jot down an Arab name which Suttum supplied.

In camp that night he was in a contemplative mood: "On all sides, as far as the eye could reach, rose the grass-covered heaps marking the sites of ancient habitations. The great tide of civilization had long since ebbed, leaving these scattered wrecks upon the solitary shore. Are those waters to flow again, bearing back the seeds of knowledge and of wealth that they have wafted to the West? We wanderers were seeking what they had left behind, as children gather up the colored shells on the deserted sands."

A detour was made to call upon Sheikh Rishwan, Suttum's father, who was encamped near the Sinjar Hills. Layard and his European guests were honored in the traditional fashion by a huge feast of boiled mutton and rice; afterward Suttum, with an embarrassed air, drew Layard aside. Such diffidence seemed out of character in this intelligent, fierce-looking young man, who, although lame from an old thigh wound, bore himself proudly as befitted a true aristocrat. Suttum wished to know if he might bring his wife, Rathaiyah, for the remainder of the excursion. Layard was to learn that this was not a marriage of love on Suttum's part; Rathaiyah had done the proposing, and he had accepted for the sake of a tribal alliance with her powerful father. As her price, Rathaiyah had forced Suttum to put away Adla, the wife he loved, who had already borne him a child. Adla, who was Suttum's cousin, had returned to her father, Moghamis, and was even now in his tents by the Khabur. No wonder then that Rathaiyah would not allow her husband to go there unaccompanied.

Rathaiyah was one of those imperious desert queens whom Layard described so graphically: "To the Arabs she was perfection, for all the resources of their art had been exhausted to complete what nature had begun. Her lips were dyed deep blue, her eyebrows were continued in indigo until they united over the nose; her cheeks and forehead were spotted with beauty-marks, her eyelashes darkened by Kohl; and on her legs and bosom could be seen the tattooed ends of flowers and fanciful ornaments, which were carried in festoons and network over her whole body. Hanging from each ear, and reaching to her waist, was an enormous earring of gold, terminating in a tablet of the same material, carved and ornamented with four turquoises. Her nose was also adorned with a prodigious ring, set with jewels, of such ample dimensions that it covered the mouth, and was to be removed when the lady ate."

Rathaiyah, jingling with earrings and silver bangles on wrist and ankle, was mounted on the riding dromedary behind her husband when the party started off. Two evenings later as camp was being set up, Suttum came to Layard with a long face. His wife had declared that the white tent in which she was expected to sleep was unbecoming to the wife and daughter of a Bedouin, and fit only for a city lady like Mrs. Roland. "So determined is she, in the matter," said Suttum, "that, Billah! she deserted my bed last night and slept in the grass, and now she swears she will leave me and return on foot to her kindred unless I save her from the indignity of sleeping in a white tent." It was clear that he would not have objected to her absence, but could not run the risk of an insult to her family. Although Layard found the whims of this Bedouin princess a great nuisance, he allowed her to take for herself the black goat-wool kitchen tent, open at the sides, in which she could breathe freely.

Otherwise all was harmony in the caravan. "Thus we rode joyously over the plain," writes Layard, happy as a boy on holiday. Hormuzd Rassam marched at the head of the Jebur workmen, improvising suitable words to their war chants; and the men answered in chorus, danced instead of walking, and waved handkerchiefs as flags upon their spear points. Suttum's tribesmen smiled scornfully at such antics, worthy only of those who touched the plough. At night the party camped beside a spring, and the Europeans dined on game birds supplied by Suttum and his hunting hawk. When the Khabur was sighted winding like a glittering snake between green banks, all let out a yell of joy; the horsemen raced each other to the water; the Jeburs again began to prance and shout, and the Chaldeans shot off their guns. Herds of sheep and camels belonging to both Jebur and Shammar browsed in the lush meadows for miles around. Mohammed Emin and his sons rode out to greet the new arrivals through wild flowers which reached to their horses' knees. Layard and Rassam dismounted, embraced the sheikh, and exchanged presents with him, before riding on to set up their tents. Moghamis, the Shammar sheikh, arrived shortly, bringing as gift a well-trained falcon named Fahaz, which was placed on a stand in the middle of Layard's tent. Tribesmen crowded in with milk, curds, butter, and other presents. Layard ordered dinner to be prepared for all. And so the first night on the Khabur was celebrated.

Mohammed Emin's tents were pitched on the ancient site of Arban, among the ruined canals, several of which his people had cleared out to irrigate their barley crop. Layard made his camp close-by, beneath the principal mound. In the middle of the camp was his *musif*, which could hold two hundred at a sitting and was always open to guests in the Bedouin fashion. Some yards to the rear was his private tent, and behind that, the other sleeping tents and one set up by Dr. Sandwich as a clinic. The desert Arabs, who had never before seen a European, swarmed over the camp, examining everything, especially Mrs. Roland. Later they brought her small *jerboas* (desert mice) as pets.

The "idols" were a pair of human-headed bulls which had suddenly appeared on the mound when winter rains and flooding river had washed away the surrounding soil. They were quite different from those at Nineveh; the wings were small in proportion to the bodies, the heads had human ears in addition to bulls' ears on the caps, the noses were big and flat, the lips thick, and the workmanship rather crude. On the fifth day of excavating, a second pair of bulls was dug out. Layard could not trace the walls which should have adjoined them, or any walls at all. The diggers subsequently found a sculptured lion, and a human figure in bas-relief, many Egyptian scarabs, and small objects from the city which, long after Assyrian times, had stood at Arban. The results were disappointing compared to Nimrud and Kuyunjik, but they proved to Layard's satisfaction that the Assyrian Empire had extended as far west as the Khabur (which is in present-day Syria). His supposition has been confirmed by modern scholarship: Arban was originally a Mitannian fortress; then Ashurnasirpal had probably occupied it; the curious bulls and the lion show Hittite influence. But there is much still to be learned from Arban.[1]

In the evenings as he sat by the door of his tent facing the river, Layard, like Ezekiel, was given to visions. He pictured the unhappy children of Israel pitching their tents and pasturing their flocks around Arban, even as the Bedouin now. Then it had been a prosperous city with a palace temple standing on the mound, and the river valley had supported many thriving villages. Some of the captives might have lingered on to form the nucleus of the Jewish communities at Ras-al-Ain and Carchemish which Benjamin of Tudela visited in the twelfth century. But now, from its source to its mouth, there was no permanent settlement upon the Khabur.

Layard found the country beautiful, and its wandering population, both human and animal, endlessly fascinating. He kept a detailed journal:

"*Monday, 8th of April.* One of my servants caught a turtle in the river measuring three feet in length. The Arabs have many stories of the voracity of these animals, which attain, I am assured, to even a larger size, and Suttum declared that a man had been pulled under water and devoured by one, probably an Arab exaggeration.

"A Bedouin, who had been attacked by a lion while resting, about five miles down the river, came to our encampment. He escaped with the loss of his mare. The lion is not uncommon in the jungles of the Khabur.

"*April 9th.* A Bedouin youth, thin and sickly, though of a daring and resolute countenance, sat in my guest tent. His only clothing was a kerchief, very dirty and torn, falling over his head, and a ragged cloak, which he drew tightly around him, allowing the end of a knotted club to appear above its folds. His story, which he was at length induced to tell, was characteristic of Bedouin education. His father was too poor to equip him with mare and spear, and he was ashamed to be seen by the Arabs on foot and unarmed. He had now become a man, for he was about fourteen years old, and he resolved to trust to his own skill for his outfit as a warrior. Without communicating his plans, he bent his way to the Euphrates. For three months he had lived in the river jungle, feeding on roots and herbs, hiding himself during the day in the thickets, and prowling at night round the tents of the Anazeh in search of a mare that might have strayed, or might be less carefully guarded than usual. At length the object of his ambition was found, and such a mare had never been seen before; but, alas! her legs were bound with iron shackles, and he had brought no file with him. He was now on his way back to his tents, intending to set forth again on new adventures in search of a mare and a spear, promising to be wiser in the future and carry a file under his cloak. Suttum seemed very proud of his relative, and introduced him to me as a promising, if not distinguished, character.

"*April 11th*. The Jeburs killed four beavers, and brought three of their young to us alive. The Arabs eat the flesh, and it was cooked for us, but proved coarse and tough. The young we kept for some days on milk, but they eventually died. Their cry resembled that of a newborn infant.

"*April 12th*. Mohammed Emin, with two of his sons, the horsemen of the tribe, and the sheikhs who were his guests, started out on their ghazou. I accompanied them as far as a large ruin called Shemshani. Suttum came with us carrying his hawk, Hattab, on his wrist. Game abounded, and the falcon soon flew towards a bustard, which his piercing eye had seen lurking in the long grass. The sun was high in the heavens; already soaring in the sky, was the enemy of the trained hawk, the 'agab' a kind of kite or eagle. Although far beyond our ken, he soon saw Hattab, and darted upon him with one swoop. The affrighted falcon immediately turned from his quarry, and with shrill cries of distress flew towards us. After circling round, unable from fear to alight, he turned towards the Desert, still followed by his relentless enemy. In vain his master, following as long as his mare could carry him, waved the lure, and called the hawk by his name; he saw him no more. Whether the noble bird escaped, or fell victim to the 'butcher,' we never knew.

"Suttum was inconsolable at his loss. He wept when he returned without his falcon on his wrist, and for days he would suddenly exclaim, 'O bej! Billah! Hattab was not a bird, he was my brother.'

"*April 18th*. The face of the Desert was as burnished gold. Its last change was to flowers of the brightest yellow hue, and the whole plain was dressed with them. Suttum rioted in the luxuriant herbage and the scented air. I never saw him so exhilerated. 'What *Kef* [delight]' he continually exclaimed, as his mare waded through the flowers, 'has God given us equal to this? It is the only thing worth living for. Ya Bej! what do the dwellers in cities know of true happiness, they have never seen grass or flowers? May God have pity on them!' "

Layard, part anthropologist and part Romantic, collected so much material on the customs of the *Bedu* that only a fraction can be repeated here. He noted that Moghamis and Mohammed Emin, though they had absolute power over their followers, had as many duties as privileges. They were responsible for feeding the tribesmen in time of want, even if it took their entire personal income. It was a lucky day when they could replenish tribal supplies by holding up a grain caravan. The common Bedouin ate little meat, living on bread with butter or truffles, asparagus, or garlic, all of which grew wild in the desert in spring. Curds, or *leben*, made from sheep's milk, was a staple; fresh milk, except from a camel, was unhealthy. A man could milk a camel without dishonor, but it was degrading, a woman's job, to milk sheep and goats. Cows were the impedimenta of decadent tribes that had given up their freedom to settle on the land.

The Children of the Desert were extremely healthy on this meager diet. Though many faces were scarred with smallpox, fatal epidemics were rare. Rheumatism and bellyaches were treated with a red-hot poker applied to the seat of the pain (still a custom in the East). There were few medicines, no opiates or sedatives. Dr. Sandwich asked what was done for a Bedouin who could not sleep. "Ho! We make use of him and set him to watch the camels," said Suttum. Women gave birth easily, causing no delay when the tribe was on the march. The birth rate was not high, one of the reasons being that the children were breast-fed for two or three years. Several wives had been necessary to bless Mohammed Emin with his sixteen off-spring. But Bedouin women, often very pretty when young, aged rapidly, growing haggard of face and sagging of body after a number of childbirths.

Soon after the arrival at the Khabur, Adla, Suttum's first wife, came with her child to ask Layard's advice. Younger than Rathaiyah and still beautiful, with olive skin, large almond-shaped eyes and luxuriant curly black hair, she was much beloved by Suttum, and she herself wished only to have him back. Rassam persuaded Rathaiyah to receive Adla in her tent, but she, considering this humiliating, refused, and was dragged there, protesting loudly, by the peacemaker. A reconciliation of all parties took place, but Layard could see trouble in store for Suttum when European eyewitnesses were no longer present. Such were the trials of married life in the desert.

Mijwell, Suttum's brother, was scornful of the whole affair, considering Suttum weak and hen-pecked. He himself was married to his cousin, Adla's sister, betrothed to a second maiden, and in love with a third, whom he had never seen. He had heard of her charms through the verses of a wandering Arab poet; the fact that she was the daughter of an Anazeh sheikh, his mortal enemy, added an extra fillip to the romance. He was already exchanging secret messages through an intermediary with the lady, whom eventually he would abduct.

From Mijwell, who, though he could neither read nor write, had been chosen by his father to be the tribal Cadi, Layard learned of the complicated Bedouin laws based on ancient practice: *Thar*, the law of blood vengeance and family responsibility for murder; *Dakheel* and *Dakhal*, the laws of the protector and the protected. The laws which perhaps interested him most were those covering the ownership and exchange of horseflesh. He was a great admirer of the Arab horse, and a fine horseman himself. Wallis Budge, no admirer of Layard, writes that forty years later the old men of the tribes along the Khabur and in the Sinjar still told tales of Layard's ability and physical endurance. "The Sheikh of Baibuk remembered him and compared him to Antar, a very famous warrior and horseman. They told me also that he treated his horses as if they were his 'maternal brother's children'—i.e. his cousins—

that he fed them more carefully than he fed himself, and that he understood the 'tongue of horses' and could converse with them."

Arab horses are an ancient breed, unchanged in appearance from those portrayed in the Assyrian sculptures. Though small, they are swift, spirited, and so sturdy that they can perform on a minimum of food and water, and never have to be under cover, summer or winter. They seldom had their saddles removed, and never were cleaned, curried or groomed. "Noble and fierce horses are the true riches," said the Prophet. Bedouin horses were divided into five strains descended from his five favorite mares. The most famous of all belonged to the Shammar and the Anazeh, and since these tribes were constantly robbing each other, their horses were always changing hands. The victors in a ghazou could safely send an envoy to the enemy tents to ask the bloodlines of the horses that had been taken; there were no written pedigrees, and the unpardonable crime was to give false information. A desert sheikh who could hardly feed his own family frequently turned down a large sum of money for his favorite animal; he had no use for money, but without his mare he was lost. "Give him the desert, his mare, and his spear," writes Layard, "and he will not envy the wealth and power of the greatest of the earth." One wonders if the oil-rich sheikhs of today enjoy their Cadillacs half as much.

After three weeks at Arban, the Shammar and the Jebur began to move on, for the grass around their encampments had been nibbled down to the roots, and the flocks would have to be taken to fresh pastures further along the river. Tents were struck, and for a whole morning Layard could see sheep and camels, men, women and children trekking off across the plain. By midday the place where the tribes had camped was marked only by burned-out fires and rubbish heaps. The hot weather was drawing near too, and Layard did not feel that the finds at Arban justified a longer stay. On April 19 he struck his own tents and turned eastward. The caravan returned through limestone foothills where the ravines were blood red with poppies and anemonies. The Arabs decorated their camels and horses with the flowers, twisted them in their own headdresses and belts. "As we journeyed chanting an Arab war song, we resembled the return of a festive procession from some sacrifice of old. During our weary marches under the burning sun, it required some such episodes to keep up the drooping spirits of the men who toiled on foot by our sides. Poetry and flowers are the wine and spirits of the Arab; a couplet is equal to a bottle, and a rose to a dram."

Layard reached Mosul on May 10. He wrote to Sir Stratford Canning: "I hope our journey has proved useful in several respects. The tribes have now been accustomed to the presence of an European and this will be an opening for future travellers. I was able to assist several of the principal tribes and to prevent bloodshed and disorder."

Suttum bade him farewell two days after their arrival in Mosul. He had invited Layard to join a grand ghazou into the Nejd (in Saudi Arabia), where excellent horses and the best riding dromedaries were bred. He expected to be gone for thirty days and to bring back a great spoil. "But I had long renounced such evil habits, and other occupations kept me in Mosul," Layard writes. "Finding that I was not to be persuaded, and that the time was at length come for us to part, he embraced me, crammed the presents we had made to himself and his wives into his saddle-bags, and, mounting his *deloul*, rode off with Mijwell towards the Desert."

Chapter XXII

RECORDS IN CLAY AND STONE
(May–July 1850)

Toma Shishman reported that during Layard's absence some interesting things had turned up in Sennacherib's palace. Bas-reliefs of kings, battles, deities and the like were by now a commonplace, but here was something new: two doorways formed by giant figures, half man, half fish. Layard owned a cylinder seal engraved with an identical image: it was Dagon, fish-god of the Philistines—the god whose temple Samson had pulled down upon himself at Gaza, a god that was worshiped in many countries under many names. But the real find was in two small chambers behind one of the fish-god doorways. Piled on the floor more than a foot deep, as if thrown down in haste, were hundreds of clay tablets of various sizes and shapes, broken and whole, covered with clear-cut, minute cuneiform symbols. The tablets ranged from rectangular ones flat on one side, convex on the other, and as large as nine inches by six and a half, to tiny ones not more than an inch square with only a line or two on them.

A few such tablets had turned up here and there before this, among them a hexagonal prism which had been used as a candlestick by a poor family living near the tomb of Jonah, and a similar prism in Colonel Taylor's collection. Studying these with a magnifying glass, Layard had recognized names of kings and texts similar to those in the palaces.[1] He wrote to Sir Stratford Canning on May 26: "We have found an immense accumulation of inscribed terra-cotta tablets—which appear to be the archives of some of the Nineveh kings. I have already six cases full and the room is not half-emptied. This is a highly valuable addition to our collection of Assyrian antiquities." Many more tablets were found scattered along a corridor leading from the chambers to the river, and still others littered the river front where they had been dropped or kicked in the frantic scramble to escape from the burning palace. Three years later Hormuzd Rassam, following in Layard's footsteps as the excavator of Kuyunjik, found a second large cache of clay books in the palace of Sennacherib's grandson, Ashurbanipal.

Over twenty-five thousand tablets reached the British Museum in 1854 and 1855, to be examined by Rawlinson, Hincks, and other scholars; some of them are still being deciphered. Known as the Kuyunjik Collection, they are the foundation of the science of Assyriology, as Layard foresaw: "We cannot over-rate their value. They furnish us with materials for the complete decipherment of the cuneiform character, for restoring the language, and history of Assyria, and for inquiring into the customs, sciences, and, we may perhaps add, literature of its people." He appends a characteristic footnote: "According to a tradition, Seth wrote the history and wisdom of the ages preceding the Deluge on burnt and unburnt bricks, or tablets, that they might never perish; for if water destroyed the unburnt, the burnt would remain; but if fire destroyed the baked tablets, those which had not been exposed to heat would only become hardened."

It was soon recognized that the tablets were of several kinds. One was a sort of dictionary of cuneiform symbols which was a key to much of the rest. Many were historical records, royal decrees, businesslike accounts of temple offerings, lists of the gods. There were five hundred tablets on medical practice, with excellent prescriptions employing several hundred drugs; names of plants, with their uses; chemical data; instructions for making glass and ceramic glazes. A catalogue of the stars, revised from an earlier Babylonian work, was applied to astrology rather than to astronomy, but it confirmed Layard's prediction at Bavian: the Assyrians kept accurate track of time and dated events in their history from a fixed point. Their literature, also, was in the main a re-rendering of Babylonian themes.

Several tablets had colophons inscribed or scratched upon them and had belonged to the library of the temple of Nebo (or Nabu) the Divine Scribe, god of art, science, and writing. Others came from the private library of Ashurbanipal, known to the Bible as "the great and noble Asnapper"; the one Assyrian monarch to take an interest in culture as well as war and the chase. Ashurbanipal sent his royal scribes to the older cities—Babylon, Nippur, and Erech— to bring back copies of ancient works. The uniformity of the script and the absence of mistakes suggest that he may have set up a sort of publishing house with himself as editor, because he was, most unusual in a king, a scribe. "I, Ashurbanipal . . . understood the wisdom of Nebo, all the art of writing of every craftsman of every kind, I made myself master of them all," he announces in his Annals, inscribed on a ten-sided prism found by Rassam.[2] The texts in his library were systematically collected and arranged in a numbered series as in a modern library. Some are catalogued on separate clay tablets.

In 1866, George Smith, who was helping Rawlinson to go over the immense body of work, discovered the fragments, in twelve tablets, of the Epic of Gilgamesh, which had come down to the Assyrians from their forerunners in Sumer and Akkad. Seven years later at Kuyunjik, Smith miraculously found the missing pieces of the eleventh tablet, which is the Babylonian account of the Flood. Uta-napishtim, the Babylonian Noah, tells his descendant, Gilgamesh:

> *I made to go up into the ship all my family and kinsfolk,*
> *The cattle of the field, the beasts of the field, all*
> *   handicraftsmen,*
> *I made them go up into it . . .*

When the storm had abated, and the ship had come to rest:

> *. . . the fifth day, the sixth day, the mountain of Nisir*
> *   held the ship and let it not move,*
> *When the seventh day had come*

I brought out a dove and let her go free.
The dove flew away and came back,
Because she had no place to alight, she came back.

Primitive peoples in various parts of the world have related legends
of a great flood, but there are enough similarities between the
Assyrian tablets, the Sumerian account from which it was taken,
and the story of Noah, to make it plain that Father Abraham carried the myth with him when he "went forth from Ur of the Chaldees to go unto the land of Canaan." The genesis of all three ver-
sions of the Deluge may have been a serious and prolonged flood
in lower Babylonia—an extraordinary storm accompanied by an
earthquake and tidal wave from the Persian Gulf, which extended
much further north in Sumerian times. This covered with water all
of the world which was known to the early inhabitants of the land.

By the time the translation of the Assyrian Flood tablet was published, Layard had left the field of Assyriology, but he must have
been pleased to note once again the close connection between the
Assyrian documents and Scripture.

Though the sea has receded since Noah's day, the Tigris-
Euphrates valley throughout its history has been constantly threatened by the flooding of those two great rivers. When Layard returned to Nimrud after the discovery of the so-called Royal Library,
another spring deluge had swamped the plain. Houses had been
swept away; his own was falling in, and the mound stood above
the brown waters like the mountain of Nisir (or Biblical Ararat).
Work went on as usual as the waters gradually subsided. The diggers
had opened trenches in a ravine between the Northwest Palace and
the mysterious pyramid, and had come upon what appeared to be
a small temple built against the eastern and southern face of the
"brick tower" (the ziggurat). In addition to a lion portal there was
a second entrance flanked by unusual sculptures. One was a monster combining a feathered body, wings and tail, with a wolf-like
head, the forefeet of a lion, and the hind feet of an eagle. The second figure was a winged man hurling tridents or thunderbolts at the
monster. Layard interpreted the pair as the conflict between the

spirits of good and evil—one of the earliest subjects for religious art. To the right of this portal stood a fine bas-relief of the North-west Palace king set in an arched frame similar to the rock tablets at Bavian. Before it was a three-footed altar. Layard took this to mean that the Assyrians, like many ancient peoples, deified their kings and heroes after death. The explanation is rather that it was customary for prominent citizens, including the monarch, to erect their images in a temple together with tables for votive offerings. The king was not the deity, but his high priest, who linked in his person the temple, which was the god's dwelling place, with his own dwelling place, the palace.

An inner chamber was paved with a huge monolithic slab inscribed with the annals of the king on both upper and lower surfaces as if to make sure that, if one side was defaced, another record of the king's great deeds would survive. While this temple was being excavated, Layard one day smelled the sweet odor of burning cedar. The workmen had dug out a beam brought from the forests of Lebanon almost three thousand years before, and set fire to it to warm themselves. They were only completing earlier destruction; the chamber was choked with charcoal from this same wood, which had probably lined its walls and ceiling.

A hundred feet east of the first temple was a second, also paved with a gigantic monolithic inscribed slab. The unusual discovery here was a statue of the king in the round—the only perfect Assyrian royal statue of this sort to be found. Upon its breast was an inscription with the name, titles, and genealogy of Ashurnasirpal, and his proud boast: "the conqueror from the upper passage of the Tigris to Lebanon and the Great Sea, who all countries, from the rising of the sun to the going down thereof, has reduced to his authority." This pompous little character was only three feet four inches high, one of the easiest sculptures to move.

Layard was busy packing and shipping material from both sites. The river was so swollen that the bridge at Mosul could not be used, and to avoid the nuisance of crossing twice a day in one of the primitive boats, he lived in a tent on the mound of Kuyunjik. His work was now much discussed abroad, and distinguished gentlemen frequently came to see him. From sunrise to sunset everyone went below to avoid the heat, the visitors choosing some convenient spot in the underground passages where they could sit and watch the digging parties. After dark, Layard and his guests dined outside his tent and afterwards reclined upon their carpets, watching the moonlight on the river and the flickering lights in the huts of men who guarded the cucumber and melon patches at the foot of the mound. Occasionally one of these watchmen would break the quiet by firing his rifle to frighten off the wild boars. The foremen of the workmen would come to consult Layard about the next day's schedule, and to talk over the latest happenings until late into the night. Then all would fall asleep under the open sky.

By July this romantic life had begun to pall. The violent change in temperature between the sun-baked surface of the mound and the dim underground passages was far from healthy. One by one Layard's companions succumbed to fever; Cooper and Dr. Sandwich were shipped off to the mountains; guests departed. Layard and Rassam managed to hold out for a while, thinking themselves fortunate if they had their severest fever attacks on alternate days so that one of them at least could be in charge of the work. The first large collection of sculptures from Kuyunjik went off down the river on July 11; as soon as he had seen it go, Layard climbed on his horse, half delirious with fever, and left Mosul for his summer travels. Rassam, the Bairakdar, and his old servants went with him; they picked up Cooper and Dr. Sandwich along the way.

The objective this time was Lake Van, in Turkish Armenia. Layard planned to take a route through districts of Kurdistan unknown to Europeans, where there might be unexplored Assyrian ruins and uncopied inscriptions. Of course there were odd people to visit and interrogate as well: Kurdish chiefs, all more or less of bad repute, who entertained the Franks with "sweets, savoury dishes, sherbets and Persian delicacies"; the Armenian Patriarch; a Nestorian Bishop, and less distinguished Christians of various sects. As the way led up through the forest to snow-capped peaks, the nights grew very cold. Many of the party, including the servants, suffered from chills and fever, but they dared not stop for shelter and rest. Not far away a small glade had been pointed out where a traveler named Schulz had been murdered by a Kurdish chief a few years before. Schulz had aroused suspicion by his habit of inveterate note-taking, which he had not bothered to conceal.

The party did rest for a day at Bash-Kalah, formerly (but no longer) the headquarters of Schulz's murderer. On leaving there, at an altitude of over nine thousand feet, they came upon the encampment of a curious people. "The flocks had been driven down from the higher pastures, and were gathered together to be milked before the black tents. A party of women already crouched round their sheep. Their long hair was platted in tresses ending in tassels mingled with gold coins. From a high turban of gay colors, also adorned with coins, a thin white veil fell over their shoulders, and their flowing garments were of bright silk. The children ran to and fro with wooden bowls, and a girl standing near sang a plaintive air, beating the measure on a tambourine. The features of the women, and of the men, who came out of their tents as we rode up, as well as the tongue in which they addressed one another, showed at once that they were not Kurds. They were Jews, shepherds and wanderers of the stock, maybe, of those who, with their high priest Hyrcanus, were carried away captive from Jerusalem by Tigranes in the second century of our era, and placed in the city and neighborhood of Van." Layard pitched his tents near the Jewish nomads that night, hoping to learn more of their curious history. They could tell him only that they paid taxes to the Turkish governor of the district, as their fathers had done before them, and that there were many more Jewish shepherds, and many Jews among the villages too, in this part of Kurdistan.

In a few more days Layard and his party reached the lake and the town of Van, which was said to have been founded by Queen Semiramis as a summer refuge from the heat of Nineveh. The ancient settlement had been on the summit of an acropolis which rose abruptly above the newer town. In 1827, the unfortunate Schulz, the first European to visit Van in many years, had copied a few of the inscriptions which were engraved on the steep-sided cliffs in letters so large and clear that, with the use of a spyglass, they could be distinguished from below. They are written in Vannic (sometimes called Urartu), a rare form of cuneiform which was adapted from the Assyrian by the kings of Urartu (Ararat) and inscribed upon monuments scattered from Van to Erzerum. Layard, during his stay at Van, copied twenty-five of the texts carved on the cliffs, as well as various others which he came upon in the vicinity. Some thirty-eight years later, A. H. Sayce, professor of Assyriology and Philology at Oxford, deciphered Vannic from Layard's copies.

In his usual way, Layard took considerable interest in the contemporary inhabitants of Van, particularly the Armenian Christians, whose schools, he notes, had recently been much influenced for the good by the work of Protestant missionaries from the United States. He left the city on August 10, for an Armenian convent in the hills where Cooper and Dr. Sandwich, still severely ill, had taken refuge. He found them planning, for reasons of health, to return to Europe at once. Layard wrote to Sir Stratford Canning that they would soon be in Constantinople, and added that neither had been qualified for duties in the East. He had received small assistance from them. "I have indeed good cause to complain of the shabby and careless manner in which the whole thing has been done in England and nothing would induce me to remain out here another year." He had been disgusted before, angry and even depressed, but now he was literally fed up. He felt that his achievements at Nineveh were not appreciated, nor were his personal sacrifices of money and health. He was a proud man and his pride was hurt; it did not make him any better humored to be suffering, as both he and Hormuzd Rassam were suffering, from constant malarial attacks. They were quite as sick as the other two, but being tougher, or more stubborn, they kept going as before. Actually Layard was rather relieved to be rid of the weaker members of the party, who had made the rough journey up to Lake Van even more difficult than it would otherwise have been.

The return through unexplored territory to the south was not easy either. But there were compensations: old Armenian churches, inscriptions (some interesting, others a waste of time), flowery upland meadows, hospitable shepherds—and one awe-inspiring sight worth all the discomforts. To the north, above a dark jumble of mountains, Layard saw a single white, dazzling cone—Mount Ararat, a hundred and forty-five miles away.[3] It seemed a fit anchorage for the last survivors of a world catastrophe. This country, if one looks down upon it from the air en route from Istanbul to Teheran, presents a formidable landscape: jagged rocks and crumpled brown valleys barren of all life. There is something terrifying, ruthless, and primeval about it. Yet Layard and Rassam found their way through this wilderness, met people living in it, and seem to have enjoyed its stark grandeur. Slowly they jogged on down a narrow gorge, struggled over a cruel pass at eleven thousand feet, to emerge at last among the familiar foothills and reach the burning plain. Layard returned to Mosul on August 30, after a holiday, if one can call it that, of seven weeks.

Chapter XXIII

BABYLON AND NINEVEH
(September 1850–April 1851)

At the end of September Layard wrote to Lord Palmerston asking for leave to return to England in the spring. His second season
of excavation, though it was bound to lack the excitement and
enchantment of brand new discovery, had been even more fruitful
than the first. Nor had he lost interest in the ancient Assyrians.
His expeditions to the Khabur, Kurdistan, and Lake Van had all
been part of a master plan to learn as much as possible about them,
but the Trustees had objected to being charged with the costs, and
he had paid for the trips himself. This misunderstanding was a
new affront to his pride. He was determined for this to be his last
winter of digging in Mesopotamia. Among the puzzles still unan-
swered were several he particularly wished to solve before leaving.
What, for instance, was Nebbi Yunus?

Rawlinson believed it to be the real site of Nineveh, and
Kuyunjik merely a latter-day palace built in the environs. All attempts to excavate at Nebbi Yunus had bogged down in threats
of religious riots. None but a True Believer might enter the tomb
of Jonah (who had somehow turned into a Moslem saint), much
less disturb the sacred soil on which it stood or dig beneath the
village and the Moslem cemetery upon the mound. Through the
friendship of one of the tomb's guardians, Layard had been permitted, in disguise, to take a peak at the sarcophagus, decorated
with a green cloth and dangling ostrich eggs. He did not really care
whether it was the Prophet's tomb or not (it obviously was not);
his interests lay deeper down, and he finally devised a means of

satisfying them. Informed by his spies that a family in the village would like a *sordaub*, he had Toma Shishman offer to dig it gratis in return for any antiquities (other than gold ones) that might be found by the diggers.

He wrote to Sir Henry Ellis: "I am happy to inform you that I have at length succeeded in opening a trench or two in the mound occupied by the Mosque of the Prophet Jonah. Slabs have been discovered and I hope in the course of today to receive a paper impression of an inscription on the back of one of them. This will, I hope, set at rest the question of the comparative antiquity of this ruin and its identification with Nineveh. I shall endeavor to carry my researches a little further and I have information of a spot where sculptures are said to exist. But I cannot visit the mound as it is a very delicate matter and the place is considered so holy that were it known that a Frank were digging there it might lead to unpleasant results." The researches could *not* be carried further, but the inscription gave a tantalizing hint of the mound's possibilities. The palace of at least one Assyrian king existed there. For the present Layard had to be content to know that the name, titles and genealogy of the Nebbi Yunus king were identical with those on the broken bulls in the Southwest Palace at Nimrud.

Next he proposed to examine the mounds in Babylonia and southern Mesopotamia, though he had neither the time nor money to make more than a superficial investigation of them. He wrote to Sir Stratford Canning: "The ruins which I shall explore are so extensive that even many years labor would not suffice for their examination and all I can do is to obtain sufficient data from them to determine their age and to illustrate disputed points of geography and history. As for specimens, all I could carry away would be a *mere fraction* in comparison with what remained. At Nimrud, for instance, there is enough remaining to fill twenty museums, and from the numerous halls which have been uncovered at Kuyunjik, I shall scarcely take away a dozen bas-reliefs as specimens."

The last shipment of sculptures for the British Museum—nearly one hundred cases—was embarked for Baghdad in mid-October.

With it on the rafts went Layard, Hormuzd Rassam, and the thirty best-trained Jebur diggers. In Baghdad Layard learned that the country to the south was in a worse state of disorder than usual—a familiar story by now. He refused to call off his plans, procured letters from the right people in Baghdad to the right sheikhs in the south, and after some delay set out, regretfully leaving Rassam behind, sick in bed. At Hilla, the nearest town to the ruins of Babylon, a spacious and once lovely house had been made ready for him—more or less. With the winter wind whistling through its broken windows, it was itself not much better than a Babylonian ruin. The Pasha of Hilla was ill, but his twelve-year-old son made as good and efficient a governor as Layard had ever seen, arriving promptly with his entourage of secretaries, slaves and other attendants, to welcome the Frank: "We trust that it has pleased God to preserve your Excellency's health," the boy said. "Our town is yours as well as our house. Our harem begs your Excellency's acceptance of sour milk and francolins. May we show that we are your slaves by ordering the irregular troops to accompany you on your ride; your person is more precious to us than our eyes, and there are evil men, enemies of our Lord the Sultan, abroad in the desert."

So evil indeed that Layard's workmen refused to set up camp near the abandoned ruins of Babylon. A sense of mystery and dread hung over the crumbling heaps of brick and sand. Like Nineveh, it had been cursed by the Hebrew prophets. "And Babylon, the glory of kingdoms, the beauty of the Chaldees' excellency, shall be as when God overthrew Sodom and Gomorra," warned Isaiah. "It shall never be inhabited, neither shall it be dwelt in from generation to generation . . . But wild beasts of the desert shall lie there; and their houses shall be full of doleful creatures; and owls shall dwell there, and satyrs shall dance there." The owl's hoot and the lion's roar were still heard in the ruins of Babylon; men far more ferocious than satyrs haunted the underground passages. Not a blade of grass would grow in the peculiar soil, blanched as if with a deadly poison, and the reedy swamps round about breathed a miasma of fever. Alexander the Great, who had intended to rebuild Babylon, had instead been one of its victims.

In 1811 Claudius Rich and his wife, Mary, with a considerable escort to see to their comfort and safety, had spent ten days at Hilla, riding out every day to Babylon. Rich sketched, measured, and employed a few workmen to dig in the temples and palaces of the inner city, on the left bank of the Euphrates. He investigated with little success the great square mound, more like a natural hill than the work of men's hands, which the Arabs named the Tower of Babel. He also visited its rival for that title, Birs Nimrud, another huge heap of brick and potsherds a mile or so from the main ruins. He collected many inscribed bricks for his collection, and made notes for the survey that was to arouse so much interest in Europe, and which remained the basis for the exploration of Babylon for many years to come.

Layard collected a good many small objects at Babylon but accomplished little else. He agreed with Rich that the dimensions of the walls given by Herodotus (480 stadia, or nearly 60 miles in circumference) did not tally with the present remains, and that the temples, palaces and bridges attributed by the Greek writer to the fabled queens Semiramis and Nicrotis were more likely to have been built in the second period of Babylonian power under Nebuchadnezzar. There had been a cemetery among the ruins for ages past; he reopened several passages in the Babel mound and found coffins similar to one discovered by Rich. The corpses smelled so frightful that even the Arab workmen could not stand it; they were not very antique. He found bowls, painted with Hebrew characters, which probably dated from the time when the Jewish exiles sat by the waters of Babylon and wept. There were also many relics of Alexander and the Seleucids. Since there were no stone quarries nearby, there were no sculptured slabs; the walls had been decorated with enameled bricks in bright colors. Ordinary bricks were stamped with the builder's name in a manner prophetic of printing, instead of being incised with a sharp instrument in the Assyrian manner. All Babylon was a vast brick heap, which was beyond Layard's patience, skill, or financial capacity to explore properly. He wrote to Sir Henry Ellis that the chances of finding inscriptions in these spread-out ruins, already tunneled in so many directions, did not justify the amount that a thorough search would cost. He estimated that £25,000 ($125,000) would be required to excavate Babylon, and remarked that if Parliament should assign such a sum, he "would solicit the favour of not being charged with its application." His pessimism was not disproved till Dr. Koldewey and his German team, who excavated at Babylon from 1899 to 1914, developed their technique of tracing mud-brick walls, and drew the picture, for the world to see, of what Nebuchadnezzar's Babylon had looked like. The "Ishtar Gate," brilliantly reconstructed, stands today in Berlin's *Staatliche Museen*.

Layard visited Birs Nimrud only briefly. Due to the state of the country, no workmen could be induced to excavate there. Early Christian and Jewish travelers, including Benjamin of Tudela, believed it the original Tower of Babel, and pointed to the mass of oxidized brick and slag at the base of the mound as proof that the Lord, angry at his people's presumption, had sent a thunderbolt to split the tower to its foundations. Layard thought Birs Nimrud the wrong shape for a tower, and too solidly constructed to be a palace. He proposed that it had consisted of a series of terraces, rising one above the other, with broad flights of steps or inclined ramps carried up the center of each stage—not a bad description of a ziggurat, which this was. Rawlinson later found inscribed on a brick from Birs Nimrud the name Borsippa, which he knew to be "a high-place of Chaldean worship." It was to the ziggurat of Borsippa that the god Nabu descended from heaven; and from thence, once a year, he went to visit his father-god, Marduk, in the ziggurat at Babylon—the other mound rumored to be the Tower of Babel. According to Herodotus, a room at the very top of the tower was furnished with a golden table and a large bed, to which was brought a beautiful Babylonian woman to be Marduk's mate for one night.

From the summit of Birs Nimrud, Layard looked out over the malarial swampland called by the Arabs "the Desert of Waters." In the distance could faintly be seen reed huts planted on small islands which swarmed with people who looked, from this distance, like the swarming insects which constantly plagued them. Ancient Babylon, built on both sides of the Euphrates, had been defended by marshes, but also supported by land drained to become fertile farms. After the city's fall, the great engineering works of Babylonia were neglected, the irrigation canals became choked up, and the rivers overflowed. Abandoned cities crumbled away on patches of barren sand between the desert and the swamp, and were known now only by their Arab names: Niffer, Warka, Al Muqayyar (where Woolley later excavated Ur, Abraham's home city). Difficult as this country was to cross, a few Europeans had ventured into it: first of all Baillie-Fraser, whose books Layard had admired as a youth, and more recently, William Kennett Loftus, geological member of the Turco-Persian Border Commission. Loftus, with an escort of troops, had gone overland from Baghdad to join the other members at Basrah, and, with the backing of the Commission, had returned later to make some small excavations at Warka.

Much interested by Loftus' report, Layard wished to see these sites for himself. Accordingly, he sent a message to Agab, Sheikh of the Afaij Arabs who lived in the marshes fifty miles south of Babylon, requesting protection and guides. On January 15 he left Hilla with his workmen and two Afaij guides who insisted on making a long, tedious detour toward the center of the Mesopotamian desert in order to avoid the hostile tribes that usually congregated along the river. But at last, on a cold winter day of crystal clearness, the mirage of a mountain range rose out of the bright green swamp grass before them—the 180-acre complex of low sandy mounds that covered Niffer (ancient Nippur). From the edge of the swamp, primitive boats of rushes coated with black tar transported Layard through a labyrinth of waterways to the headquarters of Sheikh Agab, a village of yellow reed huts shaped like boilers cut in half. The huts and the mud-built bazaar stood on a low island, in a jungle of marsh grass; even a minor flood would wipe out the village. Buffalo wallowed in mire along its banks; ducks and geese quacked and honked about its doorsteps; kingfishers swung on the tasseled rushes or plunged with a splash into the water. It was all very reminiscent of Sheikh Thamer's settlement further south, and of those sad but exciting days with Mehemet Taki Khan and the lovely Khanumi.

Sheikh Agab, dark-skinned, friendly, gowned in red silk and a gold-embroidered cloak, found a dry spot for Layard's tent, and in less than an hour raised straw cabins for the workmen. He would by no means allow his guests to camp at Niffer, where Jinns and evil spirits swarmed out of the ruins after dark, to say nothing of Bedouin cut-throats. So for the three weeks during which Layard explored Niffer, he was forced to commute six miles by slow boat, morning and evening. The finds were unimportant: broken jars and bowls and some curious post-Babylonian sarcophagi of blue-green faïence that Loftus had also reported. Again Layard's failure would be reversed by the scientific methods and greater financial resources of a later day. The field director of the expedition sponsored by the Museum of the University of Pennsylvania in 1897 lacked one valuable asset which Layard possessed *par excellence*—tact with the Arabs. The first season of the Pennsylvania expedition ended with the burning and looting of its camp by the Afaij, whom the director had offended. In the three seasons, however, over thirty thousand inscribed tablets were found, including the largest known number of Sumerian mythological and literary texts. The Sumerian legends of Paradise, the Fall of Man, and the Flood, probably set down in the beginning of the second millennium from an older oral tradition, were the forerunners of the Assyrian stories discovered at Nineveh. They, too, present parallels to the Bible. Another expedition to Nippur, sent by the Oriental Institute of the University of Chicago a little over a hundred years after Layard's visit, worked back through layers to the twenty-fourth century B.C., revealing twenty cities superimposed upon each other.

Warka has also been excavated; it is the site of Biblical Erech, one of the earliest cities of Sumer, with a radio-carbon dating of about 4000 B.C. Layard was obliged to give up the idea of investigating Warka. Sheikh Agab and other tribal leaders who gathered nightly in the *musif* to offer the Frank their advice, strongly urged him not to try it. Agab had no control over the outlaw bands that infested the Desert of Waters and could not protect Layard from their depredations. In fact the country was in such a state that he begged his guest to return to Baghdad as soon as possible, else he would be cut off from it by the marauding Bedouin. Layard might have been stubborn enough to disregard advice as he had done so often in the past, but this time he was too ill to insist on having his own way. Agab's movable capital in the swamp was not the healthiest place for one suffering from chronic malaria. It was the rainy season, and Layard's tent leaked. Even though he took heroic measures, doctoring himself with a "blistering fluid" meant for injured horses, he was completely knocked out. When Hormuzd Rassam, recovered from his own bout, arrived, Layard managed somehow to hoist himself into the saddle and depart. He had only enough strength to reach the gates of Baghdad before collapsing. Such was his stamina that after a few days of medical care and comforts he was ready for fresh adventures. But, he wrote to Sir Henry Ellis regretfully, it would be months before any full exploration of the ruins in southern Mesopotamia would be possible. "I had some difficulty in getting back to Baghdad. Eight of the workmen who accompanied me from Mosul, having remained behind on the road, were stripped to the skin, beaten, and two wounded."

Between Baghdad and Mosul, he stopped off at Kalah Sherghat to check on what had been accomplished by a party of Jeburs whom he had sent there to excavate. When he and Rassam rode down over the shoulder of the Gebel Makhul to the mound beside the Tigris, the workmen scattered in terror, taking them for Bedouin raiders. This part of the desert was in armed rebellion also. The danger and expense were not justified by the finds; Layard shortly withdrew his men. Here again later excavators reaped the success that evaded him. The *Deutsche Orient Gesellschaft*, mostly under the directorship of Dr. Walter Andrae, excavated at Kalah Sherghat from 1902 till the start of the World War I, and identified it as Ashur, the first capital of Assyria.

On his return to Mosul, Layard was delighted to find there
T. S. Bell, the artist whom he had requested as replacement for
Cooper. Bell was young, inexperienced, and, it turned out, fool-
hardy. (Some months later he was drowned while swimming in
the mountain torrent at Bavian, where he had been sent to copy
inscriptions.) Accompanied by Bell, Layard rode to Kuyunjik to
examine discoveries made in his absence. Among them, by a curious
coincidence, was a series of bas-reliefs illustrating a campaign
against marsh people, with a background of wicker boats identical
with those of the Afaij, the same jungle of reeds and date-palms,
the same waterways teeming with fish and crabs. Another series
of bas-reliefs represented the conquest of Susiana or Elam, and
still another, the fall of a city in southern Babylonia. Chamber
after chamber at Kuyunjik was lined with a recital in sculpture and
inscription of Sennacherib's victories and the horrors he inflicted
upon the vanquished: burning, beheading, flaying, ripping out of
tongues. Layard, as he walked through those halls, was reminded
of how Isaiah had begged the Lord to turn away the hand of this
king of Assyria, who had "laid waste all the nations" from His city
of Jerusalem.

And so it came to pass. Less than a century later, Nineveh itself
had been laid waste. Mixed with hundreds of Assyrian artifacts
which were scattered through the passageways of the palace, was
the spoor of all the armies—Persian, Greek, Roman, Sassanian—
which since its fall had camped among the ruins of Nineveh. The
small village on Kuyunjik described by Benjamin of Tudela had
been wiped out by Timur's hordes at the end of the fourteenth
century, and after that men dwelt there no longer. Dust covered
all, and Zepheniah's prophecy was fulfilled:

*And he will stretch out his hand against the north, and destroy
Assyria; and will make Nineveh a desolation, and dry like a wilderness . . . This is the rejoicing city that dwelt carelessly, that said in
her heart, I am, and there is none beside me: how is she become a
desolation, a place for beasts to lie down in! And everyone that
passeth by her shall hiss, and wag his hand.*

So the ruins of Nineveh, sealed beneath the earth, remained undisturbed through the centuries. In spite of the legends, no one had bothered to investigate the mounds until Henry Layard, inquisitive, romantic, and determined, pried into their secret. By his own calculations, he had unearthed nearly two miles of bas-reliefs at Kuyunjik alone, and twenty-seven portals formed by colossal beasts. He had opened up seventy-one rooms, most of them paneled with sculptures and inscriptions. He had found the first great collection of cuneiform tablets. A big task lay before him still: to set down in book form the significance of his discoveries. Others, among them his assistant and good friend Hormuzd Rassam, would take up the spade which he had laid down.

That he felt some bitterness over the opportunities he had been obliged to forego is indicated by the briefness of his concluding remarks: "The time was drawing near for my departure. Once more I was about to leave the ruins amidst which I had spent so many happy hours, and to which I was bound by so many pleasant and solemn ties; and probably to return no more. On the 28th of April I bid a last farewell to my faithful Arab friends, and with a heavy heart turned from the ruins of ancient Nineveh."

Chapter XXIV

EPILOGUE

(1851–1894)

Henry Layard's welcome home was quite different from that of four years before. The popular success of *Nineveh and Its Remains* had made his name well known in England; the public had followed his more recent discoveries step by step. Among those eager to receive him were Benjamin and Sara Austen. He quietly ignored them and went straight to the home of Lady Guest. He makes no mention in his published works either of the Austens' earlier lack of sympathy or their changed attitude once he was a celebrity. He continued to call upon Sara Austen at intervals till the day she died. She lived to be ninety-two, and must often have regretted her mistaken judgment of the nephew who might have made her salons a success. Even Benjamin Disraeli had deserted her as he went up in the world—but Henry Layard, the boy he had snubbed, was to be rewarded by him with an important diplomatic post and the Grand Cross of the Bath.

Honors were not long in reaching the man who had discovered Nineveh. The public came in droves to see the "Nineveh Court" at the great Crystal Palace Exhibition of 1851. In this glorification of commercial empire under Good Queen Victoria and her Prince Consort, the grandiose reconstruction of an Assyrian Palace was one of the most popular shows. As described in the pamphlet that Layard wrote for the occasion, it had a lower façade copied from what was known of the palaces at Kuyunjik and Khorsabad, embellished with winged, human-headed bulls and giant figures of Gilgamesh (still not known by that name). All were plaster casts except two Khorsabad bulls at the main entrance, which Rawlinson had been able to buy from the French. Above the façade were battlements and columns with capitals of kneeling bulls copied from Persepolis (not Assyrian at all). A portal leading into a central hall was formed by two bulls modeled on those at Nimrud. Around the walls were casts of the bas-reliefs, and a frieze of glazed brick copied from Khorsabad. The taste of the architect (not Layard) was eclectic, to say the least.

Layard brought out a popular abridgment of *Nineveh and Its Remains* soon after his return to England. This, the Crystal Palace Exhibition, and the idea of the Assyrian discoveries in general fired the public imagination to a degree hardly surpassed by the furor over "King Tut's" tomb in the 1920s. Nineveh was the subject for prize essays in schools, the theme of contemporary poems, including a fulsome bit of praise by the notorious figure whom Layard had admired in his youth, Walter Savage Landor:

> . . . *My song shall rise,*
> *Altho' none heed or hear it; rise it shall,*
> *And swell along the wastes of Nineveh*
> *And Babylon, until it reach to thee,*
> *Layard! who raisest cities from the dust,*
> *Who driest Lethe up and her shades,*
> *And pourest a fresh stream on arid sands,*
> *And rescuest thrones and nations, fanes and gods*
> *From conquering Time; he sees thee and turns back.*

The figures of an earlier poet's imagination—Byron's Assyrian cohorts "gleaming with purple and gold"—came to life in fascinating detail in engravings and sketches in the daily papers. There was something for everybody in the Assyrian sculptures. The elaborate, patterned costumes and accessories accorded well with Victorian taste. The faces and bodies of the Assyrians had a brutal power that came as a thrilling shock to those accustomed to the sentimental in art. Yet the gigantic bulls were as solid and dignified as John Bull himself. There was a fascination for the conventional Victorians in the wicked, especially since the wicked got their just deserts. The prudish, however, were not *too* shocked; though debauchery and the "degrading" worship of Ishtar were hinted at, there was "an absence of unseemly symbols on the Assyrian monuments." And for the devout there was the satisfaction of seeing Bible history proved true. "Nineveh, in point of fact, was no longer a waste," writes R. Campbell Thompson, one of its later excavators, "and its ruins over which the Hebrew prophet had so exulted were known to far more inhabitants of the globe in the middle of the last century than the teeming, living city itself in the very heyday of its imperial dominance."[1]

The young man responsible for this did not know, a few months after his return home, what to do next or how to support himself. "I shall certainly not leave England again if I can help it," he wrote to H. J. Ross, now commercial partner of the British Consul at Samsun, "but I may be forced to do so, as, at present, at any rate, I have no means of making ends meet without some employment." *Nineveh and Its Remains* continued to bring in a little income, but not enough. The writing of his new book went slowly, impeded by Layard's conviction that his reputation as a writer had been much exaggerated, and that he would never be able to live up to his first success. *Discoveries in the Ruins of Nineveh and Babylon* came out in 1853, and by July of that year almost twelve thousand copies had been sold. Layard was gratified, but as it had been brought out at a reasonable rate, it did not give him a large return. A *Second Series of the Monuments of Nineveh*, engraved from the drawings of Layard, Cooper, and Bell, was also issued in 1853, a beautiful and expensive art folio which few could afford to buy. Layard had in any case no intention of making his living as a professional writer, even though as a boy he had briefly cherished that ambition.

He had always been interested in social welfare and in politics; he was, among other things, a reformer at heart. "I should like to get into Parliament in England, and think that, if once there, I could push my way," he wrote to Ross. He had done no more than think about entering politics when, to everyone's surprise including his own, he was offered an appointment by Earl Granville, the Foreign Secretary. "I have just been named Under-Secretary of State for Foreign Affairs," he wrote in a letter on February 11, 1852. "I enter upon duties of such great importance with a deep conviction of the immense responsibility imposed upon me, and an earnest desire to discharge them to the good of my country . . . You know I have never sought for advancement, and I owe nothing to interest and connection." This was true; he had come a long way from being a penniless law clerk, without asking for favors or pulling strings. His first step in politics barely got inside the door; six days later the Liberal government fell. Layard however was asked to stay under the short-lived Tory administration of Lord Derby. When Parliament was dissolved, it seemed to Layard an opportune moment for him to seek a seat. He had several offers, and after due thought, decided to run as Liberal candidate for Aylesbury, to which he had sentimental attachments. His parents had lived there, his father had died there, he knew at least some of his future constituents. Though Aylesbury was considered safely Tory, he was elected by a large majority, carrying the other Liberal candidate in with him. "I never saw such a scene of triumph as our chairing procession," Layard writes from Canford on July 9, 1852. "Every window was full of well-dressed ladies, showering down bouquets of flowers, sending cakes and wine, waving flags, etc." He continued to represent Aylesbury till 1857. Meanwhile other honors descended upon him. He received the freedom of the City of London in 1853, and the honorary post of Lord Rector of Aberdeen University in 1855.

In the spring of 1853, at the request of the Grand Elchi (now Lord Stratford de Redcliffe) he returned briefly to Constantinople, which was more of a storm center than ever. The trouble between Russia and Turkey, of which he had written years before, was now threatening the peace in earnest. Layard's experience in that part of the world should have made him valuable to the British Ambassador, but for some reason they no longer saw eye to eye. Layard returned to England, and tried in a series of questions and a speech in the House to awaken the government to the dangers involved—dangers which would soon erupt into the Crimean War. This did not endear him to Prime Minister Gladstone and members of his non-interventionist Cabinet. When war was declared in the following year, Layard went out to the Crimea to see it himself, and witnessed the battle of Alma from the main top of H.M.S. *Agamemnon*. Although he spoke out in Parliament in favor of a vote of thanks to the soldiers and sailors who had fought so bravely, he gained fresh disapproval by declaring publicly that maladministration and social favoritism had cost many English lives.

Among others, he criticized the Commander-in-chief of the fleet, in a letter inadvertently published, which caused a scandal and drew angry retaliation from the Admiral's friends. The tact with which he had handled primitive tribesmen so superbly quite deserted him in dealing with his political peers. If Henry Layard took up a cause, he pursued it with the same reckless stubbornness that he had exhibited in his search for ancient ruins. Naturally a kind man, his manner grew vehement and brusque when he was opposed. Of course, he was right about the conduct of the Crimean War, as history has proved. Ross, at Samsun and Constantinople, had a close view of affairs because his firm did a big business in provisions and animals for the Army. He wrote to his sister Mary (January 17, 1855): "Our men are dying of famine and exposure at a frightful rate; and all might have been averted by the simplest foresight and care . . . From Alison and another member of the Embassy I was glad to hear that they consider Layard's position a good one; that he is playing a high and difficult game, but with a fair chance of winning it. To have obtained the name he has got, without making more enemies, is alone a great point."

He had enemies enough. Public life in England, he wrote to Ross, was a tempestuous sea, in which it was difficult to steer clear of the rocks and sandbanks. He was too truculent, too uncompromising to make a successful politician. Few of his own class would agree with him and with Ross that "the power of our aristocracy must go and men be chosen for their fitness." Layard was too liberal for his own Liberal Party, while the Opposition certainly did not approve of him. But the people did. One of his targets—

Sir Charles Augustus Murray, a British diplomat accused of a scandal in Persia—referred to him waspishly as "Mr. Oracle Layard, whom the public in England look upon as an oracle in all political questions in Asia because he was the energetic excavator of antiquities at Nineveh."

During a meeting at the Drury Lane Theatre which he organized to protest the conduct of the Crimean War, the hit of the evening was a supporting speech by Mr. Charles Dickens. The two had met in Naples during the summer of 1853 while Dickens was on holiday after finishing *Bleak House.* "We ascended Vesuvius in the sunlight and came down in the moonlight, talking merrily," says Dickens. Both being "new men," both reformers, they had much to talk about; these conversations probably influenced *Hard Times,* the book that Dickens was then planning. Dickens backed Layard's attempt to press for Administrative Reform in his own periodical, *Household Words,* and by speaking to the editors of *Punch,* the *Weekly Chronicle,* and the *Illustrated London News.* But in Parliament Lord Palmerston did everything to block the motion which Layard wished to present. When he finally got it before the House, it was defeated 359 to 46.

The friendship between Layard and Dickens was not always on such a serious level. Among Layard's private papers are numerous notes and invitations from Dickens, including one asking him to dine "at a quarter after six, and see the New Year in with such extemporaneous follies of an exploded sort (in genteel society) as may occur to us." In summer Layard frequently visited Dickens in the country, where one of their amusements was to play "a violent game of croquet." Among his intimates Layard was affectionately known as "Mr. Bull." His friends were drawn, as one would expect, from among the well-established writers and painters of his day. Being handsome, single, charming, and now famous, he was also much lionized by society, and liked to repay his dinner-party and week-end hostesses with a bit of Assyrian art. For this he has been severely criticized, but he had shipped so much that the Museum could not use it all, and in those days, helping oneself to a bit of what one dug up was considered no crime.

After failing in his efforts to reorganize the War Office and institute Administrative Reform, he was soon hot on another trail. In March 1857, when he was not returned to Parliament, he traveled East again, to investigate the Indian Mutiny. His letters show unusual insight (for that time) into conditions which years later would bring about the end of British rule in India. Layard, dubbed "a Liberal imperialist" by his friends, was not in favor of so drastic a change as Indian independence, but he recognized the Indians' hatred of their British rulers, and feared it would not be ameliorated by transfer of authority from the East India Company to the Crown. The Mutiny, he realized, had been a general rebellion rather than a mere military uprising. "We differ from the people in everything which might form a bond of sympathy between a conquered people and their rulers; in language, religion, manners, habits and feelings," he wrote to Mrs. Austen. "We have done nothing to form any other bond of sympathy, or to create mutual interests. The people we govern are treated like a distinct race, inferior to us—more, indeed, as if they were a lower order of creatures; not always actually unkindly, though in too many instances with brutality, but with that sort of kindness which would be shown to a pet animal. They are excluded from all share of government, they can never rise to anything beyond the most inferior posts. We have Sanitary Commissioners and Boards interfering with all their private and domestic affairs, no doubt all for their own good, although they won't understand it. All we have really given them in return is perfect security, and that is certainly a great boon. Under it, money-lenders and fat Parsees and Baboos can make their fortunes and enjoy them; but the cultivators—and there is no one else in India, our rule having utterly destroyed the native gentry—are reduced to the utmost poverty."

Such statements were not calculated to make Layard popular with the usual Foreign Service official, who did not regard Asians as anything other than the White Man's Burden. Layard stood for Parliament again (representing York) in 1859; he was unsuccessful but later was elected for Southwark. In spite of the remarks which had gained him enemies in some quarters, he had made such a name for himself that in 1861 Lord Palmerston appointed him to his former post of Under-Secretary for Foreign Affairs, a term of office which lasted till the fall of his Government in 1866. Among the troublesome affairs which came up during this period was the Abyssinian War. King Theodore of Abyssinia had imprisoned in chains a number of English missionaries and consular officers; Layard recommended that Hormuzd Rassam, who had always been so wise in dealing with "natives," be sent to negotiate. Rassam showed great patience and courage, but the only result was that the mad king threw him in chains also. Liberation of the prisoners was finally accomplished by an English expedition against Abyssinia.

When Gladstone became Prime Minister in 1868, Layard was appointed Chief Commissioner of Works and admitted to the Privy Council. The appointment was a tribute to his taste, since one of the duties was to supervise the erection of new public buildings. Delighted, Layard declared they would be embellished in the best Italian style. This immediately involved him in a dispute with the Parliamentary Secretary of the Treasury, who did not think public money should be squandered on "painters, sculpturers, architects, and market-gardeners." Mr. Gladstone solved the embarrassing struggle between two strong-minded members of his administration by appointing Layard Minister Plenipotentiary at the Court of Madrid. A *Punch* cartoon shows "Don Layardos in Madrid"—a dignified bearded gentleman in diplomatic uniform and plumed hat, riding a Nineveh bull, to cheers of "Bravo Toro!" from the Spanish populace.

In that same year, 1859, he married Enid Guest,* daughter of his first cousin, Lady Charlotte Guest of Canford Manor. A marble bust in the British Museum shows her to be a lovely young woman, with a classic style of beauty. She was tall, stately, blue-eyed, and half the age of her distinguished second cousin. Layard was then fifty-two, only five years younger than his mother-in-law to be. In

---

* She signed herself with this name and was known by it all her life, though officially listed in the National Dictionary of Biography as Mary Evelyn Guest.

spite of his long-standing friendship with the parents, they at first opposed the marriage, but Enid got her way by threatening to go into a decline. The age difference was not at all unusual in those days; Sir Henry Rawlinson and H. J. Ross also married younger women when they had finished their sojourns in the East. Layard was a robust personality who remained active and youthful in his enthusiasms; the marriage was a singularly happy one.

Canford, a former medieval ruin, had been remodeled by Sir John Guest into a neo-Gothic castle, and to this was now added the Nineveh Porch—actually a small museum, with an entrance flanked by a winged bull and a winged lion, and with bas-reliefs within; all surplus Assyrian sculpture presented by Layard to his father-in-law. When, in 1914, a descendant of Sir John sold the estate, the colossal beasts were acquired for the Metropolitan Museum of Art in New York, where they now stand on either side of a reconstructed Assyrian portal. Correctly there should be two beasts of one kind, but the twins of the Metropolitan's bull and lion are in the British Museum; they are the two that Layard moved from Nimrud first, with so much stress and celebration. Canford subsequently became a boys' school; in 1956 Sir Leonard Woolley spotted on the walls of the "tuck-shop," whitewashed over and hidden behind packets of cereal and piles of cricket shirts, seven bas-reliefs from the palace of Sennacherib at Nineveh. Sold in 1959 for fourteen thousand pounds, these were dispersed to Oxford, Switzerland, the United States, and the British Museum.[2]

Layard was appointed a Trustee of the Museum in 1866, but he did not get along any better with his fellow Trustees than with his political colleagues. After his marriage, the study of Italian art became more and more of a major interest, and he gradually withdrew from Assyriology. For some years he had been in the habit of taking a holiday abroad each summer, mostly in Italy, as in his youth, and there he discovered a new amusement: to make tracings of details in the Italian frescoes. For four successive years thereafter, he contributed monographs on the fourteenth- and fifteenth-century masters of fresco to the annual publication of the Arundel Society, an association for the appreciation of art. The Society had been dying, for lack of appreciative members; Layard's popular monographs, with their splendid reproductions in chromo-lithography, set it on its feet again. His companions on his holiday travels read like a Who's Who of the arts: there was the famous painter Sir John Millais; Sir Edward Bulwer Lytton, the novelist; Sir Charles Eastlake, president of the Royal Academy; Tom Taylor, editor of *Punch*; the latter's sister-in-law, Miss Parker, who sketched while Layard traced, and other congenial souls who passed the time "most agreeably" visiting Italian villas, museums and churches, with Layard as cicerone. He bought a painting for himself, a female head attributed to Palma Vecchio. Being in Italy in 1859, and being Layard, a man who could never be without one or more causes, he became involved emotionally and intellectually if not physically, in the upheavals attendant on the unification of the country under Victor Emmanuel. "I have so much to do with politics, that I have had little time for the arts," he wrote to Mrs. Austen.

In 1877 Layard was appointed ambassador to Turkey. Although a Liberal, his political opinions on Eastern Europe agreed with those of the Conservative Prime Minister, Lord Beaconsfield, whom, in his boyhood, he had known as the eccentric young writer Benjamin Disraeli. In the following year, on Beaconsfield's recommendation, he was knighted and received the G. C. B. Sayce, then a young Oxford don, dined at the British Embassy in Constantinople in 1879, and was regaled by the Ambassador with a number of tales not included in his published works. When Sayce remarked on the brilliant company at dinner, Sir Henry answered: "I owe it all to my old friend Grace who is sitting opposite us; when I first visited Constantinople, I often did not know where to look for a dinner." He explained that, before he became connected with the Embassy, Sir Stratford Canning had recommended him as dragoman for young Grace, the son of a rich Alexandrian merchant, who wished to tour Asia Minor. The Ambassador also told a story of being captured by the Bedouin East of Jordan and kept as a slave for six months. One suspects Sir Henry of pulling the leg of the scholar who was on his way "East at last," and as starry-eyed about it as the young Layard had been. Sayce gives us no report on Lady Layard other than to say that she did not appear at dinner due to a severe illness from which all the company suffered somewhat as a result of eating a delicious-looking (though greenish) cake prepared by an Embassy cook who had a grudge against one of the tea party.[3]

Ahmed Vefyk Pasha, who, at seventeen, had declared that he would some day be Grand Vizier, was promoted (still quoting Pickwick) to that post during Layard's tenure of office. Their long-standing friendship could hardly have been to the Ambassador's disadvantage. "Sir Henry had stepped into the position formerly held by 'the Great Elchi' Lord Stratford de Redcliffe, and was now omnipotent in Turkey," writes Sayce. "The Turks regarded him as a friend; he was acquainted with their language, habits, manners and ideas; he was, moreover, a man of extraordinary vigor, who had made his own way in the world, unspoilt by the debilitating atmosphere of the British diplomatic service. Just now he was called upon to carry out the conditions of the convention with Turkey which would give us possession of Cyprus."

While ambassador, Layard paid a return visit to Damascus, where, almost forty years before, he had arrived penniless, ragged, a fugitive from the Turkish quarantine guards, at the home of the British Consul. This time the whole population turned out to line the streets and cheer him as he entered the city: Christians, Jews, Turks, Arabs—a reception such as no other European, whatever his rank, had ever received in Turkish territory, a spontaneous tribute which pleased and flattered him.

Sir Henry Layard left public life on Gladstone's return to power in 1880. It cannot be said that he "retired." He was in his early sixties, Lady Layard not yet forty. Both enjoyed social life and shuttled back and forth between England and Italy according to the season and social events. Lady Layard has left a journal describing those busy years. They made their headquarters in Venice, where Sir Henry collected paintings, mostly of the Venetian School, and wrote on art. Even in this, he was not a conservative like most men of his age. He became a close friend and, in

matters of art, a disciple of Giovanni Morelli, Italian patriot, supporter of Cavour, proponent of the theory of art criticism diametrically opposed to the views of his most distinguished
contemporaries. Morelli claimed that judgment of paintings must
be scientific, based on reason and analysis of the pictures themselves. Historical, documentary, and traditional knowledge should
be secondary. Academic as this sounds to us, Morelli's theories
caused a furor. When he died in 1891, Layard contributed a bio-
graphical sketch to the first English translation of Morelli's studies.
In the same year he brought out his revision, according to Morelli's
ideas, of Kugler's *Handbook of Painting, the Italian Schools*. His
own delightful travelbook, written from old journals and notes,
Early Adventures in Persia, Susiana and Babylonia, had been published in 1887.

In 1893, at the age of seventy-six, Layard appeared in a London
courtroom as witness in a lawsuit which had the Trustees of the
British Museum and most of the intelligentsia of the city by the
ears. His former assistant, Hormuzd Rassam, had excavated in
Assyria and Babylonia on behalf of the Museum during two separate periods: the first immediately following Layard's departure
from Mosul, the second, from 1878 to 1882, when Layard, as Ambassador to the Porte, had been largely responsible for his appointment. Rassam, though sincere in his aims, was inexperienced as a
director and too ambitious; dozens of sites were opened on his
orders without his personal supervision; many were superficially
excavated and then abandoned. It is not surprising that antiquities
(cuneiform tablets in particular) began to find their way into the
commercial market instead of to the British Museum. In 1888,
Ernest Wallis Budge, then an assistant in the Museum's Department of Oriental Antiquities, was sent out to investigate. On his
return, Budge declared that the best antiquities were passing into
the hands of the dealers through Hormuzd Rassam's negligence if
not his connivance. Rassam sued Budge for slander; Layard, naturally, rallied to the side of his friend and assistant, whom he had
always trusted, and with whom he had shared so many dangers of
the road, bouts of fever, and all the irritations and frustrations

of the work at Nineveh. At the conclusion of the case, the *Daily
News* reported: "Mr. Rassam has obtained a verdict for fifty
pounds in his action against Mr. Budge of the British Museum.
It is enough . . . Sir Henry Layard and Mr. Renouf gave evidence
on behalf of Mr. Rassam, and the trial was in some respects a
sort of antiquarian festival. These distinguished persons have not
been in the intimacy of Ashurbanipal for nothing. Their measures
of time are not as our measures. Otherwise the better part of a
week would hardly have been devoted to such a case."

Austen Henry Layard died in London on July 5, 1894. H. J.
Ross's wife, Janet, wrote on this occasion: "A sentence in one of
his letters to me as a young girl: 'I *am* always getting into hot
water!' was only too true. He had many enemies, but far more
friends who loved him deeply, and felt how much sunshine had
gone out from their lives with the loss of his handsome, cheery
face, with those kind blue eyes, and the hearty shake of his helpful
hand."[4]

Chapter XXV

A SUMMING UP

The last chapter of *Nineveh and Babylon* (published in 1853)
is a beginning chapter in the study of Assyriology. In it Layard
sums up what had been learned of the ancient Assyrians in the ten
years since Botta's message from Khorsabad. He calls it a sketch,
and that is what it is, for the whole story was still not known. The
deciphering of Assyrio-Babylonian cuneiform, though much advanced since the publication of *Nineveh and Its Remains* in 1849
was not, and would not be for many years, completely solved. The
Babylonian inscription from Behistun had provided a key to it, and
Layard's *Inscriptions in the Cuneiform Character*, ninety-eight
plates issued in 1851, made available much more material for study.
In addition there were the many original inscribed slabs and
clay tablets now safely deposited in the British Museum.

Writing in 1851–53, when the meaning of many of the texts
had only been guessed at, Layard made some accurate deductions.
The names of Ashurnasirpal and other kings not mentioned in
Scripture were still uncertain; their cuneiform symbols could be
recognized by eye, but could not be reproduced phonetically with
any degree of accuracy. Layard's reasoning is intricate and lengthy;
for the contemporary reader, a sample should suffice: "The earliest
king of whom we have any detailed account [Ashurnasirpal] was
the builder of the Northwest Palace at Nimrud, the most ancient
edifice hitherto discovered in Assyria. His records, with other inscriptions, furnish the names of five, if not seven, of his predecessors, some of whom, there is reason to believe, erected palaces at

Nineveh, and originally founded those which were only rebuilt by
subsequent monarchs . . . His son, we know, built the central
palace at Nimrud, and raised the obelisk, now in the British
Museum, inscribing upon it the principal events of his reign. The
names of the subject kings who paid him tribute are duly recorded
on the obelisk . . . Amongst those kings was one who has been
identified by Dr. Hincks and Col. Rawlinson with Jehu, king of
Israel . . . Jehu ascended the throne about 885 B.C.; the accession of the Assyrian monarch must, consequently, be placed somewhere between that time and the commencement of the nineth
century B.C. and that of his father in the latter part of the tenth."
These dates are only about fifty years out of the way—a small error
actually due to the then accepted Biblical dates. Sennacherib's
accession to the throne, which Dr. Hincks dated quite accurately
as 703 B.C., taken with data from the Bavian monument, gave a
further basis for chronology. Indeed a remarkable amount *had*
been figured out in the brief period since the discovery of Khorsabad.

A paper by Rawlinson entitled *History of Assyria as collected
from the inscriptions discovered by Austen Henry Layard, Esq.,
in the ruins of Nineveh* was presented at the Royal Asiatic Society
in 1852. Layard was present to hear it read, but Rawlinson himself
was in Baghdad for his second term as Resident. In a letter dated
"at the camp, Nineveh, 11 April 1852," Rawlinson stated that the
paper had been drawn up "in great haste, amid torrents of rain,
in a little tent upon the mound of Nineveh without any aids
beyond a pocket Bible, a note-book of inscriptions, and a tolerably
retentive memory." He identified Nimrud as Calah; and Kuyunjik,
Nebbi Yunus, and their attendant ramparts as Nineveh. He found
the name of the builder of the Northwest Palace at Nimrud open
to discussion. The first of the three characters which represented it
was known to stand for Assyria and Ashur, its chief god, but as for
the whole, Dr. Hincks suggested Ashurakbal, while Rawlinson
preferred Assardanbal, or Sardanapalus. (One can hardly blame
those nineteenth-century experts for stumbling over a name which
only recently has been changed in scholarly works from the long-

accepted Ashurnasirpal to Aššûr-nasir-apli, meaning "Ashur [is] the protector of the heir.")[1]

Although still subject to revision, particularly in the matter of dates, the history of the Land between the Rivers, like that of Greece and Rome, is now a textbook affair. This long story, almost unknown when Layard began to dig at Nimrud in 1845, grows longer each year, as his successors, the field archaeologists, and Rawlinson's successors, the philologists, push back the frontiers of knowledge. Out of the deserts, malarial swamps, and haunts of the wild Bedouin, which caused such trouble for Layard, diggers have raised the cities of Sumer and Akkad: Nippur, Erech, Ur, Larsa, Kish, and innumerable layers of prehistory stretching thousands of years further back in time.

The fourth millennium B.C. marks the rise of civilization in Mesopotamia; the Sumerians drained the swamps, irrigated the deserts, developed foreign trade, and invented a form of writing (perhaps the earliest in the world). For some centuries, power seesawed back and forth between the kings of Sumer and the kings of Akkad and Babylon. Ashur (Kala Sherghat) was a city by 3500 B.C. or earlier, populated by colonists from Sumer, or perhaps by Hittites. About 2070 B.C. the first ruler of Ashur is mentioned in the inscriptions (his name is Puzur-Ashur, "the tenant farmer of Ashur"), and from then on there is a nearly complete list of rulers' names. In the middle of the second millennium, at a time of foreign invasion and general disruption, the kings of Ashur broke away completely from southern domination and set out on their militarist and imperialist course.

For the next eight centuries they relentlessly pursued this aim. Their preoccupation with war may have been forced upon them by a weak geographical position, but it became their glory and their way of life. Every spring the armies of the Assyrian kings marched out of the walled cities to subjugate another people, until the empire extended to the Mediterranean on the west, as far north as Lake Van, and deep into Babylonia. For a while, the forward march was halted by internal strife and weak rulers; nomads poured over the borders, vassal provinces broke away, and

Assyria was reduced to its nucleus: a triangle formed by the Tigris, the Lesser Zab, and the mountains of Kurdistan. In the ninth century B.C. a new strong man arose—Ashurnasirpal II—who led the armies out year after year until Egypt and most of near Asia paid him tribute. For another two hundred years or so, Assyria was a terror to her neighbors, but then, drained of her life blood in continuous war with nothing to show for it but royal spoil, the final decline set in. The Assyrians were a vigorous race of hardy farmers, and, under wiser monarchs, might have been a great nation. In the last years, Assyria's art developed in a remarkable way, producing such sculptures as the dying lioness and the wild horses in the bas-reliefs of Ashurbanipal's palace. But the constant lust for conquest, the insatiable demand for more fighting men, more treasure to build more palaces broke the back of Assyria. After Ashurbanipal came two weak kings—the prototypes of Sardanapalus, who, according to Diodorus Siculus, "exceeded all his predecessors in Sloth and Luxury." Nineveh was then an easy prey to the combined forces of the Medes, Scythians, and a revived Babylon. With the fall of Nineveh and the defeat of the Army, the Assyrians disappeared as a nation.

Fascinated as he was by the civilization he had raised from the earth, Layard did not approve the conduct of the Assyrian kings. The monuments of Nineveh, he wrote, proved that the Assyrian monarch was a thorough Eastern despot. The records of Nineveh were a "dry narrative of military campaigns, spoliations and cruelties," while the historical books of the Old Testament, in addition to similar tales of blood and war, contained "interesting private episodes and sublime moral lessons." The Biblical prophets not only answered the Assyrian boasts with prophecies of doom, but described the Assyrians in passages completely verified by bas-reliefs in the palaces of Ashurnasirpal and Sennacherib. These words of Nahum, for instance:

The noise of a whip, and the noise of the rattling of the wheels, and of the prancing horses, and of the jumping chariots. The horseman lifteth up both the bright sword and the glittering spear: and

there is a multitude of slain, and a great number of carcases; and
there is none end of their corpses; they stumble upon their
corpses . . . Behold, I am against thee, saith the Lord of hosts.

Perhaps a personal feeling for Nimrud, his first discovery, caused
Layard to cling for a time to the theory that it was part of Nineveh,
even though Rawlinson disagreed. He rationalized this claim by
arguing that the different names inscribed on the bricks found in
the various mounds signified merely different fortified palaces. He
was to admit his error shortly. Nineveh, as we know it today, bears
out Rawlinson's interpretation, being the quadrangle on the east
side of the Tigris enclosed by ramparts. The entire enclosure had
been filled with houses, but only the palaces on their raised platforms have survived. To satisfy those who take the word of the
prophet as exact truth, one can say that Jonah had in mind the
city and its suburbs—Greater Nineveh, as it were. It may be purely
fortuitous that a three-day caravan journey would just about cir-
cumambulate the heartland of Assyria, marked by its three capital
cities: Ashur, Calah, and Nineveh.

The seat of government rotated among the three, though the
Assyrian kings, like the wealthy of any age, had residences in more
than one. Ashurnasirpal II moved the capital forty miles north
from Ashur to Calah, or Kalhu (Nimrud) and built his principal
palace over the ruined dwelling of a much earlier king, Shalmaneser
I. The brilliant success of later excavations at Nimrud are in themselves a tribute to Austen Henry Layard, who pointed the way.
Most recent is the work of the British School of Archaeology in
Iraq from 1949 to 1958 under the directorship of Sir Max Mallowan. The Biblical tribute to Calah as a "great" city, which so puzzled Layard, proved to be well justified. Aerial photography, a tool
he never dreamed of, revealed a 900-acre complex surrounded by
defensive walls which could be spotted only from the air. The
great mound, sixty acres in area, was merely the fortified acropolis
of a city which supported seventy thousand souls. Most of Layard's
excavations were in the palaces and temples on the western rim of

the acropolis, in Ashurnasirpal's palace in particular. This was the first example of a classic type which developed from the private house, laid out in a series of rectangular courts surrounded by narrow rooms; it covered six and a half acres. Layard dug out the central block, which was used for ceremonials and contained most of the bas-reliefs. Around and around the walls, repeated many times, perhaps for magical reasons, ran the standard inscription, which has now been deciphered. After listing the king's lineage, titles, and conquests, it reads in part as follows:

Ashurnasirpal, the exalted prince, who fears the great gods, the powerful lord, conqueror of cities and mountains to their farthest border, the king of lords, who consumes the wicked, who is crowned with splendor, who is fearless in battle, the unsparing leader, the destroyer of opposition, the king of glory, the shepherd, the protector of the [four] quarters [of the world]; the king, the word of whose mouth destroys mountains and seas, who by his lordly attack has forced mighty and merciless kings from the rising to the setting sun to acknowledge one rule.

The former city of Calah, which Shalmaneser, king of Assyria, a prince who lived before me, had built, that city had fallen into ruins and lay prostrate. That city I built anew, and the peoples whom my hand had conquered, from the lands which I had brought under my sway . . . I took and I settled them therein. The ancient mound I destroyed, and I dug down to the water level, I went down 120 tipki. A palace of cedar, cypress, juniper, boxwood, mulberry, pistachio-wood, and tamarisk, for my royal dwelling and for my lordly pleasure for all time I founded therein. Beasts of the mountains and of the seas of white limestone and alabaster I fashioned, and set them up in its gates, I adorned it, I made it glorious, and put copper knobs all around it. Door-leaves of cedar, cypress, juniper, and mulberry I hung in the gates thereof; and silver, gold, lead, copper, and iron, the spoil of my hand from the lands which I had brought under my sway, in great quantities I took and placed therein.[2]

There was, in fact, a well going down to water level in one corner of the room in Ashurnasirpal's palace that Rawlinson had believed to be a kitchen, and Layard a storeroom. Mallowan had the well pumped out, and found, mixed with the sludge at the bottom, a collection of exquisite ivory ornaments. Perhaps they had been thrown into the well as a hiding place from an approaching enemy army. Still other ivories were found in the so-called "Burnt Palace" at the southeast corner of the mound. The richest cache of all was found in the building dubbed by its excavators "Fort Shalmaneser," where certain rooms were used to store surplus royal furniture. The Egyptian-type designs which Layard puzzled over were importations or the work of foreign craftsmen employed at Calah, for high society in Assyria was by now cosmopolitan in its tastes. They were Egyptian in inspiration, probably executed by Phoenician craftsmen, since many ivories show traces of both influences.

At the north end of the palace was an administrative wing, and to the south a domestic wing or harem. There was a second, outer court which linked the palace with the ziggurat and temples of Ishtar Kidmuri, and of Ninurta, patron god of Calah.

What did the city as a whole look like? At the top of the acropolis there was an open space large enough to accommodate thousands of spectators for ceremonials, the reception of tribute and captives. Around this space were the palaces with their towering portals guarded by great winged beasts; quarters for the court, the harem, and the nobles; and treasure houses lined with stone and securely bolted. Near the center of the upper city, where Layard found the broken bulls and the Black Obelisk of Shalmaneser III, may have stood his palace (though some scholars think instead there was only an avenue of monuments and obelisks). Nearby was the palace of Tiglath-Pileser III, of which the sole traces found were the slabs stacked ready for reuse by Esarhaddon. In the northwest corner of the acropolis, adjoining the palace of Ashurnasirpal, was the great stepped ziggurat, and in the southeast, near the palace of Sargon, the temple of Nabu, a god more fashionable than Ninurta in the latter days of Assyria. Also on the acropolis was a zoological garden for animals received as tribute or taken in the royal hunt: lions, wild bulls, ostriches, apes and elephants.

The walls of the palaces along the western rim of the acropolis dropped sheer to the river, forty feet below, where stood a massive quay of stone waterproofed with bitumen. Xenophon reported seeing the quay wall when he marched his ten thousand Greeks along the dry riverbed two hundred years after the fall of Assyria, but the city was in ruins and deserted; he thought it Larissa. Layard recognized the mound of Nimrud at first sight from Xenophon's description, though he did not find (in fact never looked for) the quay.

Northeast of the acropolis, on the plain where black tents and grazing horses had so delighted Layard's eyes, lay the outer city of Kalhu. The only entrance so far discovered is in the 100-foot-thick eastern wall. It is an ancient cobbled way rutted by chariot wheels and flanked by bas-reliefs inscribed with the name of Shalmaneser III. Built against the citadel walls in the northeast quarter was a residential section where the Mallowan expedition excavated seven private houses and the warehouse of a rich merchant, containing tablets with the records of his transactions for forty years. In the northwest corner of the lower city was the brick palace of Adad-Nirari III, son of no less a personage than Summuramat, who was probably the real queen behind the fabulous tales of Semiramis. She lived three hundred years before Herodotus, who wrote down the legends about her. Her son's palace is very modern, with brilliant murals of tile, and a bathroom, complete with an alabaster slab for the bather to stand on, a drain for waste, and water jars. The palace had been sacked and burned, perhaps when the king was in the middle of a bath, for some of the jars had been emptied and turned over, while others still stood upright. The fires which wrecked so many of Nimrud's palaces, changing alabaster to gypsum and ivory to cinders, did not all occur during the final destruction of the city; some were the fruit of earlier riots among the foreign artisans and slaves who made up a large part of the population.

Twelve acres of the outer city were occupied by a fortified building constructed by Shalmaneser III and rebuilt by Esarhaddon. It had drill yards, storerooms, and barracks from which the cohorts came down upon their neighbors each spring as Byron has described them, "like the wolf on the fold." Judging by the quantity of arms and armor scattered about its gates, "Fort Shalmaneser" may have seen the last stand of the Assyrian Army when Kalhu fell.[3]

Long before this, the Assyrian kings had moved the principal seat of government elsewhere. Sargon II, in addition to restoring Ashurnasirpal's palace at Kalhu, began the construction of a new town named for himself, Dûr-Sharrukin (Khorsabad). Sennacherib, Sargon's son, built his principal palace on the mound now called Kuyunjik, and ushered in Nineveh's greatest period of art and luxury. It was traditional for each Assyrian king to glorify himself by building a palace; it may also have been his ritual duty. From the middle of the second millennium till late in the seventh century B.C., thirteen kings built palaces at Nineveh. They also restored its very ancient shrine of Ishtar. This goddess of love and war has been identified with an earlier river goddess, Nina, which may account for the city's name and also for the name of Ninus, its legendary founder.

Sennacherib, who, like Ashurnasirpal, had an ample number of war captives for forced labor, redesigned the whole city, redid its water supply, enlarged it with new city walls, laid out gardens and orchards around it. The most skillful craftsmen of the day were called in to embellish his own dwelling, which he called "the Palace without a rival." In the disturbances which broke out following his assassination in 681 B.C., the palace was partly burned. Esarhaddon, his son and probable murderer, built palaces at Nimrud and Nebbi Yunus, the hill from which Jonah was said to have prophesied. Esarhaddon's son, Ashurbanipal, restored the part of his grandfather's palace in which he had lived as a boy, lining the walls with scenes of his own triumphs. He also built the new palace on the north where Hormuzd Rassam found the second big collection of clay tablets and the bas-reliefs which are considered the finest of all Assyrian sculptures, the Lion Hunt (now in the British Museum). The figure of Sardanapalus was probably a mixture of

Ashurbanipal (who died of old age in bed) and the historical suicide of Sin-shar-ishkin, last king of Assyria.

More than a century of exploration has gone on at Nineveh since Layard's time.[4] At Nebbi Yunus there has been no real excavation in the strict sense of the word. A sounding made in 1954 by the Director General of Antiquities in Iraq corroborated Layard's conviction that the mound covered an Assyrian palace probably of the time of Esarhaddon. Three statues were found of the Pharaoh Taharqa, apparently brought back from Egypt by Esarhaddon in 671 B.C.

Thus younger men have brought to light the underground palaces Layard was unable to dig up, and on the whole most of the questions he raised have been answered. He has been severely criticized (as have other early diggers) for unscientific methods, for the loss or destruction of all but the sturdiest and most portable finds. Layard himself writes, with regret, again and again, "entire when first exposed to view, it crumbled to dust when touched." He did his best to make a record of the object in sketches and detailed notes before it quite disappeared; one should not blame him because chemical preservatives were not yet known. Much was damaged or went undiscovered because the smallness of his subsidy forced him to open up chambers, take a look around, and re-bury or abandon them. His chief detractor was Ernest Wallis Budge, who had hard things to say about most of his predecessors in the Mesopotamian field. In addition, Budge had reasons of personal enmity—he had faced Layard's vehemence on the opposite side of the Rassam lawsuit, and had, by his own admission, incurred Layard's dislike. He gave it back in the form of derogation, in destruction of the older man's reputation as an archaeologist—so much so that Layard's greatness is only now beginning to emerge from under a seventy-five-year-old cloud.

There are those who argue that it would have been better if the Assyrian discoveries had been made later, when archaeology had come of age. Perhaps the sum total of well-preserved finds would have been greater, but not the number in museums where the

Western world can see them. Layard considered the date of the discoveries so fortunate that he felt almost superstitious about it. If the Assyrian sculptures had been found some years earlier, he argued, there would have been no one with enough knowledge to excavate them, and they would have been destroyed by the Moslems. If they had been found later, the Turkish Government would not have permitted their removal. Whether or not the Western museums were ethically justified in lifting so much ancient art from the land of its origin, it is lucky for scholars that the British Museum owns its collection of cuneiform tablets—the largest collection in the world. Thanks to Layard, it also has the largest and most important collection of Assyrian sculptures—so many that they are still being catalogued and published. Some are known only from Layard's drawings—and there may be more to come, for one portfolio of his priceless sketches has not yet been located.

Austen Henry Layard lived before the day of aerial surveys, before the invention of the camera, and of Carbon-14 dating—before a whole battery of devices used by contemporary archaeologists. His methods were as scientific as he was able to make them without funds or modern techniques. And he initiated certain procedures that are a must today. "He had proved incontestably that to find lost civilizations, it was necessary to dig methodically, to record or preserve your finds and to publish the results," writes Barnett. "The lesson was later not lost on Schliemann, for his friend, Mr. Calvert, the part-proprietor of Hisserlik-Troy, had read Layard."[5]

Claudius Rich was the first to arouse European interest in the lost civilization of the Assyrians; Botta the first to discover an Assyrian palace, but his contribution, through no fault of his own, was slight. It was Austen Henry Layard who followed up these first steps and, solely on his own initiative and through his own efforts, brought to light Assyrian history, culture, and way of life which had passed out of human ken for twenty-four centuries. Since he was the first to confirm the authenticity of Old Testament history through the use of the spade, he is not only the Father of Assyriology, but of Biblical Archaeology, which has become a separate discipline, with its own special researches, publications, and professors.

Layard's most engaging quality was his enthusiasm, which made it possible for him to convey vividly all that he had seen, learned and experienced. Let us join him for a last time on the mound where he first uncovered the civilization of Nineveh:

"Before leaving Nimrud and reburying its palaces, I would wish to lead the reader once more through the ruins of the principal edifice. Let us imagine ourselves issuing from my tent near the village in the plain. On approaching the mound, not a trace of building can be perceived, except a small mud hut covered with reeds, erected for the accommodation of my Chaldean workmen. We ascend this artificial hill, but still see no ruins, not a stone protruding from the soil. There is only a broad level platform before us, perhaps covered with a luxuriant crop of barley, or maybe yellow and parched, without a blade of vegetation, except here and there a scanty tuft of camel-thorn.

"We will descend into the principal trench, by a flight of steps rudely cut into the earth, near the western face of the mound. We descend about twenty feet, and suddenly find ourselves between a pair of colossal lions, winged and human-headed, forming a portal. Before those wonderful forms Ezekiel, Jonah, and others of the prophets stood, and Sennacherib bowed; even the patriarch Abraham himself may possibly have looked upon them. We issue from between the winged lions and enter the remains of the principal hall. On both sides of us are sculptured gigantic, winged figures; some with the heads of eagles, others entirely human, and carrying mysterious symbols in their hands. To the left is another portal, also formed by winged lions. One of them has, however, fallen across the entrance, and there is just room to creep beneath it. Beyond this portal is a winged figure, and two slabs with bas-reliefs; but they have been so much injured that we can scarcely trace the subject upon them. Further on there are no traces of wall, although a deep trench has been opened. The opposite side of the hall had also disappeared, and we see only a high wall of earth. On examining it attentively, we can detect the marks of masonry; and we soon find that it is a solid structure built of bricks of unbaked clay, now of the same colour as the surrounding soil, and scarcely to be distinguished from it.

"The slabs of alabaster, fallen from their original position, have, however, been raised; and we tread in the midst of a maze of small bas-reliefs, representing chariots, horsemen, battles and sieges. Perhaps the workmen are about to raise a slab for the first time; and we watch, with eager curiosity, what new event of Assyrian history, or what unknown custom or religious ceremony, may be illustrated by the sculpture beneath.

"Having walked about one hundred feet amongst those scattered monuments of ancient history and art, we reach another doorway, formed by gigantic winged bulls in yellow limestone. One is still entire; but its companion has fallen, and is broken into several pieces—the great human head is at our feet.

"We pass on without turning into the part of the building to which this portal leads. Beyond it we see another winged figure, holding a graceful flower in its hand, and apparently presenting it as an offering to the winged bull. Adjoining this sculpture we find eight fine bas-reliefs. There is the king, hunting, and triumphing over, the lion and wild bull; and the siege of the castle, with the battering ram. We have now reached the end of the hall, and find before us an elaborate and beautiful sculpture, representing two kings, standing beneath the emblem of the supreme deity, and attended by winged figures. Between them is the sacred tree. In front of this bas-relief is the great stone platform, upon which, in days of old, may have been placed the throne of the Assyrian monarch, when he received his captive enemies, or his courtiers.

"To the left of us is a fourth outlet from the hall, formed by another pair of lions. We issue from between them, and find ourselves on the edge of a deep ravine, to the north of which rises, high above us, the lofty pyramid. Figures of captives bearing objects of tribute,—ear-rings, bracelets, and monkeys,—may be seen on walls near this ravine; and two enormous bulls, and two winged figures above fourteen feet high, are lying on its very edge.

"As the ravine bounds the ruins on this side, we must return to the yellow bulls. Passing through the entrance formed by them, we enter a large chamber surrounded by eagle-headed figures: at one end of it is a doorway guarded by two priests or divinities, and in the centre another portal with winged bulls. Whichever way we turn, we find ourselves in the midst of a nest of rooms; and without an acquaintance with the intricacies of the place, we should soon lose ourselves in this labyrinth. We may wander through these galleries for an hour or two, examining the marvellous sculptures, or the numerous inscriptions that surround us. Here we meet long rows of kings, attended by their eunuchs and priests,—there lines of winged figures, carrying fir-cones and religious emblems, and seemingly in adoration before the mystic tree. At length, wearied, we issue from the buried edifice by a trench on the opposite side to that by which we entered, and find ourselves again upon the naked platform. We look around in vain for any traces of the wonderful remains we have just seen, and are half inclined to believe that we have dreamed a dream, or have been listening to some tale of Eastern romance.

"Some, who may hereafter tread on the spot when the grass again grows over the ruins of the Assyrian palaces, may indeed suspect that I have been relating a vision."

Appendix I

THE NINEVEH ROOM AT AMHERST COLLEGE
AMHERST, MASSACHUSETTS

A graduate of the Class of 1849, the Reverend Henry Lobdell, who was working in Mosul as doctor and missionary, was deeply impressed by the proof of Bible History offered by the Assyrian bas-reliefs being uncovered by Austen Henry Layard at Nimrud (then assumed to be Nineveh). Dr. Lobdell interested President Hitchcock of Amherst in the matter, and six hundred dollars was raised for transportation costs. Six reliefs were sawed off the faces of the alabaster slabs in the palace of Ashurnasirpal, sent five hundred miles across the desert by camel back, and embarked upon a sailing ship. They arrived in the United States in 1853. Three of them are now installed in Mead Art Building at Amherst, while the others are shown at intervals on movable pedestals. Those permanently on view represent the king holding a bow and libation bowl, flanked by two winged genii who are fertilizing the sacred date palm (see page 230).

NOTES

Chapter I

1. "*General Lacy and Cura Merino,*" in Walter Savage Landor, "Imaginary Conversations."

Chapter II

1. Edward Mitford, *A Land March.*

Chapter IV

1. J. W. Burgon, Newdigate Prize Poem, 1825.

Chapter VII

1. Firdausi, the *Shánáma,* translated by A. G. Warner and E. Warner.

2. Ibid.

Chapter IX

1. The quotations from Rawlinson in this chapter are taken from his paper, "A March from Zohab."

Chapter XI

1. In 1962, the New York *Times* announced a large sum in American Aid for a dam on the Dez River near the old city of Dizful, which, among other benefits, will "improve navigation in the lower Karun, the only navigable river in Iran."

2. The excavation of Susa, at Shush, was begun by William Kennett Loftus, 1852. Work has gone on there intermittently until the present. Its identification is no longer controversial.

3. H. J. Ross, *Letters from the East.*

Chapter XII

1. In the *Autobiography*, Layard says he made his explorations in the *Nicrotis*, but I have followed his longer account of the explorations in *Early Adventures*, in which he says it was the *Assyria*.

Chapter XV

1. Canon Rawlinson, *Memoir*.
2. Henry Rawlinson, *The Persian Cuneiform Inscription at Behistun*.
3. E. Wallis Budge, *By Nile and Tigris*.
4. André Parrot, *The Arts of Assyria*, and *The Great King*.

Chapter XVI

1. T. E. Lawrence, *Seven Pillars of Wisdom*.
2. Gertrude Bell, *Letters*.
3. This is not the famous Lion Hunt now in the British Museum, which was discovered later by Rassam in the Palace of Ashurbanipal, but another example of the Assyrian sculptors' skill in portraying animals.
4. The description is founded on Layard's remarks, plus Edith Porada, "The Palace and Reliefs of Ashurnasirpal II," in *The Great King*.

Chapter XVII

1. II Kings 9:10 mentions Jehu but not this incident. According to Assyrian records, when Shalmaneser defeated the king of Damascus, Hazael (also a Biblical character) in 842 B.C., Jehu, king of Israel, sent rich gifts which the Assyrian king regarded as tribute and commemorated on the obelisk.

Chapter XIX

1. Byron's poetic drama, like most accounts of Sardanapalus, was based on the *Historical Library* of Diodorus Siculus, who wrote in the time of Julius Caesar.

Chapter XX

1. The deciphering of cuneiform was to occur soon, some of it in time for inclusion in *Nineveh and Babylon* (1853) from

which this and the text of other inscriptions in this chapter are taken.

Chapter XXI

1. R. D. Barnett, *Assyrian Reliefs.*

Chapter XXII

1. Layard owned the "candlestick" prism, which proved to be the Annals of Esarhaddon; Colonel Taylor's was the Annals of Sennacherib.
2. E. Wallis Budge, *The Babylonian Story of the Deluge.*
3. Mt. Ararat, altitude 16,696 feet, lies in a corner of eastern Turkey, near the boundary of the Soviet Union and Iran.

Chapter XXIV

1. Thompson and Hutchinson, *A Century of Exploration at Nineveh.*
2. R. D. Barnett, *Canford and Cuneiform.*
3. A. H. Sayce, *Reminiscences.*
4. Janet Ross, *The Fourth Generation.*

Chapter XXV

1. Edith Porada, *The Great King.*
2. Luckenbill, *Ancient Monuments of Assyria and Babylonia.*
3. Edward Bacon, *Digging for History.*
4. Excavators at Kuyunjik since Layard: 1853, Hormuzd Rassam; 1854, William Kennett Loftus and the artist William Boutcher; 1873, George Smith; 1878–82, Hormuzd Rassam; 1903, L. W. King; 1927, R. Campbell Thompson and R. W. Hutchinson.
5. R. D. Barnett, *Canford and Cuneiform.*

BIBLIOGRAPHY

Albright, W. F. *The Archaeology of Palestine*. London: 1951.

Alexander, Constance. *Baghdad in Bygone Days*. London: 1928.

Bacon, Edward. *Digging for History, Archaeological Discoveries Throughout the World, 1945–59*. New York: 1960.

Barnett, R. D. *Assyrian Palace Reliefs and Their Influence on the Sculpture of Babylonia*. London (undated).

——. *A Catalogue of the Nimrud Ivories*. London: 1957.

——. "Canford and Cuneiform." Museum Journal #60. 1960.

Bell, Gertrude. *The Desert and the Sown*. New York: 1907.

——. *Amurath to Amurath*. London: 1911.

——. *Selected Letters*. London: 1953.

——, and Ramsey, William. *The Thousand and One Churches*. London: 1909.

Bonomi, Joseph. *Nineveh and Its Palaces*. London: 1853.

Budge, Sir Ernest A. Wallis. *By Nile and Tigris*. London: 1926.

——. *Guide to the Babylonian and Assyrian Antiquities*. British Museum. London: 1922.

——. *The Babylonian Story of the Deluge, and the Epic of Gilgamesh with an Account of the Royal Libraries of Nineveh*. British Museum. London: 1929.

Burrows, Millar. *What Mean These Stones?* New Haven: 1941.

Byron, Lord Alfred. *Hebrew Melodies*. Cambridge: 1905.

——. *Sardanapalus*. Cambridge: 1905.

Daniel, Glyn E. *A Hundred Years of Archaeology*. London: 1950.

De Burgh, W. G. *The Legacy of the Ancient World.* London: 1955.

Dickens, Charles. *The Uncommercial Traveller.* New York: 1909.

Diez, Ernst. *The Ancient Worlds of Asia.* London: 1961.

Elder, John. *Prophets, Idols and Diggers.* New York: 1960.

Firdausi. *The Shánáma.* Translated by Arthur George Warner and Edmond Warner. London: 1923.

Frankfort, Henry. *The Birth of Civilization in the Near East.* New York: 1956.

Gadd, C. J. *The Stones of Assyria.* London: 1936.

Gail, Marzieh. *Persia and the Victorians.* London: 1936.

Ghirshman, R. *Iran.* London: 1954.

Hall, Harry Reginald. *The Ancient History of the Near East.* New York: 1913.

Herodotus. *Histories.* Translated by Aubrey de Selincourt. Harmondsworth, Middlesex: 1954.

Hilprecht, H. V. *Explorations in Bible Lands.* New York: 1903.

Hurlbut, Jesse Lyman, D.D. *A Bible Atlas.* New York: 1948.

Jerman, B. R. *The Young Disraeli.* Princeton, N.J.: 1960.

Johnson, Edgar and Dickens, Charles. *His Tragedy and Triumph.* New York: 1952.

Landor, Walter Savage. "Imaginary Conversations." London: 1876.

———. "To Layard, Discoverer of Nineveh." London: 1876.

Lawrence, T. E. *Seven Pillars of Wisdom.* London: 1936.

Layard, Sir Austen Henry. "A Description of the Province of Khuzistan," read before the Royal Geographical Society, 1846.

———. *Nineveh and Its Remains:* with an Account of a Visit to the Chaldean Christians of Kurdistan, and the Yezidis, or Devil-worshippers; and an Enquiry into the Manners and Arts of the Ancient Assyrians. 2 vols. London: 1849.

———. *The Monuments of Nineveh,* From Drawings made on the Spot by A. H. Layard. Illustrated in 100 Plates. London: 1849.

———. *A Popular Account of Discoveries at Nineveh,* Abridged by the Author from his larger work. London: 1851.

―――. *Discoveries in the Ruins of Nineveh and Babylon;* with Travels in Armenia, Kurdistan and the Desert; being the result of a Second Expedition undertaken for the Trustees of the British Museum. London: 1853.

―――. *A Second Series of the Monuments of Nineveh,* made on the Spot during a Second Expedition to Assyria. London: 1853.

―――. *The Nineveh Court in the Crystal Palace,* Described by A. H. Layard. London: 1854.

―――. *Early Adventures in Persia, Susiana and Babylonia,* including a Residence among the Bakhtiyari and other Wild Tribes, before the Discovery of Nineveh. 2 vols. London: 1887.

―――. *Handbook of Painting: The Italian Schools.* Based on the Handbook of Kugler. Originally Edited by Sir Charles L. Eastlake, P.R.A. Thoroughly Revised and in part Rewritten by Austen Henry Layard, G.C.B., D.C.L., with nearly 250 illustrations. London: 1891.

―――. *Autobiography and Letters,* from his childhood until his appointment as H. M. Ambassador at Madrid, edited by the Hon. William N. Bruce, with a Chapter on his parliamentary career by the Rt. Hon. Sir Arthur Otway. New York: 1903.

―――. *The Private Papers of Sir Austen Henry Layard* (unpublished). In the manuscript collection of the British Museum, London.

Lloyd, Seton. *Foundations in the Dust.* London: 1955.

―――. *The Art of the Ancient Near East.* New York: 1861.

Luckenbill, D. D. *Ancient Records of Assyria and Babylonia.* Chicago: 1926.

Mallowan, M. E. L. *Twenty-five Years of Mesopotamian Discovery.* London: 1956.

Mitford, Edward. *A Land March from England to Ceylon Fifty Years Ago.* London: 1884.

Oppenheim, A. Leo. "The Mesopotamian Temple," in *The Biblical Archaeologist Reader.* Garden City: 1961.

Parrot, André. *The Arts of Assyria.* New York: 1961.

Petrie, Sir Charles. *The Victorians.* London: 1961.

Porada, Edith. "The Palace and Reliefs of Ashurnasirpal II" in *The Great King, King of Assyria*. Metropolitan Museum of Art, New York: 1946.

Pritchard, James B. *Ancient Near Eastern Texts Relating to the Old Testament*. Princeton, N.J.: 1955.

Rawlinson, George. *A Memoir of Major-General Sir Henry C. Rawlinson*. London: 1898.

Rawlinson, Sir Henry Creswicke. "Notes on a March from Zohab to Khuzistan," *Journal of Royal Geographical Society*. London: 1839.

———. "The Persian Cuneiform Inscriptions at Behistun," *Royal Asiatic Society Journal*. London: 1846.

———. "Outline of the History of Assyria as Collected from the Inscriptions Discovered by A. H. Layard, Esq. in Nineveh," *Royal Asiatic Society Journal*. London: 1854.

Rich, Claudius. *Narrative of a Residence in Koordistan*, edited by his widow. London: 1836.

Ross, H. J. *Letters from the East*. London: 1902.

Ross, Janet. *The Fourth Generation*. London: 1912.

Sayce, A. H. *Reminiscences*. London: 1923.

Strachey, Lytton. *Eminent Victorians*. London: 1960.

Tasso, Torquato. *Jerusalem Delivered*. Translated by John Hoole. London: 1797.

The Old Testament, King James Translation.

Thompson, R. Campbell, and Hutchinson, R. W. *A Century of Exploration at Nineveh*. London: 1929.

Waterfield, Lina. *Castle in Italy*. New York: 1961.

INDEX

L. *means* Austen Henry Layard